If You're Trying to
Get Better Grades
&
Higher Test Scores
in Reading & Language,
You've Gotta Have This Book !

Grades 6 & Up

by Imogene Forte
& Marjorie Frank

Incentive Publications, Inc.
Nashville, Tennessee

Illustrated by Kathleen Bullock
Cover by Geoffrey Brittingham
Edited by Jean K. Signor & Charlotte Bosarge

ISBN 0-86530-577-3

4   5   6   7   8   9   10   06

PRINTED IN THE UNITED STATES OF AMERICA
www.incentivepublications.com

Contents

GET SHARP . . . in Grammar, Usage, Mechanics, 67
& Spelling

—— Get Ready ——

Get ready to get smarter. Get ready to be a better student and get the grades you are capable of getting. Get ready to feel better about yourself as a student. Lots of students would like to do better in school, and lots of their parents and teachers would like them to as well! Lots of students CAN do better. But it doesn't happen overnight, and it doesn't happen without some thinking and trying. So are you ready to put some energy into getting more out of your learning efforts? Good! The first part of getting ready is *wanting* to do better—motivating yourself to get moving on this project of showing how smart you really are. The **Get Ready** part of this book will help you do just that: get inspired and motivated. It also gives you some wonderful and downright practical ways to organize yourself, your space, your time, and your homework. Even more than that, it gives you tips to use right away to make big improvements in your study habits.

—— Get Set ——

Once you've taken a good, hard look at your goals, organization, and study habits, you can move on to other skills and habits that will get you set up for more successful learning. The **Get Set** part of this book gives you ready-to-use tools for sharpening thinking skills and helping you get the most out of your brain. Then, it adds a quick and effective crash-course on finding information in the library, on the Internet, and from many other sources. Top this off with a great review of tools and skills you need for good studying. It's all right here at your fingertips—how to read carefully, listen well, summarize, outline, take notes, create reports, study for tests, and take tests. Take this section seriously, and you're bound to start making improvements immediately.

—— Get Sharp ——

Now you're ready to mix those good study habits and skills with the content that you want to learn. The **Get Sharp** sections of this book contain all kinds of facts and explanations, processes and definitions, lists, and how-to information. These sections cover the basic areas of language arts that you study in school—grammar, usage, mechanics, spelling, writing and speaking, reading, vocabulary, and word use. They are loaded with the information that you need to do your language homework. You will find this part of the book to be a great reference tool PLUS a *How-To Manual* for many language topics and assignments. Keep it handy whenever you do an assignment in the language arts.

How to Use This Book

Students

Students—this can be the ultimate homework helper for your language assignments and preparation. Use the *Get Ready* and the *Get Set* sections to strengthen your general preparation for study and sharpen your study skills. Then, have the book nearby at all times when you have language work to do at home, and use the *Get Sharp* sections to . . .

. . . reinforce a topic you've already learned.

. . . get fresh and different examples of something you've studied.

. . . check up on a fact, definition, or detail of language.

. . . get a quick answer to a language question.

. . . get clear on something you thought you knew but now aren't sure about.

. . . guide you in reading and writing processes (such as how to write an essay).

. . . check yourself to see if you've got a fact or process right.

. . . review a topic in preparation for a test.

Teachers

This book can serve multiple purposes in the classroom. Use it as . . .

. . . a reference manual for students to consult during learning activities or assignments.

. . . a reference manual for you to consult on particular rules, terms, forms, and skills.

. . . an instructional handbook for particular language topics.

. . . a remedial tool for individuals or groups who need a review of a particular language topic.

. . . a source of advice for parents and students regarding homework habits.

. . . an assessment guide to help you gauge student mastery of language processes or skills.

. . . a source of good resources for making bridges between home and school.
(For starters, send a copy of the letter on page 17 home to each parent. Use any other pages, particularly those in the "Get Ready" and "Get Set" sections, as send-home pieces.)

Parents

The *Get Ready* and *Get Set* sections of this book will help you to help your child improve study habits and sharpen study skills. It can serve as a motivator and a guide, and take the burden off you! Then, use the *Get Sharp* sections as a knowledge and process back-up guide for yourself.

It's a handbook you can consult to. . .

. . . refresh your memory about a language process, term, rule, or fact.

. . . clear up confusion about grammar rules, writing forms, reading skills, and many other language questions.

. . . provide useful homework help to your child.

. . . reinforce the good learning your child is doing in school.

. . . gain confidence that your child is doing the homework right.

GET READY →

Get Motivated

Dear Student,

Nobody can make you a better student. Nobody can even make you WANT to be a better student. But you CAN be. It's a rare kid who doesn't have some ability to learn more, do better with assignments and tests, feel more confident as a student, or get better grades. YOU CAN DO THIS! You are the one (the only one) that can get yourself motivated.

Probably, the first question is this: "WHY would you want be a better student?" If you don't have an answer to this, your chances of improving are not so hot. If you do have answers, but they're like Charlie's (page 15), your chances of improving still might be pretty slim. Charlie figured this out, and decided that these are NOT what really motivate him. Now, we don't mean to tell you that it's a bad idea to get a good report card, or get on the honor roll, or please your parents. We're not trying to say that getting into college is a poor goal or that there's anything wrong with getting ready for high school either.

But—if you are trying to motivate yourself to be a better student, the reasons need to be about YOU. The goals need to be YOUR goals for your life right now. In fact, if you are having a hard time getting motivated, maybe it is just BECAUSE you're used to hearing a lot of "shoulds" about what other people want you to be. Or maybe it's because the goals are so far off in some hazy distant future that it's impossible to stay focused on them.

So it's back to the question, "Why try to be a better student?" Consider these as possible reasons why:

- to make use of your good mind (and NOT short-change yourself by cheating yourself out of something you could learn to do or understand)

- to get involved—to change learning into something YOU DO instead of something that someone else is trying to do TO you

- to take charge and get where YOU WANT TO GO (It's YOUR life, after all)

- to learn all you can for YOURSELF—because the more you know, the more you think, and the more you understand—the more possibilities you have for what you can do or be in your life RIGHT NOW and in the future

Follow the "Get Motivated Tips" on the next page as you think about this question. Then write down a few reasons of your own to inspire you toward putting your brain to work, showing how smart you are, and getting even smarter.

Sincerely,

Imogene and Marjorie

None of these really motivate me much at all.

Why should I be a better student?

To please my parents
To please my teachers
To impress other kids
To impress my parents' friends
So people will like me better
To keep from embarrassing my parents
To do as well as my older brother
To do better than my sister
So teachers treat me better
To do as well as my mom or dad did in school
To get the money my parents offer for good grades
To get the privileges my parents offer for good grades
To get well-prepared for high school
To make a lot of money when I finish school
To get a good report card
To get into college

Get Motivated Tips

1. Think about why you'd want to do better as a student.

2. Think about what you'd gain now from doing better.

3. Get clear enough on your motivations to write them down.

4. Set some short-term goals *(something you can improve in a few weeks)*.

5. Think about what gets in the way of doing your best as a student.

6. Figure out a way to change or eliminate something that interferes.

(Use the form on page 16 to record your thoughts and goals.)

Why do I want to be a better student? What difference would it make for me, now and in the future?
(Write a few reasons.)

1._____

_____

2._____

_____

3._____

_____

What changes could I make in the near future?
(Write two short-term goals—things that, realistically, you could improve in the next month.)

1._____

2._____

What gets in the way of good grades or good studying for me?
(Name the things, conditions, or distractions that **most often** keep you from doing your best as a student.)

1._____

2._____

3._____

4._____

What distraction am I willing to eliminate ?
(Choose one of the interferences above that you'd be willing to try changing or getting rid of for the next month.)

1._____

Dear Parent:

What parent doesn't want **his/her** child to be a good student? Probably not many! But how can you help yours get motivated to do the work it takes? You can't do it for her (or him), but here are some ideas to help students as they find it within themselves to get set to be good students:

Read the letter to students (page 14). Help your son or daughter think about where she/he wants to go, what reasons make sense to her or him for getting better grades, and what benefits he/she would gain from better performance as a student.

Help your child make use of the advice on study habits. (See pages 18-28.) Reinforce the ideas, particularly those of keeping up with assignments, going to class, and turning in work on time.

Provide your child with a quiet, comfortable, well-lit place that is available consistently for study. Also provide a place to keep materials, post reminders, and display schedules.

Set family routines and schedules that allow for good blocks of study time, adequate rest, relaxing breaks, and healthy eating. Include some time to get things ready for the next school day and some ways for students to be reminded about upcoming assignments or due dates.

Demonstrate that you value learning in your household. Read. Learn new things. Show excitement about learning something new yourself. Share this with your kids.

Keep distractions to a minimum. You may not be able to control the motivations and goals of your child, but you can control the telephone, computer, Internet, and TV. These things actually have on-off switches. Use them. Set rules and schedules.

Help your child gather resources for studying, projects, papers, and reports. Try to be available to take her or him to the library, and offer help tracking down a variety of sources. Try to provide standard resources in the home (dictionaries, thesaurus, computer encyclopedia, etc.).

DO help your student with homework. This means helping straighten out confusion about a topic (when you can), getting an assignment clear, discussing a concept or skill, and perhaps working through a few examples along with the student to make sure he/she is doing it right. This kind of involvement gives a chance to extend or clarify the teaching done in the classroom. Remember that the end goal is for the student to learn. Don't be so insistent on the student "doing it himself" that you miss a good teaching or learning opportunity.

Be alert for problems, and act early. Keep contact with teachers and don't be afraid to call on them if you see any signs of slipping, confusion, or disinterest on the part of your child. It is easier to reclaim lost ground if you catch it early.

Try to keep the focus on the student's taking charge of meeting his/her own goals rather than on making you happy. This can help get you out of a nagging role and get some of the power in the hands of the student. Both of these will make for a more trusting, less hostile relationship with your child on the subject of school work. Such a relationship will go a long way toward supporting your child's self motivation to be a better student.

Sincerely,

Imogene and *Marjorie*

Get Organized

9:00 p.m. Charlie has a report on quasars due tomorrow. He hasn't written it yet.

Charlie! Get off the phone!

Goodbye, Sam. I've got to do my report.

He clears a space in the clutter and starts looking for the folder where he stuck all his notes. *(He might have left it in his locker.)*

Where is it?

He forgot to get a report folder. The printer is out of ink, his colored pencils are broken, and there are only three sheets of paper left.

I wonder if I can print on paper towels?

He needs to glue symbols on his diagram, but the dog ate his glue stick.

Maybe I could staple them on?

SLURP

Charlie may know a lot about quasars.
Maybe he's done some good research.
But he's not in a good place to show what he's learned
because he is so disorganized. Don't repeat Charlie's mistakes.

Get Your Space Organized

Find a good place to study. Choose a place that . . .

. . . is always available to you.

. . . is comfortable.

. . . is quiet and as private as possible.

. . . has good lighting.

. . . is relatively uncluttered.

. . . is relatively free of distractions.

. . . has a flat surface large enough to spread out materials.

. . . has a place to keep supplies handy. (See page 19 for suggested supplies.)

. . . has some wall space or bulletin board space for posting schedules and reminders.

Get Ready Tip # 2
Set this up before school starts each year.
Make it cozy and friendly— a safe refuge for getting work done. Put a little time into making it your own, so it's a place you like —not a place to avoid.

18

Get Your Stuff Organized

Gather things that you will need for studying or for projects, papers, and other assignments. Keep them organized in one place, so you won't have to waste time running around looking. Here are some suggestions:

Also have:
an assignment notebook (See page 22)
a notebook for every subject
a book bag or pack to carry things back and forth
a schedule for your week (or longer)

Get set with a place to keep supplies.
(a bookshelf, a file box, a paper tray, a drawer, a plastic dish pan, a plastic bucket, a carton, or plastic crate)
Keep everything in this place at all times.
Return things to it after you use them.

Get Ready Tip # 3
Have a place to put things you bring home from school. This might be a shelf, a box, or even a laundry basket. Put your school things in there every time you come in the door—so important stuff doesn't get lost in the house or moved or used by other family members.

Supplies to Have Handy
a good light
a clock or timer
bulletin board or wall *(for schedule & reminders)*
pencils, pens, erasable pens
erasers
colored pencils or crayons
markers
highlighters
notebook paper
scratch paper
drawing paper
typing-computer paper
index cards
sticky notes
poster board
folders
ruler, compass
tape, scissors
calculator
glue, rubber cement
paper clips, push pins
stapler, staples
standard references:
    dictionary
    thesaurus
    current almanac
    world maps
    language handbook
    writer's guide
    encyclopedia (set or CD)
homework hotline numbers
homework help websites

19

Get Your Time Organized

It might be easy to organize your study and space and supplies, but it is probably not quite as easy to organize your time. This takes some work. First, you have to understand how you use your time now. Then you'll need to figure out a way to make better use of your time. Here's a plan you can follow right away to help you get your time organized:

Think about how you use your time now.

1. For one week, stop at the end of each day, think back over the day, and write down what you did in each hour-long period of time for the whole day.

2. Then look at the record you've kept to see how you used your time.

   Ask yourself these questions:
   Did I have any clear schedule?
   Did I have any goals for when I would get certain things done?
   Did I ever think ahead about how I would use my time?
   How did I decide what to do first?
   Did I have a plan or did I just get things done in haphazard order?
   Did I get everything done or did I run out of time?
   How much time did I waste?

8:00 am
I overslept and rushed off without my books.

10:30 am
I wrote notes to friends during study hall.

3:30 pm
I watched "Teen Dreams" while I did homework.

7:00-8:00 pm
I read make-up tips in teen magazines.

5:00 pm
I watched TV for an hour.

9:00 pm
I played games on my gamestation.

Get Ready Tip # 4
When you plan your week's schedule, don't make it too tight or too rigid. Leave room for unexpected events.

3. Next, start fresh for the upcoming week. Make a plan. Include:
   time that will be spent at school
   after-school activities
   meals
   study time
   family activities
   fun, sports, or recreational activities
   social activities or special events
   sleep time

4. Make sure you have an assignment notebook. When you plan your weekly schedule, transfer assignments from that notebook into your study time. *(Did you leave enough time to do all these assignments?)* Keep a copy of your calendar at home *and* in a notebook that you carry to school.

5. Make a Daily *To-Do* List *(For each day, write the things that must be done by the end of that day.)*

20

Get Ready: Get Organized

Better Grades & Higher Test Scores / READING & LANGUAGE
Copyright ©2003 by Incentive Publications, Inc., Nashville, TN.

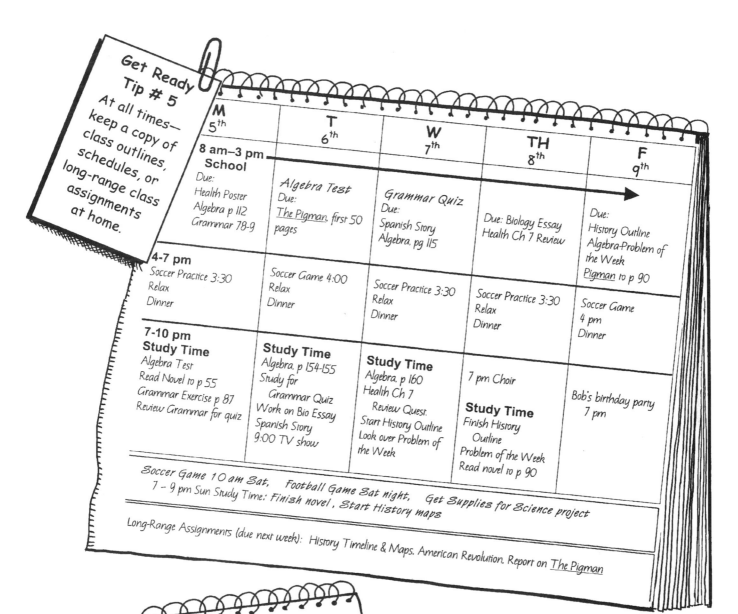

	M 5th	T 6th	W 7th	TH 8th	F 9th
8 am–3 pm School	Due: Health Poster Algebra p 112 Grammar 78-9	Algebra Test Due: The Pigman, first 50 pages	Grammar Quiz Due: Spanish Story Algebra, pg 115	Due: Biology Essay Health Ch 7 Review	Due: History Outline Algebra-Problem of the Week Pigman to p 90
4-7 pm	Soccer Practice 3:30 Relax Dinner	Soccer Game 4:00 Relax Dinner	Soccer Practice 3:30 Relax Dinner	Soccer Practice 3:30 Relax Dinner	Soccer Game 4 pm Dinner
7-10 pm Study Time	Algebra Test Read Novel to p 55 Grammar Exercise p 87 Review Grammar for quiz	**Study Time** Algebra, p 154-155 Study for Grammar Quiz Work on Bio Essay Spanish Story 9:00 TV show	**Study Time** Algebra, p 160 Health Ch 7 Review Quest. Start History Outline Look over Problem of the Week	7 pm Choir **Study Time** Finish History Outline Problem of the Week Read novel to p 90	Bob's birthday party 7 pm

Soccer Game 10 am Sat,   Football Game Sat night,   Get Supplies for Science project
7 – 9 pm Sun Study Time: Finish novel, Start History maps

Long-Range Assignments (due next week): History Timeline & Maps, American Revolution, Report on The Pigman

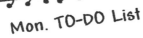

Mon. TO-DO List

Study for Algebra Test
Finish novel to page 50
Finish Grammar Exercise p 87
Review for Tues. Grammar Quiz
Call Nan to schedule weekend
     study session
Wash soccer uniform
Return library books
If Time: Check Internet for info
     for bio essay

Wed. TO-DO List

Finish Algebra p 115
Health Review Ch 7
Finish Biology Essay
Start History Outline
Look over Problem of Week
Read Pigman
Shop for Bob's present

Get Your Assignments Organized

You can't do a very good job of an assignment if you don't have a clue about what it is. You can't possibly do the assignment well if you don't understand the things you're studying. So, if you want to get smarter, get clear and organized about assignments. It takes 7 simple steps to do this:

1. Listen to the assignment.

2. Write it down in an assignment notebook.
   (Make sure you write down the due date.)

3. If you don't understand the assignment—ASK.
   (Do not leave the classroom without knowing what it is you are supposed to do.)

4. If you don't understand the material well enough to do the assignment—TALK to the teacher. *(Tell him or her that you need help getting it clear.)*

5. Take the assignment book home every day.

6. Transfer assignments to your weekly or monthly schedule at home.

7. Look at your assignment book every day.

Date	Subject	Assignment	Due Date
2/2	English	Read The Pigman	2/12
		Grammar Ex p 78-79	2/5
		Grammar Quiz	2/7
	Algebra	Unit 5 review. p 112	2/5
		Test on Unit 5	2/6
	Science	Essay on Cells & Diagram	2/8
	History	Outline-Colonial Life	2/9
	Health	Nutrition Poster	2/5
2/5	Spanish	2-paragraph story about a bus trip	2/7
	Health	Ch 7 Review Questions	2/8
	History	Timeline and Maps of the American Revolution	2/15
2/6	English	Report on The Pigman	2/14

Get Ready Tip # 6
Don't count on anyone else to listen to the assignment and get it down right. Get the assignment yourself. Find a reliable classmate to get assignments when you are absent—or contact the teacher directly.

Get Yourself Organized

Okay, so your schedule is on the wall—all neat and clear. Your study space is organized. Your study supplies are organized. You have written down all your assignments, and you've got all your lists made. Great! But do you feel rushed, frenzied, or hassled? Take some time to think about the behaviors that will help YOU feel as organized as your stuff and your schedule.

Before you leave school . . .

STOP—take a few calm, unrushed minutes to think about what books and supplies you will need at home for studying. ALWAYS take the assignment notebook home.

When you get home . . .

FIRST—put your school bag in the same spot every day, out of the way of the bustle of your family's activities.

STOP—after relaxing, or after dinner, take a few calm, unrushed minutes to look over your schedule and review what needs to be done. Review your list for the day. Plan your evening study time and set priorities. Don't wait until it is late or you are very tired.

Before you go to bed . . .

STOP—take a few calm, unrushed minutes to look over the assignment notebook and the to-do list for the next day one more time. Make sure everything is completed.

THEN—put everything you need for the next day IN the book bag. Don't wait until morning. Make sure you have all the right books and notebooks in the bag. Make sure your finished work is all in the bag. Also, pack other stuff (for gym, sports, etc) at the same time. Put everything in one consistent place, so you don't have to rush around looking for it.

In the morning . . .

STOP—take a few calm, unrushed minutes to think and review the day one more time.

THEN—eat a good breakfast.

Terri finally finished her autobiography. She worked on it for a week. She typed it perfectly. She added great photos of her life. She created a great cover and chose a smashing title. It looks fantastic. And it's due today.
Terri remembers her lunch and her gym bag.
She remembers the comic books she promised to bring to her friend Sheri.
Oh, Terri, what did you forget?

Get Ready Tip # 7
It doesn't do much good to get your homework done if you don't turn it in.

23

Get Healthy

If you are sick, or tired, or droopy, or angry, or nervous, or weak, or miserable, it is very hard to be a good student. It is hard to even use or show what you already know. Your physical and mental health is a basic MUST for doing as well as you would like to in school. So, don't ignore your health. Pay attention to how you feel. No one else can do that for you.

Get plenty of rest

If you're tired, nothing else works very well in your life. You can't think, concentrate, or pay attention, learn, remember, or study. Try to get 7 or 8 hours of sleep every night. Get plenty of rest on weekends. If you have a long evening of study ahead, take a short nap after school.

Eat well

You can't learn or function well on an empty stomach. And all that junk food (soda, sweets, chips, snacks) actually will make you more tired. Plus, it crowds the healthy foods out of your diet—the foods your brain needs to think well and your body needs to get through the day with energy. So eat a balanced diet, with lean meat, whole grains, vegetables, fruit and dairy products. Oh, and drink a lot of water—8 glasses a day is good.

Exercise

Everything in your body works better when your body gets a chance to move. Make sure your life does not get too sedentary. Do something every day to get exercise—walk, play a sport, play a game, or run. It's a good idea to get some exercise before you sit down to study, too. Exercise helps you relax, unwind, and de-stress. It's good for stimulating your brain.

Relax

Your body and your mind need rest. Do something every day to relax. Take breaks during your study time and do anything that helps you unwind.

Find Relief for Stress

Pay attention to signs of anxiety and stress. Are you nervous, worried, angry, sad? Are your muscles tense, your stomach in a knot? Is your head aching? Are you over-eating or have you lost your appetite? All these are signs of stress that can lower your success in school and interfere with your life. If you notice these signs, find a way to de-stress. Exercise and adequate rest are good for stress relief. You also might try these: stretch, take a hot bath, take a nice long shower, laugh, listen to calming music, write in a journal. If you're burdened with worries, anger, or problems, talk to someone—a good friend, or a teacher or parent or other trusted adult.

── Get a Grip (on Study Habits) ──→

Here's some good advice for getting set to improve your study habits. Check up on yourself to see how you do with each of these tips. Then set goals where you need to improve.

. . . in school:

1. Go to class.
You can't learn anything in a class if you are not there.
Go to all your classes. Show up on time.
Take your book, your notebook, your pencil and other supplies.

2. Choose your seat wisely.
Sit where you won't be distracted. Avoid people with whom you'll be tempted to chat.
Stay away from the back row. Sit where you can see and hear.

3. Pay attention.
Get everything you can out of each class.
Listen. Stay awake.
Your assignments will be easier
if you've really been present in the class.

4. Take notes.
Write down main points. If you hear it AND write it, you'll be likely to remember it.
(See pages 56-57 for note-taking advice.)

5. Ask questions.
It's the teacher's job to see that you understand the material. It's your job to ask if you don't.

6. Use your time in class.
Get as much as possible of the next day's assignment finished before you leave the class.

7. Write down assignments.
Do not leave class until you understand the assignment and have it written down clearly.

8. Turn in your homework.
If you turn in every homework assignment, you are a long way toward doing well in a class—even if you struggle with tests.

Top 10 Tips for Success
(for getting better grades)

1. Get enough rest.
2. Write down your assignments.
3. Go to class (and be on time).
4. Take notes.
5. Pay attention in class.
6. Turn off the TV.
7. Do your homework.
8. Turn in your homework.
9. Don't procrastinate.
10. Ask for help.

Better Grades & Higher Test Scores / READING & LANGUAGE
Copyright ©2003 by Incentive Publications, Inc., Nashville, TN.

Get Ready: Study Habits

. . . at home:

9. Gather your supplies.

Before you sit down to study, get all the stuff together that you'll need: assignment book, notebook, notes, textbook, study guides, paper, pencils, etc. Think ahead so that you have supplies for long-term projects. Bring those home from school or shop for those well in advance.

10. Avoid distractions.

Think of all the things that keep you from concentrating. Figure out ways to remove those from your life during study time. In other words, make a commitment to keep your study time uninterrupted. If you listen to music while studying, choose music that can be in the background, not the foreground of your mind.

11. Turn off the TV.

No matter how much you insist otherwise, you cannot study well with the TV on. Plan your TV time before or after study time.

12. Make phone calls later.

Plan a time for phone calls. Like TV watching, phoning does not mix with focusing on studies. The best way to avoid this distraction is to study in a room with no phone. Call your friends when your work is finished.

13. Hide the computer games.

Stay away from video games, computer games, email, and Internet surfing. Plan time for these when studies are complete, or before you settle into serious study time.

14. Know where you're going.

Review your weekly schedule and your assignment notebook. Be sure about what it is that needs to be done. Make a clear *To-Do* list for each day, so you will know what to study. Post notes on your wall, your refrigerator, or anywhere that will remind you about what things you need to get done!

15. Plan your time.

Think about the time you have to work each night. Make a timeline for yourself. Estimate how much time each task will take, and set some deadlines. This will keep your attention from wandering and keep you focused on the task.

16. Start early.

Start early in the evening. Don't wait until 10:00 P.M. to get underway on any assignment. When it's possible, start the day before or a few days before.

17. Do the hardest tasks first.

It's a good idea to do the hardest and most important tasks first. This keeps you from avoiding procrastination on the tough assignments. Also, you'll be doing the harder stuff when your mind is the most fresh. Study for tests and do hard problems early, when your brain is fresh. Do routine tasks later in the evening.

18. Break up long assignments.

Big projects, major papers, or test preparations can be overwhelming. Break each long task down into smaller ones, then take one small task at a time. This will make the long assignments far less intimidating, and you'll have more success more often. Never try to do a long assignment all in one sitting.

19. Take breaks.

Plan a break for your body and mind every 30-45 minutes. Get up, walk around, stretch, or do something active or relaxing; however, avoid getting caught up in any long phone conversations or TV shows. You'll never get back to the studying!

20. Cut out the excuses.

It's perfectly normal to want to avoid doing school work. Just about everybody has a whole list of techniques for work avoidance. And the excuses people give for putting off or ignoring it are so numerous, they could fill a whole book.

Excuses just take up your energy. In the time you waste convincing yourself or anyone else that you have a good reason for avoiding your studies, you could be getting some of the work done. If you want to be a better student, you'll need to dump your own list of excuses.

NO MORE EXCUSES

27

21. Plan ahead for long-range assignments.

Start early on long-range assignments, big projects, and test preparations. Don't wait until the night before anything is due. You never know what will happen that last day. You could be distracted, sick, or unexpectedly derailed. Get going on long tasks a long time before due date. Make a list of everything that needs to be done for a long-range assignment (including finding references and collecting supplies). Start from the due-date and work backwards. Make a timeline or schedule that sets a time to do each of the tasks on the list.

22. Don't get behind.

Keeping up is good. Many students slip into failure, stress, and hopelessness because they get behind. The best way to avoid all of these is—NOT to get behind. This means DO your assignments on time. If you DO get behind because of illness or something else unavoidable, do something about it. Don't get further and further into the pit! Talk to the teacher. Make a plan for catching up.

23. Get on top of problems.

Don't let small problems develop into big ones. If you are lost in a class, missed an assignment, don't understand something, or have done poorly on something—act quickly. Talk to the teacher, ask a parent to help, find another student who has the information. Do something to correct the problem before it becomes monumental.

24. Ask for help.

You don't have to solve every problem alone or learn everything by yourself. Don't count on someone noticing that you need help. Tell them. Use the adults and services around you to ask for help when you need it.

25. Reward yourself for accomplishments.

If you break your assignments down into manageable tasks, you'll have more successes more often. Congratulate and reward yourself for each task accomplished—by taking a break, getting some popcorn, bragging about what you've done to someone—or any other way you discover. Every accomplishment is worth celebrating!

GET SET →

Get Sharp with Thinking Skills

Your brain is capable of an amazing variety of accomplishments!
There are different levels and kinds of thinking—all of them necessary
to get you set for effective studying. Review these thinking skills.
Pay attention to what's possible for your mind. Then use this information
to freshen up your mental flexibility and put these skills to use as you learn
and study.

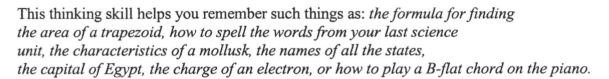

Recall – To **recall** is to know and remember specific facts, names, processes, categories, ideas, generalizations, theories, or information.

This thinking skill helps you remember such things as: *the formula for finding the area of a trapezoid, how to spell the words from your last science unit, the characteristics of a mollusk, the names of all the states, the capital of Egypt, the charge of an electron, or how to play a B-flat chord on the piano.*

Classify – To **classify** is to put things into categories. When you classify ideas, topics, or things, choose categories that fit the purpose and clearly define each category.

> ***Albania, Algeria, Angola, Afghanistan, Andorra, Armenia, Austria, Azerbaijan, Australia***
>
> These are countries that begin with *A*. *(helpful category for purposes of an alphabetizing exercise)*
>
> They are also countries that are in the eastern hemisphere. *(helpful category for a geography exercise)*

Generalize – To **generalize** is to make a broad statement about a topic based on observations or facts. A generalization should be based on plenty of evidence (facts, observations, and examples). Just one exception can prove a generalization false.

Safe Generalization:

Weather usually varies more from season to season in countries at higher latitudes than in countries at lower latitudes.

Invalid generalizations:

faulty generalization - A faulty generalization is invalid because there are exceptions.

High school students love sports and movies.

broad generalization - A broad generalization suggests something is *always* or *never* true about *all* or *none* of the members of a group. Most broad generalizations are untrue.

Teenagers always dress in sloppy, baggy clothes.

stereotypes - A stereotype describes an individual member of a group or the whole group of people with a generalization. Stereotype generalizations are invalid because people are individuals and have individual differences, no matter what group they belong to.

Children in large families suffer from lack of proper attention.
Russians hate America and French citizens are rude.

Better Grades & Higher Test Scores / READING & LANGUAGE
Copyright ©2003 by Incentive Publications, Inc., Nashville, TN.

Thinking skills are rarely used in isolation from one another. For instance, in order to predict, you'll need to make inferences.

Elaborate

Elaborate - To **elaborate** is to provide details about a situation (to explain, compare, or give examples).

When you elaborate, you might use phrases such as these: *so, because, however, but, an example of this is, on the other hand, as a result, in addition, moreover, for instance, such as, if you recall, furthermore, another reason is.*

The pizza was terrible because it was cold and soggy. To make matters worse, the sausage was rancid and the cheese smelled rotten. It tasted even lousier than the nachos.

Predict

Predict - To **predict** is to make a statement about what will happen.

Because the pizza is so lousy, Antonio's pizza shop will lose customers.

Infer

Infer - To **infer** is to make a logical guess based on information. Often writers give information and descriptions in stories and let the reader infer something about the characters or plot.

Someone reads a story wherein the writer tells these things:

1. *Jake has gone into the woods searching for his dog.*
2. *The night is pitch-black and Jake's flashlight has burned out.*
3. *Jake has taken many confusing twists and turns through the woods.*
4. *Jake's heart is pounding wildly.*

The reader infers that *Jake is lost and scared.*

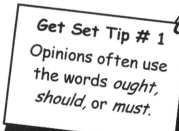

Get Set Tip # 1
Opinions often use the words *ought*, *should*, or *must*.

Distinguish Fact from Opinion

Distinguish Fact from Opinion - A **fact** is a statement that can be proven to be true.

An **opinion** is a statement that expresses personal attitudes or beliefs. Many opinions tell what a person believes or wishes should be so. It is not always easy to tell the difference between fact and opinion. Good thinkers will analyze statements carefully in order to keep from accepting opinions as fact.

During playing time, each football team is allowed to have eleven players on the field. (Fact)
The players on the Cougars' team are smarter than those on the Chargers' squad. (Opinion)
The Chargers should practice harder. (Opinion)
Next year, the Chargers will win more games than the Cougars. (Opinion)

31

Recognize Cause & Effect -
When one event occurs as the result of another event, there is a **cause-effect relationship** between the two.

Recognizing causes and effects takes skill. When reading, pay careful attention to words that give clues to cause and effect (*the reason was, because, as a result, consequently*). Some effects have several causes. Some causes lead to several effects.

Because he thought he was being followed, the man was jumpy and acted strangely.
(cause)   (effect)   (effect)

The reason he thought he was being followed was that he'd received frightening calls.
(effect)   (cause)

Hypothesize -
To **hypothesize** is to make an educated guess about a cause or effect.

A hypothesis is based on examples that support it but do not prove it. A hypothesis is something that can be—and should be—tested.

Very few of the people who ride the new roller coaster, The Black Phantom, get sick.

Extend -
To **extend** is to connect ideas or things together, or to relate one thing to something different, or to apply one idea or understanding to another situation.

You are extending when. . .

. . . *you read a poem about rain and it increases your appreciation of the next rainstorm.*

. . . *you learn the characteristics of insects, then find "bugs" that you realize are not insects.*

. . . *you recognize a character's fear in a story and identify emotionally with the character because it reminds you of a time when you were afraid.*

Compare & Contrast -
When you **compare** things, you describe the similarities. When you **contrast** things, you describe their differences.

The poems are both odes. Both are written to a show the writer's passion about someone or something. "Ode to a Lost Friend," is written to a person. It is somber and sentimental. In contrast, "Ode to My Eraser," is written to an object. It is surprising and frivolous.

Identify Bias -
A **bias** is a one-sided attitude toward something. Biased thinking does not result from facts, but from feelings or attitudes. Learn to look for bias—as biased information may not be reliable especially if it's presented as fact or nonfiction.

I would never shop at a second-hand store. The merchandise is unsanitary and of very poor quality.

Draw Conclusions - A **conclusion** is a general statement that someone makes after analyzing examples and details.

A conclusion generally involves an explanation someone has developed through reasoning.

> *Todd notices a man on the street in a trench coat with the collar turned up high covering his chin and ears. The man is wearing sunglasses and a hat pulled down over much of his face. As Todd watches, the man stops often and waits in doorways, furtively looking around. He buys a newspaper and stops every few minutes, holding the newspaper up, but peeking over the top.*
>
> *Todd concludes that the man is afraid that someone is following him.*

Analyze - To **analyze**, you must break something down into parts and determine how the parts are related to each other and how they are related to the whole.

For instance, you must analyze to . . .

. . . solve an equation.

. . . outline a passage.

. . . edit a piece of writing for proper sequence.

. . . divide an essay into paragraphs.

. . . examine an argument and decide if it is a good one.

> Ah, ha!
> I get it, now.
> I need to analyze the facts and synthesize them into the perfect report.

Synthesize - To **synthesize,** you must combine ideas or elements to create a whole.

For instance, you must synthesize to . . .

compose a poem from thoughts you've gathered.

combine facts you've researched into a timeline.

coordinate schedules in your family.

put effective diagrams, tables, and graphs into a report.

Evaluate

To **evaluate** is to make a judgment about something.

Evaluations should be based on evidence. Evaluations include opinions, but these opinions should be supported or explained by examples, experiences, observations, and other forms of evidence.

When you evaluate an argument, a position, a piece of literature or other writing, an advertisement, a performance, or a media presentation, ask questions like these:

- *Are the conclusions reached based on good examples and facts?*
- *Are the sources reliable?*
- *How effective is the argument?*

- *Is this believable?*
- *Does it make sense?*
- *Is the writer biased?*
- *Is it realistic?*

Better Grades & Higher Test Scores / READING & LANGUAGE
Copyright ©2003 by Incentive Publications, Inc., Nashville, TN.

Get Set: Thinking Skills

Inductive Reasoning

You use inductive reasoning when you reason from specific facts or examples to come up with a generalization.

The Smyth family has a dog. Their next door neighbors, the Allantras, have two dogs. The Jansens across the street have a dog.

Therefore, all the Smyth's neighbors have dogs.

Deductive Reasoning

You use deductive reasoning when you use a generalization as a basis for making statements about a specific situation.

All the families on the Smyth's block have at least one dog.

So the Allantras and the Jansens, who live in the Smyth's neighborhood, must have dogs.

Logical Thinking (or Reasoning) –

When you think **logically**, you take a statement or situation apart. You use **inductive** or **deductive reasoning** to examine the details that support a conclusion, or the generalization that leads to specific details.

Mom was the first person to come home at the end of the day. If she found the door unlocked, and Sam was the last one to leave the house in the morning, then Sam did not lock the door.

Identify Faulty Arguments –

An **argument** is **faulty** when it is based on an error in logic. This means the information is misleading, or there are exceptions to the statement, or the statement is not supported by evidence.

Once you see that movie, you'll want to become a mountain climber.

Any business that does not display a flag has owners that are unpatriotic.

People who have a lot of money are very happy.

(See also the faulty argument in the Inductive Reasoning example above.)

Identify Propaganda –

Propaganda is a form of communication intended to make listeners or readers agree with the ideas of a group. Unlike ordinary persuasive writing, propaganda often focuses on an appeal to emotions. Propaganda often uses faulty arguments, exaggeration, or information that distorts or confuses the truth.

To identify propaganda, look for faulty arguments, exaggeration, appeal to emotions, manipulation of facts, manipulation of emotions, or unsupported claims.

During Tom Gates' first term as governor, two convicted criminals committed murders while on parole. Do not re-elect Tom Gates; he's soft on crime.

A DIVERGENT THINKER IS...

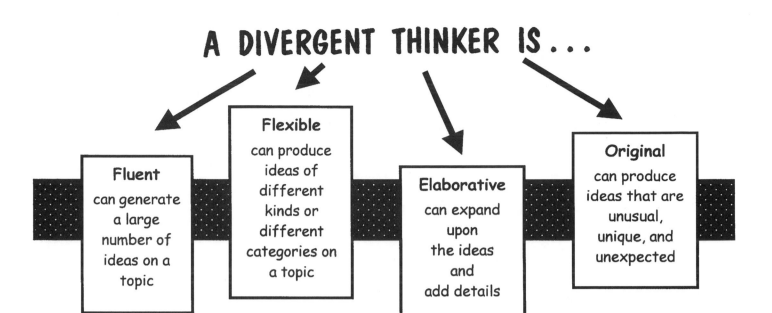

Fluent
can generate a large number of ideas on a topic

Flexible
can produce ideas of different kinds or different categories on a topic

Elaborative
can expand upon the ideas and add details

Original
can produce ideas that are unusual, unique, and unexpected

BLOOM'S TAXONOMY
(Levels of cognitive thinking from easiest to most complex)

1. **Knowledge** - remembering of specific facts and previously-learned information
   Knowledge is used to identify, label, match, name, describe, recall, reproduce, state.

2. **Comprehension** - understanding of the meaning of information
   Comprehension is used to classify, describe, discuss, explain, generalize, summarize, give examples.

3. **Application** - using previously learned information in new and real-life situations to solve problems that have single or best answers
   Application is used to collect, assess, discover, extend, implement, predict, produce, relate, show, demonstrate, teach.

4. **Analysis** - breaking down of information into parts and determining how the parts are related to each other and how they are related to the whole
   Analysis is used to distinguish, discriminate, infer, differentiate, illustrate, separate.

5. **Synthesis** - applying prior knowledge to create a new or original whole
   Synthesis is used to adapt, compare, contrast, create, communicate, integrate, modify, rearrange, revise, formulate, generate, compose, combine, integrate, plan.

6. **Evaluation** - judging the value of material based on personal values/opinions
   Evaluation is used to draw conclusions, judge, interpret, criticize, draw conclusions, decide, defend.

35

Get Brushed-Up on Information Skills

If you're going to get set to be a good student, you need sharp skills for finding and using information. You're fortunate to live in a time and place of almost unlimited resources for finding information. You can only make use of those resources well if you know what they are, and what's in them. Here's a quick review of some of the most common sources of information available for students. Get to know these references well.

Which Reference is Which?

Almanac: a yearly publication that gives information, basic facts, and statistics on many topics. Almanacs are organized with lists of information by topics. They have an alphabetical index. Much of the information is about current or recent years, but some of it is historical. Almanacs cover current events, famous people, sports, countries, geographic records, and many other categories. They usually have an index which lists information by categories.

Atlas: a book of maps. Atlases give geographical information in the forms of maps, table, graphs, and lists. They include information about geography—including population, climate, weather, elevation, vegetation, regions, topics, topography, and much more. Some maps in atlases show political information such as countries and cities.

Bibliography: a list of books, articles, and/or other resources about a certain topic. Often a bibliography is found at the end of a book or article, giving a list of the sources used in the publication.

Biographical Dictionary or Reference: a book that gives a brief summary of the lives and accomplishments of famous persons. Entries are listed alphabetically. *Contemporary Authors, The Dictionary of American Biography*, and *Who's Who in America* are examples of this kind of reference.

Dictionary: a book that lists the standard words of a particular language alphabetically, and gives their meanings and pronunciations. Many dictionaries also provide other information about the word, such as part of speech, uses, antonyms, and etymologies.

Special Dictionaries: dictionaries of words related to one subject only. There are many special dictionaries, listing such things as slang, scientific terms, historical terms, geographical features, biography, foreign words, or abbreviations.

Glossary: a listing of the important terms used in a specific book or article. A glossary is arranged alphabetically and generally located at the end of the book or article.

---

pedestal

page 599

physical

pedestal \'pe-dəs-tl\ *n* the base of an upright structure

peruse \pə-'rūz\ *v* to examine or consider in detail

pervasive \pər-'vā-siv\ *adj* that goes throughout

pesky \'pes-kē\ *adj* troublesome

peso \'pā-sō\ *n pl* pesos [*Sp.* weight] an old silver coin of Spain and Spanish America

pessimism \'pe-sə-mi-zəm\ *n* a tendency to emphasize adverse aspects, conditions, or possibilities, or to expect the worse

pesto \'pes-tõ\ *n* [*It., Fr.* pounded] a sauce made of ingredients pounded or pressed together, especially garlic, oil, pine nuts, and cheese

petite \pə-'tēt\ *adj* [*Fr.* small] having a small trim figure

petit fours \pe-tē-' fõrz\ *n* [*Fr.* small oven] a small cake cut from pound or sponge cake and frosted

pet-napping \'pet-na-ping\ *n* the act of stealing a pet, usually for profit

petrify \'pe—trə-fi\ *v* 1. to convert into stone or a stony substance 2. to make rigid or lifeless 3. to frighten

Some information you could gain from these dictionary entries:

Pedestal, peso, pessimism, pesto, petit fours and *pet-napping* are nouns.

Persuade and *petrify* are verbs.

Pesky and *petite* are adjectives.

In *petite*, the accent is on the second syllable.

Petrify has a least three different meanings.

The plural of *peso* is *pesos*.

Petit fours and *petite* are words borrowed from the French language.

In French and Italian, *pesto* means *pounded*.

Get Set Tip # 2
Guide words are a great help in using dictionaries and glossaries. All the words on a page fall alphabetically between the two guide words. Brush up your skills with guide words!

Better Grades & Higher Test Scores / READING & LANGUAGE
Copyright ©2003 by Incentive Publications, Inc., Nashville, TN.

Get Set: Information Skills

Encyclopedias: a set of books providing information on many branches of knowledge. Usually there are many volumes. Information is presented in the form of articles, and consists of a survey of the topic. The information is arranged alphabetically according to the topic or name of person, place, or event. It is best to use key words to search for a topic in an encyclopedia.

Special Encyclopedias: There are many encyclopedias that contain information about one subject rather than about many subjects (as are found in regular encyclopedias). Individual volume encyclopedias or whole sets cover such topics as science, art, music, history, and sports. Don't miss this one: *The Encyclopedia of American Facts and Dates.*

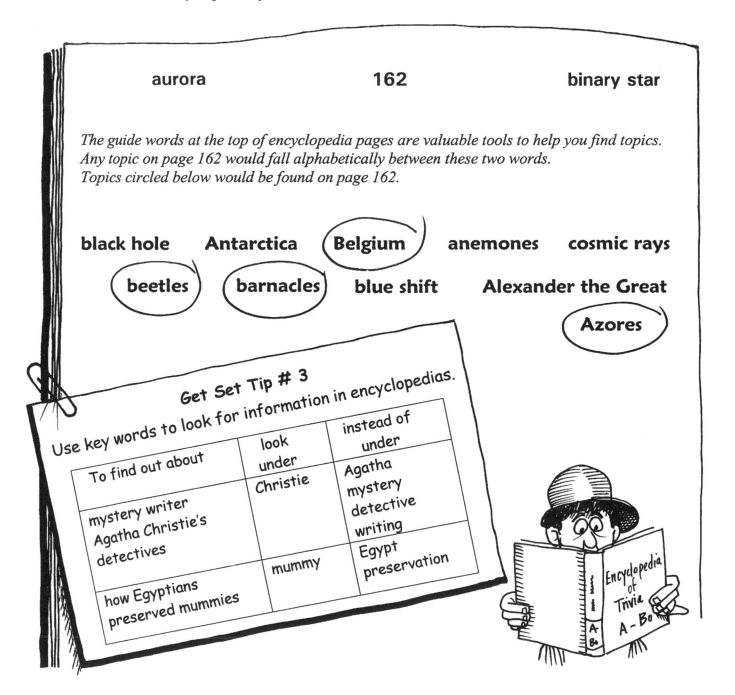

| aurora | 162 | binary star |

The guide words at the top of encyclopedia pages are valuable tools to help you find topics. Any topic on page 162 would fall alphabetically between these two words. Topics circled below would be found on page 162.

black hole   Antarctica   Belgium   anemones   cosmic rays

beetles   barnacles   blue shift   Alexander the Great

Azores

Get Set Tip # 3

Use key words to look for information in encyclopedias.

To find out about	look under	instead of under
mystery writer Agatha Christie's detectives	Christie	Agatha mystery detective writing
how Egyptians preserved mummies	mummy	Egypt preservation

Famous First Facts: a book that lists facts about firsts (first happenings, discoveries, and inventions) of many kinds in America, listed alphabetically. There is also an international version.

Gazetteer: a geographical dictionary, listing information about important places in the world. Subjects and places are listed alphabetically.

Guinness World Records: a collection of information about the best and worst, most and least, biggest and smallest, longest and shortest, and other facts and records

Index: a list of information or items found in a book, magazine, set of books, set of magazine, or other publications. The index is generally located at the end of the resource. Information is listed alphabetically.

Sometimes a resource has an index that is a separate book. A specific magazine or journal sometimes has its own index, as do most encyclopedia sets. For instance, to find articles and information that appear in the National Geographic, you would consult a *National Geographic Index* volume instead of looking in the back of each magazine. To find the volume and page location of information in a set of encyclopedias, you would consult the encyclopedia index accompanying the encyclopedia set. When a reference is on CD or online, a CD or online index accompanies the reference.

Internet: an extensive computer network that holds a huge amount of information from organizations and groups around the world as well as government agencies, libraries, schools, universities, educational organizations, and businesses. Information can be located by browsing through categories and sites assembled by your Internet service provider and by searching the web with the help of a good search engine. The Internet can connect you to information on a vast number of topics related to all sorts of subject areas.

Get Set
Tip # 4

When you find a site that gives good information, add it to your list of favorites (or bookmark it) so you can get there quickly next time.

MAXIE'S FAVORITE
SEARCH ENGINES
webcrawler.com
google.com
ask.com
hotbot.com
yahoo.com
yahooligans.com
dogpile.com

39

Library Card Catalog: a file of cards that has three cards for every book in the library. These cards are filed separately. There is an author card, which is filed alphabetically by the author's last name; a subject card, which is filed alphabetically according to the subject of the book, and a title card, which is filed alphabetically according to the title of the book. In many libraries, card catalog information is now found on computers.

Library Computer Catalog: a computer file of author, title, and subject listings for all books (and other materials) in a library.

Periodicals: publications that are issued at regular intervals, such as daily, weekly, monthly, quarterly, or annually. Magazines, newspapers, and scholarly journals are types of periodicals. Periodicals are an excellent source of current news and information.

Periodical Index: a book or computer database that lists the subjects and titles of articles in a particular magazine or newspaper, or a particular group of magazines or newspapers.

Newspapers: a valuable periodical published frequently, containing current information on national, international and local news. Newspapers also provide a wealth of information on sports, financial information, book reviews, editorial comments, reviews of film, theater and other entertainment events. Other features such as classified ads, comics, puzzles, TV-radio-movie listings, restaurant reviews, recipes, and horoscopes add to the list of information available in newspapers.

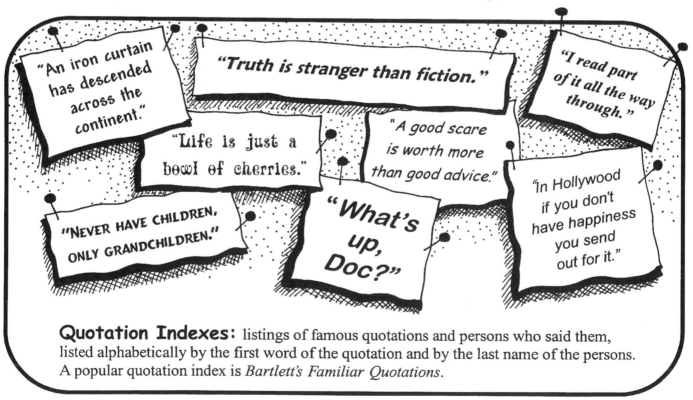

"An iron curtain has descended across the continent."

"Truth is stranger than fiction."

"I read part of it all the way through."

"Life is just a bowl of cherries."

"A good scare is worth more than good advice."

"In Hollywood if you don't have happiness you send out for it."

"NEVER HAVE CHILDREN, ONLY GRANDCHILDREN."

"What's up, Doc?"

Quotation Indexes: listings of famous quotations and persons who said them, listed alphabetically by the first word of the quotation and by the last name of the persons. A popular quotation index is *Bartlett's Familiar Quotations*.

Better Grades & Higher Test Scores / READING & LANGUAGE
Copyright ©2003 by Incentive Publications, Inc., Nashville, TN.

Table of Contents: an outline of the information contained in a book, listed in order that the information occurs in the book.

The Table of Contents is found at the beginning of the book.

Thesaurus: a reference book that groups synonyms or words with similar meanings. A thesaurus is sometimes organized by idea or theme with an alphabetical index. Other versions organize the words like a dictionary. Some thesaurus editions contain antonyms as well as synonyms.

Yearbook: a book that gives up-to-date information about recent events or findings, or that reviews events of a particular year. One such yearbook is the *World Book Yearbook of Facts*. Many encyclopedia sets publish a yearbook to update the set each year. This reduces the need to update the entire set to keep information current.

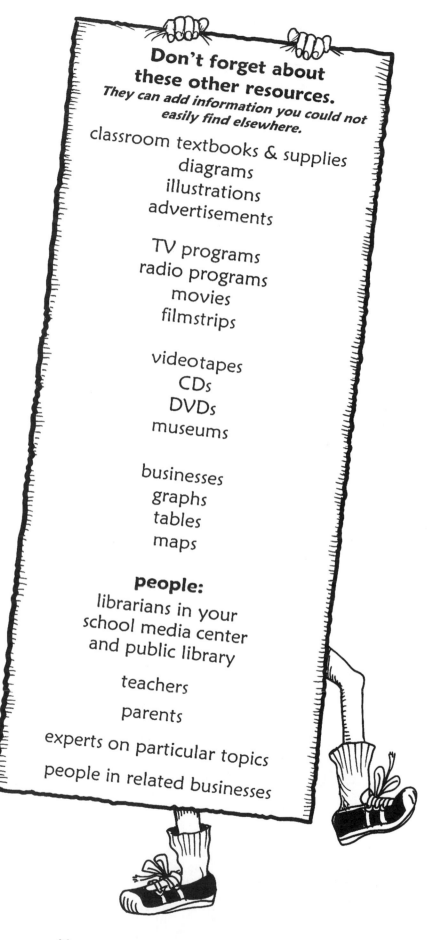

Don't forget about these other resources.
They can add information you could not easily find elsewhere.

classroom textbooks & supplies
diagrams
illustrations
advertisements

TV programs
radio programs
movies
filmstrips

videotapes
CDs
DVDs
museums

businesses
graphs
tables
maps

people:
librarians in your school media center and public library

teachers

parents

experts on particular topics

people in related businesses

Get Set: Information Skills

How the Library is Organized

When you're getting set to be a better student, you may need to brush up on your library skills. How well do you know your way around the library? Here's a review of your library's organization. Every book in a library has a unique number called a *call number*. These numbers are used to organize the books. The call number is on the spine of each book. Most school libraries and public libraries use the Dewey Decimal System as a classification system for nonfiction books.

How Nonfiction is Organized

The Dewey Decimal System has ten major subject area divisions. (See the chart below.) Nonfiction books are grouped by subject. Each subject and subdivision of the subject has a decimal number. Letters from the last name of the author also are a part of the call number.

The Dewey Decimal System

000-099 General Works References	**300-399** Social Sciences	**700-799** Fine Arts Sports
100-199 Philosophy Psychology	**400-499** Language	**800-899** Literature
	500-599 Pure Science Mathematics	
200-299 Religion	**600-699** Uses of Science Technology	**900-999** History Geography Biography

How Biographies are Organized

Biographies are nonfiction books, so they are classified as a part of the Dewey Decimal System. Within the 900 section of the Dewey Decimal System, biographies and autobiographies are organized according to the name of the person who is the subject of the biography. These last names are organized alphabetically. The author's name is not a part of the organization.

Here is a sample of call numbers and organization of some biographies.

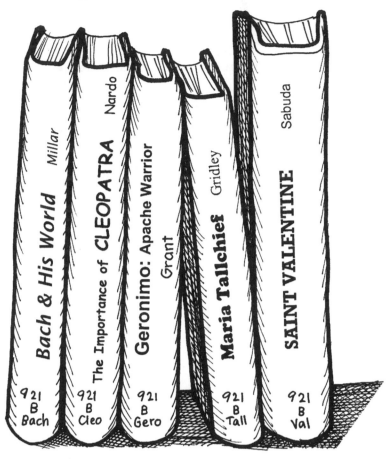

How Fiction is Organized

Fiction is organized according to the authors of the books. Fiction books are shelved alphabetically by the last name of the author. If there are authors with the same last names, then the first name comes into use as a part of the organization. If there is more than one book by an author, then the books are organized within that author's section by title, alphabetically. *(In titles beginning with articles such as a, an, or the, the article is dropped when alphabetizing.)*

The call number consists of the letter **F** and some letters from the author's last name.

Better Grades & Higher Test Scores / READING & LANGUAGE
Copyright ©2003 by Incentive Publications, Inc., Nashville, TN.

Get Set: Information Skills

Finding Information in the Library

A **library card catalog** contains three cards for each book in the library—a **subject** card, a **title** card, and an **author** card. The cards are alphabetized by subject, first main word in the title, and last name of the author.

When you look for a book in the library, look under the title or author if you know either of these. Otherwise, search for the subject you want to research.

Each card shows the call number so you can locate the book. In addition, the card shows quite a bit of information about each book: author, title, illustrator, publisher, copyright date, number of pages, and whether the book has illustrations.

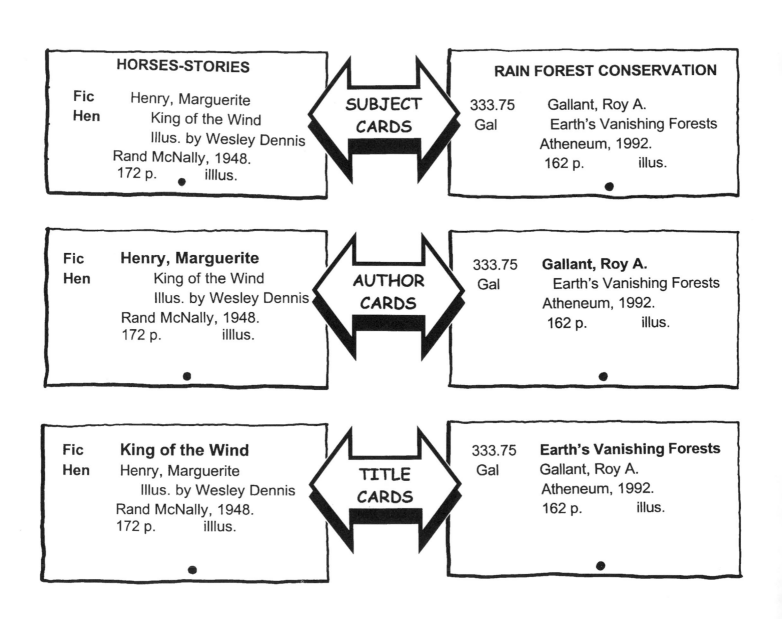

HORSES-STORIES	**RAIN FOREST CONSERVATION**
Fic Hen — Henry, Marguerite / King of the Wind / Illus. by Wesley Dennis / Rand McNally, 1948. / 172 p. illlus.	333.75 Gal — Gallant, Roy A. / Earth's Vanishing Forests / Atheneum, 1992. / 162 p. illus.

SUBJECT CARDS

Fic Hen — **Henry, Marguerite** / King of the Wind / Illus. by Wesley Dennis / Rand McNally, 1948. / 172 p. illlus.	333.75 Gal — **Gallant, Roy A.** / Earth's Vanishing Forests / Atheneum, 1992. / 162 p. illus.

AUTHOR CARDS

Fic Hen — **King of the Wind** / Henry, Marguerite / Illus. by Wesley Dennis / Rand McNally, 1948. / 172 p. illlus.	333.75 Gal — **Earth's Vanishing Forests** / Gallant, Roy A. / Atheneum, 1992. / 162 p. illus.

TITLE CARDS

Many libraries list all the materials held on a **computer system**. The computer catalog holds the same information as the card catalog. You can search for a book on the computer system by doing a title search, an author search, or a subject search. You can type in a key word (or more than one word) to a title or subject search to find books that have that word in the title.

In many libraries, the computer screen also will tell you if the library has the book on the shelf or when it will be available.

SPORTS-ANECDOTES

796 **Not So Great Moments in Sports**
Pe   By Pellowski, Michael
        Illus. by Myron Miller
        N.Y.: Sterling Pub Co, 1994
        95 p.   illlus.

I want to do research on the life of Sandra Day O'Connor, my role model.

- Do a subject search. Type in **O'Connor.** You'll get a list of books about her.

Dude, I need to find something on the subject of asteroids.

- Do a subject search. Type in **asteroids.** You'll get a list of books on the topic. If this yields nothing, type in **space.**

I'm looking for a collection of poems by John Ciardi.

- Do an author search. Type in **Ciardi, John.** You'll see a listing of his books.

I'm looking for a book called, **Earthworms, Dirt, and Rotten Leaves.**

- Do a title search. Type in the whole title. You'll find the book if the library has it.

I want to find the **Dictionary of Imaginary Places.**

- Do a title search. Type in the whole title.

I can't remember the title of a book I want, but I know the word danger is in the title.

Do a title search. Type in the word **Danger.** You'll get a list of books with **Danger** in the title. Scan the list to see if you find the one you wanted.

Finding Information on the Internet

It's a skill to use the Internet well for finding reliable information. It takes practice. Here's some good advice for smart use of the Internet.

Browse—Your Internet provider gathers pages on general topics. These give you quick access to information on several of the most popular topics, such as news, weather, health travel, music, and sports. Most providers also offer quick links to kids' pages and reference materials.

Search—For a more advanced search, use a good search engine such as google.com or yahoo.com. Try different engines until you find your favorite. To use a search engine, type in a key word (such as *snowboarding*). To make your search more specific, type in a phrase (such as *snowboarding records*) or more than one word connected by AND (*snowboarding* AND *Olympics*).

Good Questions to Ask About a Web Site

- *Is it clear who sponsors the page?*
- *Is the sponsor an established organization?*
- *Is there useful information?*
- *Are sources given for the facts?*
- *Does the author appear to be qualified?*
- *Is the material and site up to date?*
- *Is the material easy to use and understand?*

Be selective—Use your time wisely to get the best information by choosing reputable sites. Sites from the government, established companies or organizations, and universities are usually reliable (Examples: National Hockey League www.nhl.com; Field Museum www.fmnh.org; NASA www.nasa.gov; National Geographic for Kids www.nationalgeographic.com/kids/).

Be smart—Learn to evaluate the websites you visit, and don't waste time on sites that won't yield information that is reliable or in-depth enough.

Be cautious—If you download information, beware of viruses. Download information only from sites that seem reputable. If you are going to download software, it is safest to do it directly from the company that publishes the software. Be very careful what you download from individuals. Never open an email or download a file unless you know the source of the document. Keep a good anti-virus program on your computer. Keep the program updated.

Be safe—NEVER give away any personal information on the Internet.

Internet Terms to Know

bookmark – a shortcut option that allows you to get to a site without typing in the address

BPS – *(bits per second)* – how fast information moves from one place to another

browser – a software tool that is used to view sites on the Internet

chatting – "talking" with other people on the Internet (usually by typing)

chat rooms *(or chat groups)* – addresses online where many people can talk to each other

cookie – little bits of text or code that a web server leaves on your computer to track information about your personal preferences

cyberspace – refers to all the resources available on the Internet

domain name – the name that identifies an Internet site

download – to copy files or programs or information from Internet sites

email – *(electronic mail)* – mail that is sent over the Internet between persons

GIF – *(graphics interchange format)* – graphics format frequently used in Internet programs

hacker – a person very skilled with computers and Internet use, who is therefore able to get into computer programs

HTML – *(hyper-text mark-up language)* – the computer code used to create web pages

hyperlink – addresses, words, or graphics that are inserted into documents on the World Wide Web (A click on the link leads to another web page.)

That's a Good Question!

When should I NOT use the Internet to get information?

ANSWER:
Stay OFF the web when you can get the same information faster with a walk to your bookshelf!

hypertext – a word or group of words that form a hyperlink

ISP – *(Internet service provider)* – a company that sells connections to the Internet

keyword – a word that is typed into a search engine

login or logon – to connect to the Internet

logoff – to disconnect from the Internet

mailbox – a place where the ISP keeps email for a user

netiquette – suggested guidelines for good online behavior by Internet users

net surfing – visiting sites on the Internet

offline – not connected to the Internet

online – connected to the Internet

post – to place a message in a newsgroup or discussion group

search – to explore the Internet for information on a specific topic

search engine – program that searches for Web pages that contain specific words

server – a computer that provides an Internet service to clients

SPAM - *(sending particularly annoying messages)* - junk email or postings in discussion groups

upload – to send files or information from your computer to another computer, usually through a modem or higher-speed connection

URL – *(universal resource locator)* – the address for an Internet location

Web page – a computer document written in HTML code, placed for Internet access

Website – a collection of Web pages set up by a person, group, or organization

— 47 —

Listening for Information

Keep your ears wide open! You can gain a great amount of information if you know how to listen well—to a speech, lecture, explanation, tape, TV program, or reading. Here are some tips for smart listening. They can help you get involved in the listening process so that you take in more good information through your ears.

1. Appreciate the Value

You listen for information to get

. . . details.
. . . instructions.
. . . directions.
. . . facts.
. . . examples.
. . . hazards.

You listen for understanding to
. . . be able to discuss what you heard.
. . . be able to process what you heard.
. . . be able to relate it to your own experience.
. . . be able to test what you heard.

2. Recognize the Obstacles

Tiredness
Surrounding noise
Uncomfortable setting
Personal concerns, thoughts, or worries
Wandering attention
Too many things to hear at once
Missing the beginning
Missing the end
Talking (yourself)
Speaker talks too fast
Speaker's presentation is expressionless

3. Make a Commitment to Improve

You can't always control all obstacles (such as the comfort of the setting or the quality of the speaker's presentation), but there are things you can control.

Put these to work to gain more from your listening:
. . . Get enough rest.
. . . Do your best to be comfortable while you listen.
. . . Cut out as many distractions as possible.
. . . Keep your mind focused on what is being said.
. . . Look directly at the speaker.
. . . Take notes.
. . . As the speaker talks, think of examples or relate the information to your life.
. . . Don't miss the beginning or ending.
. . . Pay special attention to opening and closing remarks.
. . . Pay special attention to anything that is repeated.
. . . As soon as possible after listening, summarize what you have heard.
. . . Write the summary into your notes.

Get Set
Tip # 5
Stop talking!
(You can't listen while you talk.)

Reading for Information

To find information in written passages, you need to make use of many different reading skills. Some information can be gained quickly, by scanning or skimming a list, definition, description, or other passage. To get other kinds of information, you need to give a close reading, paying attention to each detail. Before you read a passage, get clear about the purpose of your reading. How much detail do you need to get?

An urgent call came into the *Discreet Inquiries Detective Agency* at 6:30 P.M. "My business is ruined!" screamed the agitated caller. "Help! Mice! There are mice everywhere! They are falling from the sky!"

Detective Cici Sharp calmed the troubled restaurant owner to get the story. This is what the detective learned. Just at the height of the busy dinner hour at the elegant *Les Manages* restaurant, dozens of mice floated down from the sky wearing tiny parachutes. A red shoelace fastened a parachute to each mouse. The mice landed on the outdoor dining patio of the restaurant, then began racing around the floor and across the tables.

Les Manages is located next to a pet shop. The restaurant owner, Patrice, explained that he had recently filed a suit against the pet shop because the odors from the shop harmed his restaurant's business. Then Patrice went back to frenetically describing the incident: "They just came out of nowhere. We heard no airplanes. We saw nothing in the sky. I was just serving cream of leek soup to a large group of guests. All of a sudden, a hundred tiny red parachutes were overhead. We heard squeaking. Then they landed. One mouse landed in a customer's soup. The mice started eating the salads. They were so disgusting. All my guests ran away screaming." Frantically waving his arms, he added, "What shall I do? No one will ever come back to my restaurant!"

Skimming

By skimming the passage, the reader can quickly gain the main ideas of the passage:

Mice parachuted into a restaurant, frightening away the customers.

The frantic restaurant owner called in a detective agency for help.

There had been some issue between the restaurant owner and the pet shop next door.

Close Reading

With a closer, slower reading, the reader will discover such specific details as:

the time of the call for help
the name of the detective
the name of the agency
the name of the restaurant
an approximate number of mice
where the mice landed
how the parachutes were fastened
the nature of the disagreement with the pet shop
what the guests were eating
what the mice ate

Get Serious about Study Skills

Let's face it—good learning and good grades don't happen without some sharp study skills. Take advantage of every opportunity you get to strengthen skills like the ones described on pages 50-66.

Summarizing & Paraphrasing

WHAT'S THE DIFFERENCE?

Hey sis, what's the difference between a **summary** and a **paraphrase**?

A **paraphrase** is a restatement of someone else's ideas in your own words.

A **summary** is a short statement of the main ideas of a speech or piece of writing.

The concert was sold out months ago. Everybody in the city was wild about the hot new group, *Gravity*. We were so lucky to get tickets.

The big night finally arrived. And, oh, what a disappointment! This was not what we expected for the amount of money we spent. First of all, the seats were much farther from the stage than we had been told by the ticket agent. We were so high up in the arena that we were experiencing a shortage of oxygen. Then the concert started two hours late. (This time was not added onto the end.) However, the concert was so awful, who could have stood it another two hours anyway? The sound system screeched the whole time. The group sang off tune. The leader, G.G. Force, was in a terrible mood. He sang badly, and in between songs, he complained about the weather, the arena, and our city. He scolded the crowd for not cheering loud enough. The group never even sang their big hit song, "Leaving the Planet". No wonder they're called *Gravity*—their performance is such a ***letdown***!

— Summary: —

We had looked forward for months to the Gravity concert, but everything about the concert was a huge disappointment, and it certainly was not worth the money.

— Paraphrase: —

We were fortunate to get tickets for the Gravity concert, because the concert was a sell-out. The concert was not nearly as good as we expected, especially considering the cost of the tickets. The seats were high and far from the stage. Besides starting late, the concert was really bad and Gravity never even sang their biggest hit. Everything about it was poor: the singing, the sound quality, and the mood of the leader. He insulted the crowd and criticized the city. Maybe the band is called Gravity because they're so <u>down</u>-right lousy.

BACKWOODS REVIEW
Friday, April 28

Bigfoot

An ape-like creature reported to live in the Pacific Northwest. Sasquatch, as the Canadians call it, has been reported most often in the mountainous regions of California, Oregon, Washington, and British Columbia. Stories about Bigfoot are similar to those told about the Abominable Snowman of the Himalayan Mountains in central and northeast Asia.

Hundreds of people have reported seeing Bigfoot, or its footprints. The creature is described as ape-like, standing upright, from 7-10 feet tall, and weighing more than 500 pounds. It has thick fur, powerful arms and shoulders, and a short neck. Its footprints measure about 16 inches long by 6 inches wide.

Most scientists are not convinced of Bigfoot's existence. Many believe that some of the evidence, including the footprints and photos, is fake.

Somebody *doubts* my existence?

Summary:

There have been many reported sightings of a large ape-like creature called Bigfoot (or Sasquatch) in the Pacific Northwest. There is uncertainty about the existence of Bigfoot, with some skeptics believing that any "evidence" such as photos or footprints, are phony.

Paraphrase:

Bigfoot, or Sasquatch (as named by Canadians) is a large creature reportedly sighted in the mountains of the Pacific Northwest United States. The stories of Bigfoot are somewhat akin to the legend of the Yeti, a creature supposedly living in mountains of Asia. There have been numerous reports about seeing the Sasquatch or finding footprints. According to the stories, Bigfoot is a 500-pound, 7-10 foot tall upright creature with heavy fur and strong shoulders and arms. Claims have been made of footprints that measure as long as 16 inches and as wide as 6 inches.

The existence of Bigfoot is disbelieved by most scientists. The evidence of its existence, such as footprints or photographs, is also suspect.

Get Set: Study Skills

Outlining

An outline is a way to organize ideas or information into main ideas and sub-ideas (or supporting details). If you want to get set to improve as a student, it's a good idea to polish your outlining skills. You will find outlining very helpful for many study situations.

You can use an outline to

· organize ideas to prepare a speech
· organize ideas for a piece of writing
· plan a project
· record and review information from a textbook
· get ready to re-tell a story
· take notes in class
· take notes from a textbook assignment
· prepare to give or write a report
· write a story
· write a speech
· study a passage

An outline can be formal or informal. It can contain single words, phrases, or sentences, depending on its purpose.

I'm going to use this outline to plan steps for a project that I'll be starting soon.

Starting a Detective Business

I. Decide on details of the business
  A. Clarify business purpose
  B. Choose specialty and type of client
  C. Choose name and location
  D. Decide on number/kind of employees

II. Look into supplies and costs
  A. Look for supplies
    1. Office supplies and furniture
    2. Clothing, disguises
    3. Cameras, surveillance equipment
  B. Make a price/cost list
    1. Office supplies and equipment
    2. Detecting supplies and equipment
    3. Personnel and expenses
  C. Make a budget

III. Learn about detecting
  A. Read books
  B. Search the Internet
  C. Interview other detectives and agencies
    1. Getting clients
    2. Getting information, tracking
    3. Surveillance
    4. Problems and risks

IV. Develop system
  A. Getting clients
  B. Assigning cases
  C. Gathering information
  D. Keeping records on cases

V. Set up business
  A. Advertise
  B. Phone, utilities
  C. Office hours
  D. Office signs

FINAL REPORT: MY CASES
by Student Detective Maxie Sharp

I.   Introduction
    A. Number of cases over time period
    B. Kinds of cases; time spent
    C. Summary of four major cases

II.   The Surf Shop Swindle
    A. Description of the Swindle
    B. Interviews with surfers
    C. Catching the Swindler
       1. How we caught the impostor
       2. Where we found the money

III. The Case of the Stolen Bagels
    A. The doughy crime scene
    B. Following the cream cheese tracks
    C. Catching the hungry thieves

IV.   The Piggy Bank Robbery
    A. Clues about the crime
       1. Fingerprints on the broken china
       2. Coins in the suspect's pockets
    B. Questioning the suspect
    C. The arrest

V.   The Case of the Missing Boa Constrictor
    A. Snake on the loose
    B. Report of snake sightings
    C. Capturing the snake
    D. Catching the culprit

VI.   What I learned
    A. Tracking; surveillance
       1. Following suspects
       2. Listening and watching
    B. New skills
       1. Internet detecting
       2. Patience
       3. Library research

I'll use this outline to get organized for a writing assignment. This report will summarize my cases from my training and tell what I learned from the experience.

How to Track a Suspect

1. **Learn about the suspect**
   --*Favorite places*
   --*Daily schedules*
   --*Daily routes and routines*
2. **Make a plan for following**
   --*The stake-out places*
   --*Timeline*
3. **Getting ready**
   --*Disguises, clothing*
     --*Wig*
     --*Trench coat*
     --*Dark glasses*
   --*Equipment*
     --*Camera*
     --*Tape recorder*
     --*Listening devices*

4. **Following**
   --*Starting the tracking*
   --*Keeping a low profile*
   --*Using equipment*
     --*Taking pictures*
     --*Eavesdropping*
   --*What to do
      if discovered*
   ---*When to give up*
   ---*Keeping yourself safe*
5. **Keeping records**
   --*Things to note*
   --*Timeline*
   --*Final report*

Here I used a casual outline to organize main points and details I'll cover when making a speech.

This outline was created to organize facts I gathered from my research. Later, I will do further study on each piece of information to expand the facts into a presentation on famous mystery writers.

Mystery Writers

I. Mystery Writers
  A. Early (1841-1900)
    1. Edgar Allen Poe
    2. Charles Dickens
    3. Wilke Collins
    4. Arthur Conan Doyle
  B. Early 1900s
    1. R. Austin Freeman
    2. Agatha Christie
    3. Dashiell Hammett
    4. G. K. Chesterton
    5. Ellery Queen
    6. Dorothy Sayers
    7. Raymond Chandler
  C. Recent
    1. British
     a. Anne Perry
     b. Dick Francis
     c. P.D. James
     d. Elizabeth George
     e. James McClure
    2. American
     a. Sue Grafton
     b. Tony Hillerman
     c. Ross MacDonald
     d. Sara Paretsky
     e. Robert B. Parker
     f. Martha Grimes
     g. Mickey Spillane
II. Styles of Stories
  A. Detective story
  B. Inverted detective story
  C. "Hard-boiled" mystery

54

The 1920s

I. America after the war
    A. Election of 1920
        1. 19th amendment—women had right to vote
        2. large voter turnout
        3. victory of Harding
    B. Foreign policy
        1. 5-Power Naval Treaty promised battleship constructions
        2. Open Door Policy—9 nations assured rights to trade with China
        3. Post-war isolationist mood
    C. Mood—Issues in the nation
        1. Wave of labor strikes
        2. Red Scare, Palmer Raids—fear of communism
        3. Revival of Ku Klux Klan, discrimination, race riots
        4. New immigration laws to slow flow of immigrants
            a. Emergency Quota Act
            b. National Origins Act
        5. Sacco-Vanzetti Case—result of xenophobia
        6. Prohibition—18th Amendment
        7. Growing fundamentalist movement
II. Roaring Twenties
    A. Jazz Age
    B. Cultural revitalization in Harlem
    C. Golden Age of Sports
    D. Rise in popularity of motion pictures
    E. Radio becomes giant industry
III. The Automobile Civilization
    A. Ford mass-produces car
    B. Rise of automobile leads to economic boom
    C. Expansion of road building and tourism
    D. Auto allows move to suburbs
    E. Increase in traffic and air pollution
    F. Rapid use of oil reserves

I wrote this outline as I read a section from my history textbook.

Doing the outline helped me find the main points in the assignment.

Writing the outline also helped me process and remember the information.

Taking Notes

A study skill of major importance is knowing how to take notes well and use them effectively. Good notes from classes and from reading are valuable resources to anyone who's trying to do well as a student. A lot of learning goes on while you're taking notes—you may not even realize it's happening!

Here's the basic process for taking notes:

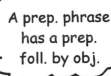

> I've got three details for each main idea.

> A prep. phrase has a prep. foll. by obj.

| 1. Write notes in formal or casual outline form. | 2. Listen for a main idea. Write it down. | 3. Indent and write examples and details given to support each main idea. | 4. Use abbreviations or shortened forms for common words. |

Here's what is happening when you take notes:

1. When you take notes, you naturally listen better. (You have to listen to get the information to write it down!)

2. When you listen for the purpose of taking notes, you naturally learn and understand the material better. Taking notes forces you to focus on what's being said or read.

3. When you sort through the information and decide what to write, you naturally think about the material and process it—making it more likely that you'll remember it.

4. The actual act of writing the notes fixes the information more firmly in your brain.

5. Having good notes in your notebook makes it possible for you to review and remember the material.

Tips for Wise Note-Taking

from a speech or lecture . . .

- Have a notebook or a notebook section for each subject.

- When the speech or lecture begins, write the topic at the top of a clean page.

- Write the date and the subject at the top before the speech or lecture begins.

- Only take notes on one side of the paper.

- Use an erasable pen for clear notes, not a pencil.

- Write neatly so you can read it later.

- Leave sizable margins to the left of the outline.

- Use these spaces to star important items or write key words.

- Leave blank space after each main idea section.

- Pay close attention to the opening and closing remarks.

- Listen more than you write.

**Get Set
Tip # 7**

When you take notes from a lecture, be alert for signals from the teacher about important ideas. Write down anything the speaker (or teacher)...
...writes on the board.
...gives as a definition.
...emphasizes with his/her voice.
...repeats.
...says is important.

from a textbook assignment . . .

- Skim through one section at a time to get the general idea (a few paragraphs or use the textbook divisions). Then go back and write down the main ideas.

- For each main idea write a few supporting details or examples.

- Notice bold or emphasized words or phrases. Write these down with definitions.

- Read captions under pictures. Pay attention to facts, tables, charts, graphs and pictures, and the explanations that go along with them. Put information in your notes if it is very important.

- Don't write too little. You won't have all the main points or enough examples.

- Don't write too much. You won't have time or interest in reviewing the notes.

Better Grades & Higher Test Scores / READING & LANGUAGE
Copyright ©2003 by Incentive Publications, Inc., Nashville, TN.

Get Set: Study Skills

Preparing a Report

Reports—they're everywhere! Students are always being asked to do a report of some kind. When you hear the word, you might immediately think of a book report or a long written paper. But the world of reports is far broader than this. There are all kinds of reports. They can be papers, posters, demonstrations, speeches, audio or visual presentations, computer projects or art projects—to name a few. They can be assigned for any subject area to cover just about any topic.

Whatever the subject or the type of report—they all have some things in common. First, you need some raw material (facts and information) as the basis for the report. To get that, you need to do some research. Then, for any report, you must select and organize the information so that it can be communicated (or reported!). Finally, a report is presented. This means you need to find a way to share with someone else what you learned about the topic.

Here are some steps to follow for any report of any kind on any topic. Page 61 gives some suggestions for creative or out-of-the ordinary kinds of reports. This will get you thinking beyond the standard written report. (For help with written reports, see pages 164-166.)

Step 1   Choose a topic

Your topic might be assigned, but usually the student has some choice. There are generally dozens of possibilities within any one subject or topic.

If you do have a choice. . .

A. Pick something that interests you.

B. Make sure your topic is not too broad. If it is, there will be too much information to manage.

C. Make sure your topic is not too narrow. If it is, you won't be able to find enough information to create a substantial report.

> **Too Broad**: Structure and Topics of Poems
> **Too Narrow**: Limericks about France
> **Just Right**: Structure and Topics of Some Short Poetry

Short Poems

Couplet
—Structure
—Rhyme
—Usual subjects
Haiku
—Structure
—Rhyme
—Usual subjects
Limerick
—Structure
—Rhyme
—Usual Subjects

Cinquain
—Structure
—Rhyme
—Usual subjects
Diamante
—Structure
—Rhyme
—Usual subjects
Ode
—Structure
—Usual subjects
OTHER

Step 2   Identify the subtopics

Make a list of the subtopics.

Then, for each subtopic, note information you'll need to find out that will support or explain that subtopic.

What do you need to know about the topic?

What categories are natural divisions for this topic?

You might use a rough outline for this step.

58

Step 3 Find information

Use as many resources as you can to find solid information on your topic. Don't limit yourself to just one source or one kind of source. (See pages 36-41.)

As you observe, listen to, or read the sources, take notes. Write ideas, key words or phrases, and examples. Use a separate note card for each source and each major idea or fact you find.

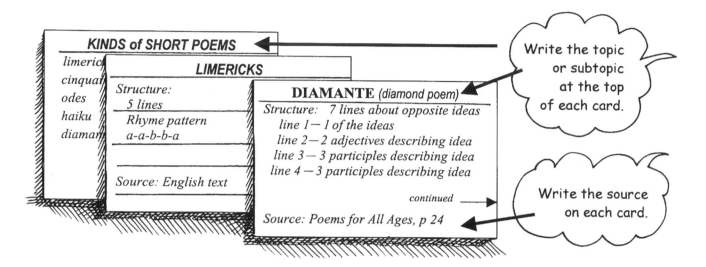

Step 4 Organize the information

Organize the information by grouping your cards into subtopics and placing them in a logical sequence. Decide what fits where.

If you have too much, or if some information doesn't quite fit, this is the time to eliminate some.

If you have subtopics that are not well supported with examples or details, this is the time to do more research and collect more information.

Step 5 Decide on the format

If you've been asked to write a paper or give a speech, then the format is already decided.

If you are free to choose a format or product, do this now.

How will you show what you have learned? Will it be a paper, a speech, a demonstration, a dance, a musical production, a broadcast, an interview, a painting, a slide show, a mime?

Decide now! The steps you follow from this point on depend greatly on the format you choose.

Step 6 Begin to put the report together

If your report will be spoken or written, you'll begin writing sentences and paragraphs, making sure each paragraph covers a subtopic with supporting details.

If your report follows a different format, you still need to decide how to communicate each idea and its supporting examples or details.

Get Set: Study Skills

Step 7   Review and edit your work

This is the time to look at your work. This is also a time to ask someone else to give a response. (Exactly how you review the work will depend on the format of the report.)

Ask questions such as this about the "rough draft" of your report, whatever form it takes:

Are the main ideas covered?

Is the information clear?

Is the information complete?

Does the manner of presentation make sense?

Does the report have a clear introduction and conclusion?

Is there a logical order for the presentation?

Is the material interesting? Is the presentation interesting?

If written, does the piece flow along well?

If written, are the mechanics and grammar correct?

After you and another person (or persons) have reviewed it, make revisions that are necessary.

> **Get Set Tip # 8**
> Avoid these common problems with reports:
> • Topic too broad
> • Topic too narrow
> • Missing some subtopics
> • Not enough information on some subtopics
> • Poor presentation of final product

Step 8   Put the final product together

Whatever the format, this is the time to prepare the final product. Add extra materials at this time too (drawings, diagrams, lists, charts, maps, graphs, time lines, tables, surveys).

Step 9   Present the report

How will you share the information? **Turn it in? Hang it up? Sing it? Dance it? Show it? Read it? Perform it? Mail it? Publish it?** This is the time to do it!

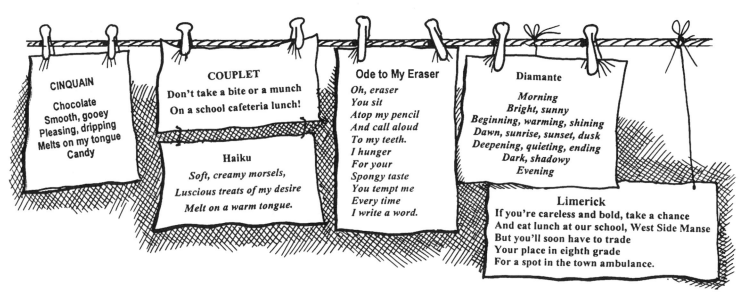

CINQUAIN

Chocolate
Smooth, gooey
Pleasing, dripping
Melts on my tongue
Candy

COUPLET

Don't take a bite or a munch
On a school cafeteria lunch!

Haiku

Soft, creamy morsels,
Luscious treats of my desire
Melt on a warm tongue.

Ode to My Eraser

Oh, eraser
You sit
Atop my pencil
And call aloud
To my teeth.
I hunger
For your
Spongy taste
You tempt me
Every time
I write a word.

Diamante

Morning
Bright, sunny
Beginning, warming, shining
Dawn, sunrise, sunset, dusk
Deepening, quieting, ending
Dark, shadowy
Evening

Limerick

If you're careless and bold, take a chance
And eat lunch at our school, West Side Manse
But you'll soon have to trade
Your place in eighth grade
For a spot in the town ambulance.

Creative Reporting

When you think about a **report**, think about the many ways a report can be structured and shared. It might take a little creativity (or a lot), but nearly any body of information can be presented in a number of different or unexpected ways. Here are just a few options for preparing and giving a report.

Reports that Combine Writing & Art

- children's picture book
- advertisement
- an original CD
- travel brochure
- a map
- cartoons
- time line
- game
- a book cover
- a music album cover
- an original song
- slide presentation
- instructive poster
- How-To Handbook
- A Guide Book to _____
- collage of pictures and words
- illustrated dictionary of terms

Other Reports

- mime performance
- painting or drawing
- sculpture
- dance
- demonstration
- model
- scavenger hunt
- drama

Written or Spoken Reports

- viewpoint (or different viewpoint)
- cause-effect account
- group of short poems

- letter
- editorial
- diary
- narrative poem
- photo essay
- a protest
- a dialogue
- an argument

- interview questions
- radio broadcast
- series of riddles

- a book of crossword puzzles
- clues to unravel a mystery
- words & phrases cut from magazines
- fictionalized account of an event

- The Fact Book About _____
- The ABC Book of _____
- event told as a news report
- A Top 10 List of _____

- 10 Facts & 10 Fables About _____
- A Day In the Life of _____
- The Truth About _____
- Myths About _____ Debunked

- 20 Questions & Answers About _____
- Strange & Amazing Facts About _____
- Future Predictions About _____

Get Set: Study Skills

How to Prepare for a Test

Good test preparation does not begin the night before the test.

The time to get ready for a test starts long before this night.

Here are some tips to help you get ready —weeks before the test and right up to test time.

1. **Start your test preparation at the beginning of the year— or at least as soon as the material is first taught in the class.**

   The purpose of a test is to give a picture of what you are learning in the class. Learning doesn't start 12 hours before the test. It starts when you start attending the class. Think of test preparation this way, and you'll be able to be less overwhelmed or anxious about an upcoming test.

   You'll be much better prepared for a test *(even one that is several days or weeks away)* if you . . .

   Get Set
   Tip # 9
   Don't wait until the last minute to study for a test.

   - *pay attention in class*
   - *take good notes*
   - *keep your notes and class handouts organized*
   - *read all your assignments*
   - *do your homework regularly*
   - *make up any work you miss when you're absent*
   - *ask questions in class about anything you don't understand*
   - *review notes and handouts regularly*

2. **Once you know the date of the test, make a study plan.**

   Look over your schedule and plan time to start organizing and reviewing material.

   Allow plenty of time to go through all the material.

   Your brain will retain more if you review it a few times and spread the studying out over several days.

   Ooooohhh, I should have paid attention in class!

3. **Get all the information you can about the test.**

   Write down everything the teacher says about the test.

   Get clear about what material will be covered.

   If you can, find out about the format of the test.

   Get any study guides the teacher distributes.

   Make sure you listen well to any in-class reviews.

4. Use your study time effectively.

Don't:	Do:
spend your study time blankly staring at your notebook or mindlessly leafing through your textbook	gather and organize all the notes and handouts you have
	review your text, paying attention to bold words and statements
	review the questions at the end of text sections; practice answering them
study with someone else unless that person actually helps you learn material better	review your notes, using a highlighter to emphasize important points
	review the study guides provided by the teacher
study in blocks of time so long that you get tired, bored, or distracted	review any previous quizzes on the same material
	predict the questions that may be asked; think about how you would answer them
	make a list of important points with brief reminders about each one
	make sets of cards with key vocabulary words, terms and definitions, main concepts, or other brief bits of information you need to remember
	ask someone (reliable) to quiz you on the main points and terms

5. Get yourself and your supplies ready.

Do these things the night before the test (not too late):

Gather all the supplies you need for taking the test (good pencils with erasers, erasable pens, scratch paper). Put these supplies in your school bag.

Gather your study guides, notes, and text into your school bag.

Get a good night of rest.

In the morning:

Eat a healthy breakfast.

Look over your study guides and note card reminders.

Relax and be confident that your preparation will pay off.

Get Set: Study Skills

How to Take a Test

Before the test begins

Try to get a little exercise before class to help you relax.

Go to the bathroom and get a drink.

Arrive at the class on time (or a bit early).

Get settled into your seat; get your supplies out.

If there's time, you might glance over your study guides while you wait.

To relax, take some deep breaths; exhale slowly.

When you get the test

Put your name on all pages.

Before you write anything, scan over the test to see how long it is, what kinds of questions it has, and generally what it includes.

Think about your time and quickly plan how much time you can spend on each section.

Read each set of directions twice.

Circle key words in the directions.

Answer all the short-answer questions. Do not leave any blanks.

If you are not sure of an answer, make a smart guess.

Don't change an answer unless you are absolutely sure it is wrong.

Get Set Tip # 10

Research shows that your first answer is correct more often than not! So stick with it unless you are sure you know the right answer.

Max is not sure of the answer. So he makes a smart guess. He puts an **X** by the question so he will remember to come back to it later.

When he comes back to the question, he is still not sure, so he stays with his first answer.

More Test-Taking Tips

Tips for Answering Multiple Choice Questions

Multiple choice questions give you several answers from which to choose.

Read the question through.

Before you look at the choices, close your eyes and answer the question. Then look for that answer.

Read all the choices through before you circle an answer.

If you are not absolutely sure, cross out answers that are obviously incorrect.

Choose the answer that is most complete or most accurate.

If you are not absolutely sure, choose one of the answers that has not been ruled out.

Do not change an answer unless you are absolutely sure of the correct answer.

Tips for Answering Matching Questions

Matching questions ask you to recognize facts or definitions in one column that match facts, definitions, or descriptions in a second column.

Read through both columns to familiarize yourself with the choices.

Do the easy matches first.

Cross off answers as you use them.

Match the left-over items last.

If you don't know the answer, make a smart guess.

Get Set
Tip # 11
On all questions, on any test—
always read the directions through twice.

Tips for Answering Fill-in-the Blank Questions

Fill-in-the-blank questions ask you to write a word that completes the sentence.

Read through each question. Answer it the best you can.

If you don't know an answer, mark the question with an **X**. Go on to answer the ones you know.

Go back to the questions you marked with **X**. If you don't know the exact answer, write a similar word or definition. Come as close as you can to the correct answer.

If you have no idea of the answer, make a smart guess.

Tips for Answering True-False Questions

True-false questions ask you to tell whether a statement is true or false.

Watch for words like *most, some,* and *often.* Usually statements with these words are TRUE.

Watch for words like *all, always, only, none, nobody,* and *never.* Usually statements with these words are FALSE.

If any part of a statement is false, then the item is FALSE.

Get Set: Study Skills

Even More Test-Taking Tips

Tips for Solving Analogies

An **analogy question** asks you to choose an answer by finding the relationship between a pair of words.

This symbol **:** in an analogy means *is to*. This symbol **::** means *as*.

glove : hand :: sock : _____

a. fingers   **b. shoe**   **c. toes**   **d. foot**

So the above analogy reads: glove is to hand as sock is to _____

First, you must establish the relationship between the first two words.

Try to state a sentence that relates the words: *A glove is a fabric item that covers the hand.*

Second, find the word that shows the same relationship between the second pair.

Try to finish a similar sentence about the other word: *A sock is a fabric item that covers the ___.*

Tips for Answering Reading Comprehension Tests

Reading comprehension tests ask you to read a piece of writing and answer questions about it.

Read through the questions before you read the passage.

Keep the questions in mind as you read the passage.

Read each question carefully.

Skim back through the passage to look for key words that are related to the question.

Re-read that section carefully.

Eliminate any answers that cannot be correct.

Choose the correct answer.

Tips for Answering Essay Questions

Essay questions ask you to write a short answer (usually a few paragraphs) about a subject.

Make sure you are clear about what the question is asking.

Think ahead to your answer. Sketch out a rough outline of the main points you will make and details supporting each point.

Write an introduction which briefly states a summarized version of your answer.

Write a body that states the main ideas clearly.

Reinforce each main idea with details and examples.

Write a summarizing sentence that restates the main idea.

GET SHARP →

in

GRAMMAR, USAGE, MECHANICS, and SPELLING

Nouns

A noun is a word that names a person, place, thing, or idea.

common noun - any noun which does not name a specific person, place, thing, or idea

    persons*: brother, governor, clowns, violinist, baker, gymnast, plumber*

    places: *wilderness, circus, street, park, school, garage, cities, kitchen, subway*

    things: *motorcycle, pancreas, measles, skateboard, tortilla, crutches*

    ideas: *truth, compassion, freedom, honesty, immaturity, confusion, evil*

proper noun - the name of a specific person, place, thing, or idea
Grandma Wiggles, Lake Superior, Golden Gate Bridge, Times Square, Goofy

concrete noun - names a thing that is tangible or physical (can be touched or seen)
ukulele, sister, hamburger, computer, writers, aardvark, sidewalk

abstract noun - names something you can think about but cannot see or touch
superiority, love, poverty, progress, pride, fear, democracy, friendship

compound noun - made up of two or more words, two words, or hyphenated words
football, jellybean, high school, maid of honor, father-in-law, seventh-graders

collective noun - names a collection of persons, animals, places, or things
team, tribe, herd, flock, jury, committee, United Nations, orchestra, bunch, gang

singular noun - names one person, place, thing, or idea
fingernail, fox, veto, goose, knife, city, tooth, alto, jealousy

plural noun - names more than one person, place, thing, or idea
fingernails, foxes, vetoes, geese, knives, cities, teeth, altos, jealousies

Nouns have gender, you know.

Get outta here!

It's true!

female – bridesmaid, aunt, actress, doe, hostess

male – rooster, brother, fireman, bull, actor

neutral – gymnasium, lottery, avenue, appendicitis

indefinite – gorilla, president, dentist, lamb, conductor

Get Sharp: Grammar Guide

Better Grades & Higher Test Scores / READING & LANGUAGE
Copyright ©2003 by Incentive Publications, Inc., Nashville, TN.

Nouns are grouped into one of three cases. The **case** of a noun tells how it is related to the other words in the sentence. Here's how to tell which case is which:

nominative case - A noun is in the nominative case when it is used as the subject of the verb.

*Yesterday, a rare **diamond** disappeared right out of a locked vault.*

*Right after the incident, numerous **detectives** came running.*

*How did the **culprit** manage to get away with the diamond?*

possessive case - A noun is in the possessive case when it shows possession or ownership.

*How many people knew the **vault's** combination?*

*So far, the **diamond's** true value has been kept a secret.*

*News reporters were anxious to hear the **detectives'** stories.*

objective case - A noun is in the objective case when it is used as the direct object, the indirect object, or the object of the preposition.

*Detective Snoop interviewed three **suspects**. (direct object)*

*Miss Quiche brought the **investigators** lunch. (indirect object)*

*She gave the biggest burrito to her **boss**. (object of a preposition)*

Be positive about appositives!

An **appositive** is a noun placed next to another noun or pronoun to add information about it. An appositive may be a noun alone, or it may have other words that modify it.

*Slim Slipperyfingers, **the renowned diamond thief,** was not in town this week.*

*No one knows the whereabouts of his partner **Lefty**.*

*The detectives got a lucky break, an **anonymous tip**.*

*The lead detective, **Sgt. Scrutiny**, was optimistic about solving the case.*

Get Sharp Tip # 1
Commas are used to set most appositives off from the rest of the sentence. If the appositive is essential to the meaning of the sentence, commas are not needed. *Detective Sgt. Scrutiny was the one who followed up on all the leads.*

69

---

13 Rules for Forming Plural Nouns

1. Add **s** to the singular form of most nouns.

2. Add **s** to most nouns that *end in o preceded by a vowel.*
radios, rodeos, stereos, studios

3. Add **s** to most musical terms that *end in o.*
pianos, altos, sopranos, cellos, banjos

4. Add **s** to most nouns that *end in y preceded by a vowel.*
keys, monkeys, donkeys, valleys

5. Add **s** to proper nouns that *end in y.*
O'Gradys, Savoys, Barrys

6. Add **s** to most nouns that *end in f or fe where the final f sound is still heard in the plural.*
safes, hoofs, chiefs, beliefs

7. Add **s** to the end of nouns that *end in ful.*
pailfuls, tankfuls, tablespoonfuls

8. Add **s** to the most important word in a *compound word or hyphenated word.*
commanders-in-chief, Secretaries of State, sisters-in-law, great-aunts

9. Add **es** to nouns which *end in ch, sh, s, x, or z.*
churches, lunches, bushes, foxes, buses, messes, buzzes

10. Add **es** to many nouns that *end in o preceded by a consonant.*
echoes, heroes, tomatoes, tornadoes

11. Add **es** to most nouns that *end in y preceded by a consonant.* *(Change the y to i.)*
flies, pennies, diaries, cities, fairies

12. Add **es** to nouns that *end in f or fe where the final sound becomes a v sound.*
wives, knives, leaves, calves

13. Add **'s** to *symbols, letters, figures, and words described as words.*
D's, 9's, +'s, x's; She counted the *hello's* in the dialogue.

4 Rule Breakers for Plural Nouns

1. Some plurals are formed by irregular spelling changes.
women, teeth, geese, mice, children, cacti, oxen

2. Some nouns have the same singular and plural forms.
deer, sheep, buffalo, antelope

3. Some nouns sound like plurals but have a singular meaning.
mathematics, series, mumps, physics

4. Some nouns have only a plural form.
species, scissors, slacks, clothes, measles

5 Rules for Forming Possessive Nouns

1. Add **'s** to make most singular nouns into the possessive form.
frog's legs, fish's gills, Tom's flippers, alto's song

2. Add **only an apostrophe** to make most plural nouns ending in *s* into the possessive form.
elephants' trunks, potatoes' eyes, foxes' teeth, sharks' skeletons

3. Add **'s** to make most other plural nouns into the possessive form.
women's rights, geese's feathers, mice's whiskers, children's giggles

4. Add **'s** to make most compound nouns into the possessive form.
mother-in-law's, mothers-in-law's, crackerjack's flavor

5. Add **'s** to the last noun in a series to show shared possession.
Susan, Sam, Sally, and Stan's snow fort

pizza of one teenager	teenager's pizza
two pizzas for one teenager	teenager's pizzas
pizza for several teenagers	teenagers' pizza
two pizzas for several teenagers	teenagers' pizzas

Better Grades & Higher Test Scores / READING & LANGUAGE
Copyright ©2003 by Incentive Publications, Inc., Nashville, TN.

Get Sharp: Grammar Guide

Pronouns

A **pronoun** is a word which is used in place of a noun.

personal pronoun – refers to people or things

singular personal pronouns – ***She*** *does great skateboard tricks.*
plural personal pronouns – *Do **they** worry about Jan's safety?*
first person pronoun – ***I*** *can do the same tricks!*
second person pronoun – *When did **you** learn to flip like that?*
third person pronoun – *C.J. films **them** on videotape.*

subject pronoun - used as the subject of the verb
or used in place of a predicate noun
We have never broken any bones.
*Did **they** tell mom about the bad accident?*

object pronoun- used as a direct or indirect object or object
of a preposition
*The crowd cheered **us**.* (direct object)
*Give **her** a round of applause.* (indirect object)
*Did the judge award first prize to **them**?* (object of preposition)

possessive pronoun - shows possession or ownership
*The newest snowboard is **mine**.*

reflexive pronoun - throws the action back upon the subject of
a sentence
*Cici bought **herself** a new snowboard today.*

intensive pronoun - calls special attention to a noun or pronoun,
giving it special emphasis
*Georgie **himself** painted the designs on the board.*

relative pronoun - relates one part of a sentence to a noun or pronoun
in another part of the sentence
*Some skateboarders prefer boards **that** are longer.*

indefinite pronoun - does not specifically name its antecedent
Everybody *thinks these athletes are awesome.*

interrogative pronoun - asks a question
Who *scheduled the performance for tomorrow?*
Whose *is this?*

demonstrative pronoun - points out a noun
This *was a fascinating competition.*
*Weren't **those** the best tricks ever?*

Which Pronouns are Which?

personal pronouns
    first person
    second person
    third person
	I, me, mine, my, we, our, ours, us
	you, your, yours
	he, his, him, she, her, hers, it, its, it, they, their,
	theirs, them

singular pronouns	*I, you, he, she, it, my, mine, me, your, yours, his, him,* *her, hers, its*
plural pronouns	*we, you, they, our, ours, your, yours, their, theirs,* *us, them*
subject pronouns	*I, you, he, she, it, we, you, they, who, whoever*
object pronouns	*me, you, him, her, it, us, you, them, whom, whomever*
possessive pronouns	*my, mine, your, yours, his, her, hers, its, our, ours,* *their, theirs, your, yours*
relative pronouns	*who, whose, whom, which, what, that, whoever,* *whosoever, whatever, whatsoever, whichever*
intensive & reflexive pronouns	*myself, yourself, yourselves, ourselves, himself,* *herself, itself, themselves*
interrogative pronouns	*who, whose, what, which, whoever, whatever, whom*
demonstrative pronouns	*this, that, these, those*
indefinite pronouns	*all, another, any, anybody, anything, anyone, both,* *each, either, everybody, everyone, everything, few,* *many, much, most, neither, none, nobody, no one,* *nothing, one, other, some, somebody, someone,* *several, something, such*

Get Sharp Tip # 2
Unlike possessive nouns, possessive pronouns NEVER have apostrophes.

Better Grades & Higher Test Scores / READING & LANGUAGE
Copyright ©2003 by Incentive Publications, Inc., Nashville, TN.

Get Sharp: Grammar Guide

Verbs

A verb is a word which expresses action or existence.

action verb – a word that expresses physical action or mental action
*The roller coaster **plunged** down the vertical track.* (physical)
*Ramon **regretted** choosing this ride.* (mental)

being verb – a word that describes a state of being (tells what the subject *is* or *feels*).
*After the ride, Ramon **felt** sick. He **seemed** dazed. **Is** he ready for the next ride?*

linking verb - links a subject to a noun or adjective in the predicate
*The Twister **is** the most popular ride. It **remained** closed six weeks for repairs.*

singular verb - a verb with a singular subject
*Which Ferris wheel **provides** riders with the best view?*

plural verb - a verb with a plural subject
*All three Ferris wheels **thrill** the riders with spectacular views.*

I scream in a very active voice.

points of view – form of the verb matching the person of the subject
    first person verb – *I **scream**. We **scream**.*
    second person verb – *You **scream**.*
    third person verb – *He **screams**. She **screams**. They **scream**.*

active voice – verb form used when the subject performs the action
    in a sentence
*Gravity **pulls** the Screamin' Demon cars down the track.*

passive voice – verb form used when the subject receives the action
*The Screamin' Demon cars **are pulled** down the track by gravity.*

transitive verb – a verb that transfers its action to an object
*Four teenagers **rode** The Big Splash twice.* (*The Big Splash* is the direct object)
*The ride **gave** the teenagers a thrill.* (*teenagers* is the indirect object; *thrill* is the direct object)
*All of them **were drenched** with water.* (*water* is the object of the preposition *with*)

intransitive verb – a verb that completes its action without an object
*After the ride, the kids **looked** hilarious.*
*They **laughed** boisterously.*

verb phrase – more than one word used to make up a verb; one or more helping verbs and a main verb

    main verb – in a verb phrase, the verb that expresses action or feeling

    helping verb – the verb that helps complete the meaning of the main verb

    Soon the new ride, The Terminator, **will open.** (**open** *is the main verb;* **will** *is the helping verb*)

principal verb parts – Every verb has four principal parts. These are used to form all the verb tenses.

    base form, or present - ***scream***   present participle   - *(is) screaming*

    past participle   - ***screamed***   past participle   - *(has) screamed*

verb tenses –

    present tense - expresses action that happens now or continually: *We* **scream.**

    past tense - expresses action that already happened: *We* **screamed**.

    future tense - expresses action that will take place: *We* **will scream**.

    present perfect tense - expresses action which began in the past but continues to the present:
        We **have screamed.**

    past perfect tense - expresses action which began in the past and was completed in the past:
        We **had screamed.**

    future perfect tense - expresses action which will begin in the future and will be completed
    by a specific time in the future: *We* **will have screamed.**

irregular verbs – verbs that do not follow the usual rules for forming tenses

verbal – word formed from a verb, but used as a noun, adjective, or adverb

    gerund - a verb form which ends in *ing* and is used as a noun
        Screaming *makes your throat sore.*
        Most of us were tired of **squealing**.

    participle - a verb form used as an adjective
        The **famished** *teenagers hurried to buy cotton candy.*
        The girls **gobbling** *cotton candy had sticky faces.*

    infinitive - a verb form usually introduced by *to*,
        and used as a noun, adjective, or adverb
        To ride *The Terrible Trolly was our next goal.*
        The first one **to get** *to the gate got the best seat.*

progressive form– verb form which shows that the action
    is continuing
    (The progressive form may be found in all six tenses.)
    We **are screaming** *now. We* **were screaming** *yesterday.*
        We **will be screaming** *tomorrow.*
    We **have been screaming** *all day.*
        We **had been screaming** *all day yesterday.*
    We **will have been screaming** *for hours.*

Forming Verb Tenses for Regular Verbs

To form the PRESENT TENSE. . . use the base form of the verb.
dread, swallow, complain, close, carry, worry, enjoy, eat, save

To form the PRESENT PARTICIPLE. . . add *ing* to the base form of the verb.
(Sometimes you will need to drop a final *e* or change *y* to *i* before adding *ing*.)
dreading, swallowing, complaining, closing, carrying, worrying

To form the PAST TENSE. . . add *d* or *ed* to the base form of the verb. (Sometimes you will need to change a final *y* to *i* before adding *ed*.)
dreaded, swallowed, complained, closed, carried, worried

To form the FUTURE TENSE . . . use *will* with the base form of the verb.
*We will swallow. They **will complain**. He **will worry**.*
OR . . . use time words, such as *tomorrow, later,* or *next week* with the base form.
***Tomorrow** we **close** at noon. **Later** we **eat** the cake. **Next week** we **save** our money.*

To form the PRESENT PERFECT TENSE. . . use *have* or *has* with the past form.
We have dreaded this for a long time. He has complained about the ride often.

To form the PAST PERFECT TENSE. . . use *had* with the past form.
*Until today, we had dreaded this for weeks. Ramon **had worried** about that steep drop.*

To form the future PERFECT TENSE. . . use *will have* or *shall have* with the past form.
*Andrea **will have been** here six times. We **shall have enjoyed** ourselves immensely!*

FOR PROGRESSIVE FORMS. . . combine the present participle of the verb with a form of the helping verb *be*. **The form of *be* shows the tense.**

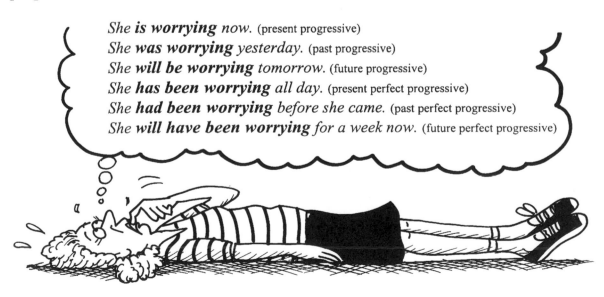

*She **is worrying** now.* (present progressive)
*She **was worrying** yesterday.* (past progressive)
*She **will be worrying** tomorrow.* (future progressive)
*She **has been worrying** all day.* (present perfect progressive)
*She **had been worrying** before she came.* (past perfect progressive)
*She **will have been worrying** for a week now.* (future perfect progressive)

Forming Verb Tenses for Irregular Verbs

Here are some verbs that do NOT follow the rules for forming tenses.
They are called **irregular verbs**.

These are just a few irregular verbs. There are many more.

present	present perfect	past	past perfect	future	future perfect
am, be	has been, have been	was, were	had been	will be, shall be	will have been, shall have been
begin	has begun	began	had begun	will begin	will have begun
blow	has blown	blew	had blown	will blow	will have blown
break	has broken	broke	had broken	will break	will have broken
bring	has brought	brought	had brought	will bring	will have brought
catch	has caught	caught	had caught	will catch	will have caught
choose	has chosen	chose	had chosen	will choose	will have chosen
come	has come	came	had come	will come	will have come
do	has done	did	had done	will do	will have done
draw	has drawn	drew	had drawn	will draw	will have drawn
drink	has drunk	drank	had drunk	will drink	will have drunk
eat	has eaten	ate	had eaten	will eat	will have eaten
fight	has fought	fought	had fought	will fight	will have fought
fly	has flown	flew	had flown	will fly	will have flown
give	has given	gave	had given	will give	will have given
go	has gone	went	had gone	will go	will have gone
grow	has grown	grew	had grown	will grow	will have grown
hide	has hidden	hid	had hidden	will hide	will have hidden
know	has known	knew	had known	will know	will have known
lie	has lain	lay	had lain	will lie	will have lain
raise	has risen	rose	had risen	will raise	will have risen
ring	has rung	rang	had rung	will ring	will have rung
run	has run	ran	had run	will run	will have run
see	has seen	saw	had seen	will see	will have seen
sing	has sung	sang	had sung	will sing	will have sung
speak	has spoken	spoke	had spoken	will speak	will have spoken
swim	has swum	swam	had swum	will swim	will have swum
take	has taken	took	had taken	will take	will have taken
throw	has thrown	threw	had thrown	will throw	will have thrown

WRITE: has written · wrote · had written · will write · will have written

Better Grades & Higher Test Scores / READING & LANGUAGE
Copyright ©2003 by Incentive Publications, Inc., Nashville, TN.

Get Sharp: Grammar Guide

Transitive & Intransitive Verbs

Transitive:

"*Once I **took** a ride on the Danger Drop Freefall,*" *bragged Gramps.*
(The verb *took* transfers action to *ride*; the object *ride* receives the action.)

Intransitive:

"*My favorite hat **blew** away before I finished the ride,*" *he sighed.*
(The verb *blew* completes its action without an object.)

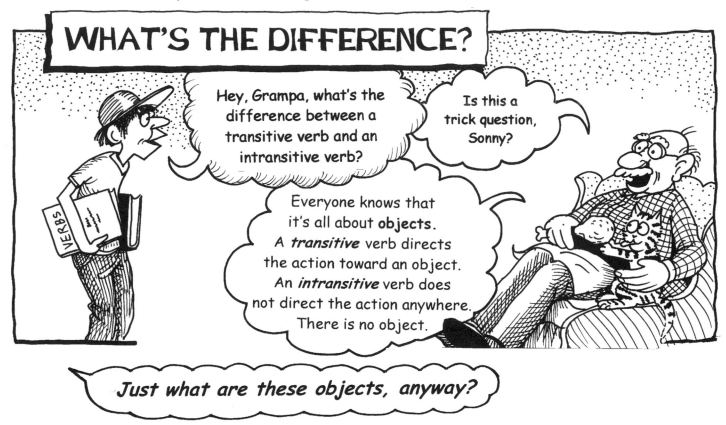

WHAT'S THE DIFFERENCE?

Hey, Grampa, what's the difference between a transitive verb and an intransitive verb?

Is this a trick question, Sonny?

Everyone knows that it's all about **objects**. A *transitive* verb directs the action toward an object. An *intransitive* verb does not direct the action anywhere. There is no object.

Just what are these objects, anyway?

A **direct object** is someone or something that receives the action of a verb.

It answers the question *whom?* or *what?*

*The Danger Drop scared **Georgio** out of his wits!* (*Georgio* is the direct object.)
*His friends shouted **cheers** and encouraging **words**.* (*Cheers* and *words* are direct objects.)
*Afterwards, he bought **tickets** for all of his friends.* (*Tickets* is the direct object.)

An **indirect object** comes between the verb and the direct object.

It answers the questions *to whom?* or *for whom?* or *to what?* or *for what?*

*Before the ride started, the ride operator gave **Georgio** instructions.*
  (*Georgio* is the indirect object. *Instructions* is the direct object.)
*The park sold freefall **riders** sixty tickets yesterday.*
  (*Riders* is the indirect object. *Tickets* is the direct object.)
*Georgio gave his **harness** a firm tug before the ride began.*
  (*Harness* is the indirect object. *Tug* is the direct object.)

78

Verbs That Link

A **linking verb** connects the subject of a sentence with a noun or adjective in the predicate.

*The foot-long hot dogs at the amusement park **taste** great!*

*Suddenly, the carousel operator **smelled** smoke.*

Link to What??

A linking verb can connect the subject to a **predicate noun** that identifies the subject.

*Charlie Chuckles **is** the **manager** of the Fun House.*

A linking verb can connect the subject to a **predicate adjective** that describes the subject.

*In his clown outfits, old Charlie always **looks** comical.*

COMMON LINKING VERBS

am	is
are	taste
were	was
appear	smell
turn	seem
sound	grow
look	turn
feel	become

Verbs That Help

A **helping verb** helps the main verb express action or helps complete the meaning of the verb.

*Charlie **has been** wanting to ride in the front car on the Double Loop Coaster.*

*He **might** grab a seat today, if he's lucky.*

COMMON HELPING VERBS

am	is	are
be	was	were
been	had	has
have	can	could
will	do	does
would	did	may
might		should

Better Grades & Higher Test Scores / READING & LANGUAGE
Copyright ©2003 by Incentive Publications, Inc., Nashville, TN.

Get Sharp: Grammar Guide

Adjectives

An **adjective** is a word that modifies, or describes, a noun or pronoun.

An adjective can modify a **noun.** *Look at those **juicy** tacos.*

OR, an adjective can modify a **pronoun.** *They are **scrumptious.***

A **predicate adjective** follows a linking verb, but always describes the subject.

*The burritos were **fat** and **dripping** with gooey cheese.*

- An adjective can tell **how many.** *I ate **forty-four** tacos.*
  most, several, few, little, many, some, much, or any number

- An adjective can tell **what kind.** *Then came the **horrendous** stomachache.*
  unexpected, endless, uncomfortable, worst, legendary, three-hour

- An adjective can tell **which one.** ***That** meal was a big mistake.*
  those, his, these, the, Amy's, which, other, her, their, our, whichever

Get Sharp: Grammar Guide   *Better Grades & Higher Test Scores / READING & LANGUAGE*
Copyright ©2003 by Incentive Publications, Inc., Nashville, TN.

Special Adjectives

simple – a one-word adjective
green, exotic, boisterous, suspicious, forty, outrageous, spicy, putrid, tiny

compound – made up of more than one word *(sometimes hyphenated)*
seafaring, knee-high, underground, mile-deep, long-term

common – any adjective that is not proper; not capitalized
rotten, tasty, dull, familiar, thirteen, furious, golden, teenage, crooked

proper – formed from a proper noun; always capitalized
Spanish, Texan, Roman, American

predicate – an adjective which follows a linking verb and describes the subject of the sentence
That story sounds ludicrous.

articles — a special group of adjectives made up of *a, an,* and *the*

A and *an* are indefinite articles because they refer to one of a general group.
A is used before words beginning with consonant sounds.
An is used before words beginning with vowel sounds.
The is a definite article because it identifies a specific person, place, thing, or idea.

an historian
a shocking story
the last ballerina
a deep mystery
an ornery child

demonstratives — an adjective that points out a specific noun: *these, those, this, that.*

(These words are adjectives only when followed by a noun.)

This pizza is tastier than that one.
Those toenails are cracked.
These students are asleep.

Better Grades & Higher Test Scores / READING & LANGUAGE
Copyright ©2003 by Incentive Publications, Inc., Nashville, TN.

Get Sharp: Grammar Guide

Adverbs

An adverb is a word that modifies, or describes, a verb, adjective, or other adverb.

An adverb can modify a **verb**. *It is a good idea to handle snakes carefully.*

An adverb can modify an **adjective**. *Very dangerous snakes should be avoided.*

An adverb can modify another **adverb**. *Poisonous snakes almost always terrify me.*

An adverb can tell **how**. *Ivy considered thoughtfully before touching the snake.*
easily, grumpily, loosely, miserably, happily, repeatedly, well, firmly

An adverb can tell **when**. *Yesterday, she insisted she would never go near a snake.*
soon, later, tomorrow, early, immediately, often, never, usually, forever, annually

An adverb can tell **where**. *This boa constrictor has lived here for years.*
here, there, everywhere, outside, inside, upstairs, below, anywhere, around

An adverb can tell **to what extent**. *(Such an adverb adds intensity to the word it modifies.)*
She was terribly anxious to show her bravery by handling the snake.
almost, extremely, least, really, terribly, very, quite, more, rather, slightly

Get Sharp Tip # 3
Consider the placement
of adverbs in your sentences.
The position may affect the meaning.

Only Ivy handled the boa constrictor.
Ivy only handled the boa constrictor.

Scarcely Sara had been around rattlesnakes.
Sara had scarcely been around rattlesnakes.

After, the snake escaped dinner.
The snake escaped after dinner.

Some adverbs that end in *ly*

early
loudly
frequently
softly
angrily
noisily
immediately
easily
usually
carelessly
casually
critically
lonely
hotly
rarely
eagerly
annoyingly
purposely
overtly
tremendously
openly
smartly
hungrily
harshly
sweetly
grumpily
arguably
secondly
tensely
shortly
eventually
totally
unlikely
supremely
peculiarly
desperately
accurately
absentmindedly

Some adverbs that do not end in *ly*

afterward
almost
already
always
never
anywhere
now
backward
often
below
seldom
before
sometimes
beneath
outside
somewhere
nowhere
better
early
soon
ever
then
least
long
farther
tomorrow
fast
there
forever
too
further
well
here
worse
inside
worst

Some adverbs used to modify adjectives & other adverbs

somewhat
almost
partly
barely
rather
extremely
really
totally
hardly
so
too
rarely
unusually
quite
just
usually
very
terribly
particularly
especially
nearly

I'm really almost always early for lunch, particularly when I'm totally ravenous.

Adjectives That Compare

Adjectives can be used to compare one or more person or thing.

A **comparative adjective** compares one person or thing with another.

A **superlative adjective** compares one person or thing with several others.

For most one-syllable adjectives (and some two-syllable adjectives), form the comparative by adding *er* and the superlative by adding *est*.

For most adjectives of two or more syllables, form the comparative by adding *more* and the superlative by adding *most*.

The words *less* and *least* are used before all adjectives to form the negative comparative and superlative forms.

Base Form	Comparative	Superlative
wild	wilder	wildest
fine	finer	finest
big	bigger	biggest
witty	wittier	wittiest
splendid	more splendid	most splendid
complicated	more complicated	most complicated
able	less able	least able

Rule-Breakers

The comparative and superlative forms of some adjectives are **irregular.** You'll have to learn these forms without the rules.

Base Form	Comparative	Superlative
good	better	best
bad	worse	worst
well	better	best
many	more	most
little	less	least
much	more	most

84

Adverbs That Compare

Adverbs can be used to compare one action or more actions.

A **comparative adverb** compares one action with another.

A **superlative adverb** compares one action with several others.

For most short adverbs, form the comparative by adding *er* and the superlative by adding *est*.

For most long adverbs (and a few short ones) form the comparative by adding *more* and the superlative by adding *most*.

The words *less* and *least* are used before all adverbs to form the negative comparative and superlative forms.

Base Form	Comparative	Superlative
soon	sooner	soonest
long	longer	longest
early	earlier	earliest
foolishly	more foolishly	most foolishly
deeply	more deeply	most deeply
smoothly	less smoothly	least smoothly
awkwardly	less awkwardly	least awkwardly

Rule-Breakers

The comparative and superlative forms of some adverbs are **irregular.** You'll have to learn these forms without the rules.

Base Form	Comparative	Superlative
badly	worse	worst
well	better	best
little	less	least
much	more	most
far (distance)	farther	farthest
far (degree)	further	furthest

Better Grades & Higher Test Scores / READING & LANGUAGE
Copyright ©2003 by Incentive Publications, Inc., Nashville, TN.

Get Sharp: Grammar Guide

Prepositions

A **preposition** is a word that shows a relationship between a noun or a pronoun and another word in the sentence.

Common Prepositions

above	because of	for	off	subsequent to
about	before	from	on	through
according to	behind	in	on account of	throughout
across	below	in addition to	on top of	till
after	beneath	in back of	out	to
against	beside	in front of	out of	toward
along	besides	in place of	outside	under
alongside	between	in spite of	outside of	underneath
amid	beyond	inside	over	until
among	but	inside of	over to	unto
apart from	by	instead of	past	up
around	despite	into	prior to	upon
aside from	down	like	round	with
as	during	near	save	within
at	except	of	since	without

In a sentence, a preposition is always followed by an **object.**

*Gracie finally flew **into** space. (**space** is the object of **into**)*

The preposition, its object, and any modifiers form a **prepositional phrase**.

*She chose to be an astronaut **instead of an electrician.***

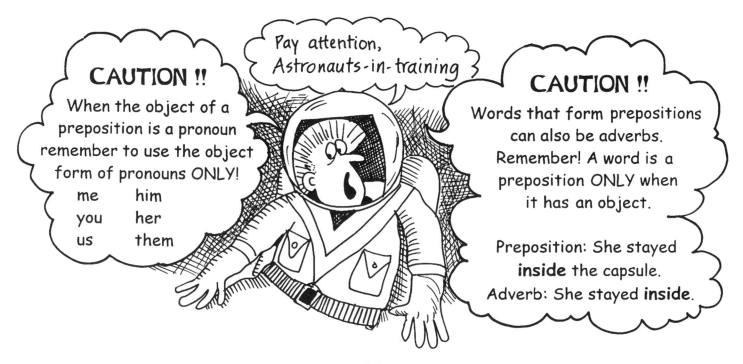

Pay attention, Astronauts-in-training

CAUTION !!
When the object of a preposition is a pronoun remember to use the object form of pronouns ONLY!

me	him
you	her
us	them

CAUTION !!
Words that form prepositions can also be adverbs. Remember! A word is a preposition ONLY when it has an object.

Preposition: She stayed **inside** the capsule.
Adverb: She stayed **inside**.

86

Conjunctions

A **conjunction** connects individual words or groups of words.

A **coordinate conjunction** connects a word to a word, a phrase to a phrase, or a clause to a clause. The words, phrases, or clauses joined by a coordinate conjunction must be equal or of the same type.

*Weather **and** mechanical problems delayed the liftoff.*
*The launch may proceed tomorrow **but** will not go today.*

Common coordinate conjunctions: and   or   not   yet   nor   but   for   so

A **subordinate conjunction** connects, and shows a relationship between, two clauses which are **not** equally important. It connects a dependent clause to an independent clause.

*The launch will proceed tomorrow **provided that** the weather has improved.*
(The second clause, the weather has improved, is the dependent clause.)

Common subordinate conjunctions:

as	after	although	as if	as long as	as soon as
if	before	even though	when	since	provided that
till	because	so that	unless	until	whenever
than	where	although	while	whatever	in order that

Correlative conjunctions are coordinate conjunctions used in pairs.
*__Neither__ the astronauts **nor** the space scientists have any control over the weather.*

Common correlative conjunctions:

either . . . or	neither . . . nor	not only . . . but also	both . . . and
whether . . . or	just . . . as	just . . . so	just . . . as

Interjections

An **interjection** is a word or short phrase included in a sentence to communicate surprise or other strong emotion.

Hooray! Gracie is finally ready to blast off into space!
Oh, no! There's trouble with the spacecraft!
Whew! Everything's okay!
There it goes! Spectacular sight!

Get Sharp Tip # 4
Punctuation for an interjection is usually an exclamation point. It usually separates the interjection from the rest of the sentence.

Phrases . . .

A phrase is a group of related words that is missing a subject, a predicate, or both.

a fast-approaching eel   *wearing her new mask*   *seventeen savage sharks*

descended thirty feet   *after the incident with the stingray*

extremely cautious divers   *A full tank of air*   *bothered by the cold*

to escape narrowly

Prepositional Phrases

A prepositional phrase . . . a preposition and its object *(along with any modifiers).*

beneath the surface
beside the sunken ship
past the largest coral reef

*The diver **in the purple wet suit** needs a different tank. (prepositional phrase used as an adjective)*
*Will the divers follow the shark **inside the shipwreck**? (prepositional phrase used as an adverb)*

Gerund Phrases

A gerund phrase . . . contains the *ing* **form of a verb used as noun**

serious searching
ruining her new fins
exploring the last cave

***Proper training** is essential to safe diving. (gerund phrase used as subject of the sentence)*
*One illegal activity is **standing on a coral reef**. (gerund phrase used as a predicate noun)*
*That diver got a ticket for **taking marine life samples**. (gerund phrase used as object of the preposition* for*)*

Infinitive Phrases

An **infinitive phrase** . . .

includes the combination of the word *to* **and the base form of a verb**

>>> *to explore the caves*
>>>> *to forget about the time*
>>>>> *to escape from danger*

To dive alone *is foolish. (infinitive phrase used as a noun—the subject of the sentence)*

They wanted **to explore the underwater caves**. *(infinitive phrase used as the direct object of the verb* wanted*)*

Are these the right fish **to photograph**? *(infinitive phrase used as an adjective—tells which* fish*)*

She hid behind the reef **to avoid the barracuda**. *(infinitive phrase used as an adverb telling why* she *hid)*

Participial Phrases

A **participial phrase** . . .

contains a verb's present, past, or perfect participle used as an adjective

>>> *a shark biting divers*
>>>> *two divers bit by a shark*
>>>>> *some divers badly bitten*

>>>> *We heard of a shark* **biting some divers**.
>>>>> *(present participial phrase describes the* shark*)*

>>>> *The diver* **bit by the shark** *was bleeding.*
>>>>> *(past participle phrase describing the* diver*)*

>>>> *Sam Slick,* **bitten by the shark,** *managed to swim to safety.*
>>>>> *(perfect participle phrase describing* Sam Slick*)*

DID YOU KNOW?

Some phrases are essential. Some are not.

An essential (or restrictive) phrase is necessary to the basic meaning of the sentence.

The expert diver **who runs the dive shop** is my brother.

A nonessential (or nonrestrictive) phrase is **not** necessary to the basic meaning.

My brother, **who runs the dive shop**, is an experienced diver.

An essential phrase needs no commas.
A nonessential phrase is set off with commas.

Clauses

A **clause** is a group of related words with a subject and a predicate.

Noun Clauses

A **noun clause** . . . a subordinate *(or dependent)* clause that functions as a noun

That she was running out of air worried the diver. *(clause used as the subject of the sentence)*

She calculated *it would take five minutes to reach the boat*. *(clause used as a direct object of the verb* take*)*

Alert *whoever is on the boat* that Beth may be in trouble. *(clause used as an indirect object of the verb* alert*)*

Did you think about *the chance that she can't make it*? *(clause used as the object of the preposition* about*)*

She will make it; that is *what the dive master predicts*. *(clause used as a predicate noun)*

Adjective Clauses

An **adjective clause** . . . a subordinate *(or dependent)* clause used as an adjective to describe any noun or pronoun

(***NOTE***: An adjective clause always begins with *who, whom, which, whose,* or *that*.)

Is the octopus *which is lurking behind the plants* headed this way? *(clause modifies the noun* octopus*)*

It's the biggest lobster *that I've seen so far*. *(clause modifies the noun* lobster*)*

Oh, it's you *who borrowed my new fins*! *(clause modifies the pronoun* you*)*

Adverb Clauses

An adverb clause . . . a subordinate *(or dependent)* clause used as an adverb

(*NOTE:* An adverb clause always begins with a subordinate conjunction such as *although, after, as, as if, before, because, if, since, so that, unless, until, where, when, which,* or *that*).

Because the visibility was poor, I decided to head for the boat. *(clause tells why for the verb* decided)

I'll leave the camera in the boat ***until we return later for lunch.*** *(clause tells when for the verb* leave)

Meet me by the cave ***where we saw the giant squid.*** *(clause tells where for the verb* meet)

I took precautions ***as if my life depended on them.*** *(clause tells how for the verb* **depended***)*

DID YOU KNOW?

Some clauses are essential. Some are not.

An essential (or restrictive) clause identifies the noun or pronoun it follows and is necessary to the basic meaning of the sentence.

*They caught that eel **which was dangerous to divers.***

A nonessential (or nonrestrictive) clause adds optional information and is **not** necessary to the basic meaning.

A huge eel, ***which was caught yesterday,*** poses a danger to divers.

An essential (or restrictive) clause needs no commas.

A nonessential (or nonrestrictive) clause is set off with commas.

Some clauses are independent. Some are not.

An independent clause expresses a complete thought and can stand alone as a sentence.

They finished the dive just as the storm was brewing. *(Independent clause is bold.)*

A subordinate clause does not express a complete thought and cannot stand alone as a sentence.

By the time the storm hit, they were safe on shore. *(Subordinate clause is bold.)*

Get Sharp: Grammar Guide

10 SENTENCE PARTS TO REMEMBER

1. SUBJECT - the part of a sentence which is doing something or about which something is said

Seven lion tamers bravely faced seven ferocious lions.

2. SIMPLE SUBJECT - the subject without the words which describe or modify it

*Seven lion **tamers** bravely faced seven ferocious lions.*

3. COMPLETE SUBJECT - the simple subject and all the words which modify it

***Seven lion tamers** bravely faced seven ferocious lions.*

4. COMPOUND SUBJECT - made up of two or more simple subjects

***Seven lions and four tigers** surrounded the brave lion tamers.*

5. PREDICATE - the part of the sentence which says something about the subject

*Seven lion tamers **bravely faced seven ferocious lions.***

6. SIMPLE PREDICATE - the predicate (verb) without the words which describe or modify it

*Seven lion tamers bravely **faced** seven ferocious lions.*

7. COMPLETE PREDICATE - the simple predicate and all the words which modify or explain it

*Seven lion tamers **bravely faced seven ferocious lions**.*

8. COMPOUND PREDICATE - composed of two or more simple predicates

*Seven lion tamers **charmed seven ferocious lions** and **entertained four feisty tigers.***

9. PHRASE - a group of related words which lacks either a subject or a predicate (or both)

Outside the ring, *the lions paced impatiently. (2 phrases)*

Were the lions **in a hurry** *to get some dinner? (3 different phrases)*

Which tigers *were growling* **during the performance***? (3 different phrases)*

10. CLAUSE – a group of words that has a subject and verb

While some of the tigers are rather tame, *others are terribly fierce. (2 clauses)*

The whip, *which the lion tamer used often,* **made a sharp cracking sound.** *(2 clauses)*

That clown is teasing the tigers; *he's not afraid at all. (2 clauses)*

8 KINDS OF SENTENCES TO REMEMBER

1. SIMPLE SENTENCE - a sentence with only one independent clause (complete thought). It may contain one or more phrases, but no dependent clauses.

Has she ever walked a tightrope before?

2. COMPOUND SENTENCE - a sentence made up of two or more simple sentences; a coordinate conjunction, punctuation, or both must join these simple sentences

Lucy can ride an elephant and she can swing from a trapeze.

3. COMPLEX SENTENCE - contains one independent clause and one or more dependent clauses

Besides her acrobatic skills, Lucy has great skills walking the tightrope.

4. COMPOUND-COMPLEX SENTENCE - contains two or more independent clauses and one or more dependent clauses

When she was a little girl, Lucy pretended that she was working for a circus.

5. DECLARATIVE SENTENCE - makes a statement

Unfortunately the high-wire walker has slipped from the wire.

6. INTERROGATIVE SENTENCE - asks a question

Was there a net below to catch him when he fell?

7. IMPERATIVE SENTENCE - makes a command (often has an understood subject—*you*)

Don't plan to have a safe life if you walk on high-wires.

8. EXCLAMATORY SENTENCE - communicates strong emotion or surprise

What an astounding performance!

Get Sharp: Grammar Guide

4 BASIC SENTENCE PATTERNS TO REMEMBER

#1   Subject + Verb

Storms raged.

Did storms rage?

Wind blew and waters rose.

Wind and waves increased.

#2   Subject + Verb + Direct Object

Waves pounded the coast.

Water damaged the beaches and highways.

Wind and waves destroyed beaches and battered businesses.

#3   Subject + Verb + Indirect Object + Direct Object

Water gave beaches a beating.

Did the storm cause the town damage?

The storm brought the area misery.

#4   Subject + Verb + Predicate Noun or Adjective

The wind was a monster.

Which storm was the hurricane?

The wind sounded deafening and terrifying.

That storm seemed worse.

Get Sharp Tip # 5
Any of the parts of each pattern may be compound.

Complicated Sentences

Some Compound Sentences

Was that a hurricane warning or was it a hurricane watch?

Cars flew through the air and power lines crashed to the ground.

The tree snapped, a branch fell, and the roof gave way.

Some Complex Sentences

Although we were watching, we never saw the tornado coming.

Since we were hiding in the basement, we didn't hear the roar until it was almost upon us.

After the tornado passed, we found a tractor stuck in a treetop.

Some Compound-Complex Sentences

My stomach sinks, and my heart beats wildly whenever I hear that roaring sound.

When tornado season arrives, we put flashlights in the basement and we stock up on food.

After floods subside and before hurricanes starts, the weather is fine and we're happy.

Better Grades & Higher Test Scores / READING & LANGUAGE
Copyright ©2003 by Incentive Publications, Inc., Nashville, TN.

Get Sharp: Grammar Guide

Subject-Verb Agreement

ASK PROFESSOR KNOW-IT-ALL
She knows a lot!

It's as easy as 1-2-3 to agree!
1. Single subjects require singular verbs.
2. Plural subjects require plural verbs.
3. Pronouns used as subjects must also agree in number with the verb.

*What about subjects that already end in **s**? Are they singular or plural?*

ANSWER: Some are singular and need a singular verb:
news
physics
mathematics
United States
Illinois
Los Angeles

*What about **scissors**?*

ANSWER: It's plural, like these:
jeans   *pants*
tweezers   *pliers*
binoculars *sunglasses*
mumps   *measles*

Thanks, doctor. I think I've got it!

Band **members** **arrive** at noon to record.

On this album, **Mara** **performs** on every song.

She **sings** beautifully.

Seven **technicians,** skilled with sound and lights, **travel** with the band.

This **band,** despite its hard rock sounds, **appeals** to all age groups.

Two **songs** from their last album **have won** major awards.

Fanatic **fans,** all eager to buy the new release, **wait** for the store to open.

Which **tune** **is playing** for the 20th time today on that radio station?

Special Cases: Compound Subjects

Compound subjects joined by **and** or by **both . . . and** require a plural verb.

Both Mara **and** the other vocalist **have** laryngitis.

Traveling **and** non-stop concerts **are** hard on a singer's health.

When compound subjects **refer to the same person or thing**, a singular verb is required.

The drummer **and** leader of the band **is** Angela.

When compound subjects are joined by **or, either . . . or**, or **neither . . . nor**, the verb agrees with the subject closest to it.

Neither illness **nor** holidays **interrupt** the schedule.

Did the guitars **or** the guitar player **miss** the plane?

Neither the lights **nor** the sound **was working** well tonight.

Special Cases: Names and Titles

A title or a name takes a singular verb form, even though it may look plural.

> *Warner and Wagoner Guitars* **sponsors** *the band.*
>
> **Is** *The British Isles home to three band members?*
>
> *The Chargers Arena* **was** *the site for last night's concert.*
>
> *Star Wars* **remains** *the favorite movie of the drummer.*

Special Cases: Collective Nouns

When a collective noun names a group acting as a single unit, it takes a singular verb.

> *What a fine sound the orchestra* **is producing***!*
>
> *The whole family* **claps** *wildly for their son, the lead singer.*
>
> *One group* **expresses** *shock at the band's outfits.*

When a collective noun refers to the individuals in a group, it takes a plural verb.

> *The* **orchestra** **are tuning** *their instruments.*
>
> *Why* **are** *the* **family** **spread** *throughout the arena?*

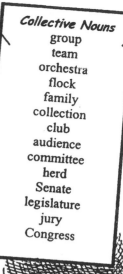

Collective Nouns
group
team
orchestra
flock
family
collection
club
audience
committee
herd
Senate
legislature
jury
Congress

Special Cases: Nouns of Amount

When thought of as a single unit, nouns of amount take a single verb.

> *Eight* **months** **seems** *a long time to be on a tour.*
>
> **Is** *twenty* **dollars** *the cost of a ticket to the concert?*

When thought of as separate units, nouns of amount take a plural verb.

> *The eight* **months** *actually* **pass** *quickly when you travel every day.*

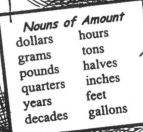

Nouns of Amount
dollars   hours
grams   tons
pounds   halves
quarters   inches
years   feet
decades   gallons

Special Cases: Indefinite Pronouns as Subjects

Indefinite pronouns do not refer to a specific person, place, or thing. They can be singular or plural.

> *Can* **anybody** *of any age* **purchase** *a concert ticket?*
>
> *No,* **everyone** **is** *not right for this audience.*
>
> **Something** *great* **happens** *for fans when this band begins to play.*
>
> *Before the concert,* **several** **hang** *around the door.*
>
> **Few** **are allowed** *backstage.*
>
> **None** *of the fans* **have** *access to the dressing rooms.*
>
> **Most** *of the concert* **sounds** *very loud.*

Singular Indefinite Pronouns
another   much
anybody   neither
anyone   nobody
anything   no one
each   nothing
either   one
everybody   somebody
everyone   someone
everything   something

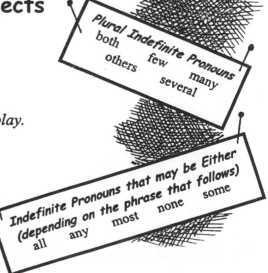

Plural Indefinite Pronouns
both   few
others   many
         several

Indefinite Pronouns that may be Either (depending on the phrase that follows)
all   any   most   none   some

Get Sharp: Usage Guide

Pronoun Particulars

1. **A pronoun must have a clear antecedent** *(noun to which it refers).*

   *When did the bass **player** finally arrive? Why was **he** late?*
   *(**Player** is the clear antecedent of **he**.)*
   *Both the bass player and the drummer missed the bus. That's why **she** was late.*
   (The antecedent is unclear—Is it player or drummer or neither?)

2. **A pronoun must agree with its antecedent** *(in person, gender, and number).*

   ***Blake** said **he** ordered tickets for himself and four friends. (second person, masculine gender)*
   ***Angela** has played the drums since **she** was three years old. (second person, feminine gender)*
   *Aren't **they** the **musicians** who had the best-selling record? (plural subject and pronoun)*
   *Only one **album** sold less than a million copies; **it** was the first **album**. (singular subject and pronoun)*

3. **An indefinite pronoun used as a subject must agree with the verb.**

   ***Somebody** needs to replace the broken guitar strings.*
   ***Nothing** ever **interferes** with the afternoon rehearsal.*
   ***Each** of the band members **memorizes** his or her parts.*
   ***Several** more strings **broke** that day.*
   ***Others** think this music is too loud, also.*
   *Few **fans** were **disappointed** in the music **they** heard.*

4. **The interrogative pronoun *who* (or *whoever*) is used as a subject of a sentence. *Whom* (or *whomever*) is used as an object.**

   ***Whoever** loves loud music will love this band! (subject)*
   ***Who** got us these great seats? (subject)*
   *To **whom** was that last song dedicated? (object)*
   *The seats are open for **whomever** gets there first. (object)*

98

Better Grades & Higher Test Scores / READING & LANGUAGE
Copyright ©2003 by Incentive Publications, Inc., Nashville, TN.

5. Use subject pronouns as subjects or predicate pronouns.

(Never use an object pronoun as a subject.)

Correct: Did **they** sell over five thousand tickets today?

It was **she** who gave away those expensive tickets.

Weren't **we** lucky to get those front row seats?

Incorrect: It was **him** who got a backstage pass.

Them are the ones who snuck into the dressing room.

Didn't **us** get the best seats?

6. Use object pronouns as direct objects or indirect objects.

(Never use a subject pronoun as an object.)

Correct: How lucky Dylan was to get autographs from all of **them**!

Every band member gave **him** a free CD.

Who was that dancing with **you** in the aisle?

Incorrect: Next week, Sara will start taking drum lessons from **I**.

Who taught **they** to dance?

Did the Cooley brothers get up to dance along with **she**?

7. In a compound subject, use subject pronouns.

Correct: **She and he** dance together all the time.

When will **Sam and they** ever get up to dance?

Unfortunately, **our friends and we** are terrible dancers.

Incorrect: **Him and her** have been taking dance lessons for years.

When **B.J. and us** started dancing, everyone laughed.

Couldn't **them and me** start our own band?

8. In a compound object, use object pronouns.

Correct: For the best pictures, entrust the camera only to **them or me**.

Please give **him and us** copies of the picture of Alonzo dancing.

When the concert was over, no one was more exhausted than **her or him**.

Incorrect: Okay, who took that terrible picture of **she and I**?

These concert tickets cost our **parents and we** over a hundred dollars.

Luckily, the evening was free for **the girls and they**.

USAGE DOs & DON'Ts

DON'T . . . use double negatives. → **DO** . . . use only one negative in a sentence.

Incorrect Usage:

*Scarcely **nobody** swims here.*
*No camping is **never** allowed on the beach.*
*No fishing is allowed **neither**.*
*Do **not** feed **nothing** to the seagulls.*
***Hardly** no one swims here.*
*You **shouldn't** take **no** coral from the reefs.*

Correct Usage:

Scarcely anybody swims here.
***No** camping is ever allowed on the beach.*
***No** fishing is allowed either.*
*Do **not** feed anything to the seagulls.*
***Hardly** anyone swims here.*
*You should take **no** coral from the reefs.*

DON'T . . . use a double subject. → **DO** . . . use either a noun or pronoun to name the subject of the sentence.

Incorrect Usage:

*Rex **he** got away from the shark.*
*It's a shame that Terri **she** got bad sunburn.*

Correct Usage:

Rex got away from the shark.
It's a shame that Terri got a bad sunburn.

DON'T . . . . . . use *of* with *would, could,* or *should*. → **DO** . . . . use *have* with *would, could,* or *should*.

Incorrect Usage:

*You would **of** screamed, too.*
*Rex could **of** been badly injured.*

Correct Usage:

*You would **have** screamed, too.*
*Todd could **have** been badly injured.*

Get Sharp: Usage Guide

Better Grades & Higher Test Scores / READING & LANGUAGE
Copyright ©2003 by Incentive Publications, Inc., Nashville, TN.

 These here rules don't apply to me.

 WRONG!

 More dos and don'ts

DON'T... use *here* or *there* with a demonstrative pronoun. DO... use demonstrative pronouns without *here* or *there*.

Incorrect Usage:

*This **here** crab is a hermit crab.*
*That **there** boy is bothering the crabs.*
*Will **those there** crabs pinch you?*

Correct Usage:

This crab is a hermit crab.
That boy is bothering the crabs.
*Will **those** crabs pinch you?*

DON'T... split infinitives. DO... try to keep the *to* next to the verb in an infinitive.

Incorrect Usage:

*She tends **to** easily **burn** in the sun.*
*Can you all remember **to** not **swim** alone?*

Correct Usage:

*She tends **to burn** easily in the sun.*
*Can you all remember not **to swim** alone?*

DON'T... use *where* after *at*. DO... use *where* without *at*.

Incorrect Usage:

***Where** is the lifeguard **at**?*
*Do you know **where** your towel is **at**?*

Correct Usage:

***Where** is the lifeguard?*
*Do you know **where** your towel is?*

DON'T... dangle participles. DO... keep the participle close to
The meaning will become unclear. the word it modifies.

Incorrect Usage:

*Sam caught a marlin **fishing from the yacht**.*
*We heard about the beached whale **eating lunch in front of the TV**.*

Correct Usage:

***Fishing from the yacht**, Sam caught a marlin.*
***While eating lunch in front of the TV**, we heard about the beached whale.*

Get Sharp: Usage Guide

Usage Mix-ups

anyway and anyways

Anyway does not need an *s* at the end. There is no such word as *anyways*!
The same is true for **anywhere, everywhere, nowhere** and **somewhere**.

Correct: *Anyway, I can't possibly ride on an elephant.*

Incorrect: *I can't see elephants **anywheres**!*

beside and besides

Beside means "next to" or "at the side of."   *Besides* means "in addition to."

between and among

Between is used to show a relationship or comparison between two persons or things,
or to compare more than two items within the same group.
Among is used to show a relationship in which more than two persons or things within
the same group.

Correct: *For lunch, the zebra alternated his eating **between** two carcasses.*
             *What was the difference **between** the two meals?*
             *When taking pictures, I couldn't decide **between** the zebra, the hippo, and the giraffe.*
             *There was confusion **among** the zebras as to whose lunch was whose.*
             *The lunch was shared **among** several zebras.*

Incorrect: *Lunch was shared **between** all members of the entire family of zebras.*
             *One zebra just couldn't choose **among** the two possibilities.*

Better Grades & Higher Test Scores / READING & LANGUAGE

set and sit

Set means "to place" or "to put." Forms of *set* are **usually** followed by a direct object.
Sit means "to place oneself in a seated position." Forms of *sit* are **not** followed by a direct object.
(Forms of *set* are *set, setting, set, set*. Forms of *sit* are *sit, sitting, sat, sat*.)

Correct:
*The zookeeper **set** the food bucket too close to the cheetah.*
*After **setting** the keys by the gate, she walked away and forgot them.*
*Which panther is **sitting** closest to the fence?*
*That's the mother; she has **sat** by that fence since dinner.*
*A rumor has it that she **sits** there waiting to snatch visitors' fingers.*

Incorrect:
*Don't **sit** that food bucket near the cheetah!*
*Why are you **setting** so close to the panther's mouth?*
*I'm sure I **sat** my hamburger right here on the fence.*

raise and rise

Raise means "to lift" or "to grow." Forms of *raise* are **usually** followed by a direct object.
Rise means "to move upward" or "get up." Forms of *rise* are **not** followed by a direct object.
(Forms of *raise* are *raise, raising, raised, raised*. Forms of *rise* are *rise, rising, rose, risen*.)

Correct:
*Will the giraffe **raise** his head to treetop?*
*Actually, he **raised** it higher than that.*
*He ate a breakfast of leaves before the sun had **risen**.*
*We watched him **rise** up on his tall legs.*

Incorrect:
*The giraffe family has **risen** four children.*
*Don't **rise** your camera up just yet.*
*Which giraffe **rose** her head up when you shouted?*

let and leave

Let means "to allow to."   *Leave* means "to go away."

Get Sharp: Usage Guide

lay and lie

Lay means "to put" or "to place." Forms of *lay* are **usually** followed by a direct object.
Lie means "to recline" or "to be positioned." Forms of *lie* are **not** followed by a direct object.
(Forms of *lay* are *lay, laying, laid, laid*. Forms of *lie* are *lie, lying, lay, lain*.)

Correct: *Why did the rhinoceros **lie** in that mud? She has **lain** there the entire afternoon.*
*Could she be **lying** there because she's sick of standing up?*
*Where did you **lay** your ticket? Oh! I think I **laid** them beside the ostrich pen!*

Incorrect: *I noticed the rhino is **laying** in the mud. Hasn't she **laid** there for hours?*
*Did you **lie** the tickets near the fountain? I'm sure you've **lain** them somewhere.*

can and may

Can is in indication of ability.
May is a request or granting of permission.

Correct: *Can the gorilla eat peanut butter sandwiches without getting sick?*
May I give the gorilla my peanut butter sandwich?

Incorrect: *Can I play with the gorilla, mom?*
Gorillas are so agile that they may climb bars.

good and well

Good is an adjective. Use it before nouns and with linking verbs to modify a subject.
Well is an adverb. Use it to modify action verbs.
Well is also used as an adjective to mean "in good health."

Correct: *I hope I can do a **good** job at my interview for the zookeeper's job.*
*You certainly did **well** performing as a gorilla.*

Incorrect: *You look **well** in that gorilla suit.*
*It's **well** that you got the job as a zookeeper.*
*Didn't I do **good** at pretending to be a gorilla?*

how come and why

How come is not good usage for asking a question. In formal writing and speech, use *why* instead.

Why did you choose to stay overnight in the cage with the python?

How come you stayed in the cage with that python?

Correct   Incorrect

bad and badly

Bad is an adjective. Use it before nouns and with linking verbs to modify a subject.
Badly is an adverb. Use it to modify action verbs.

Correct: *The **bad** bear ate all the berries. Then he felt **bad** about eating all the berries.*
            *The bear behaved **badly** when he ate all the berries.*

Incorrect: *The bear felt **badly** about the berries.*
            *The bear behaved **bad** yesterday.*

real and really

Real is an adjective. Use it before nouns and with linking verbs to modify a subject.
Don't use **real** as a substitute for the adverbs **really** or **very**.
Really is an adverb. Use it to modify action verbs, adjectives, or other adverbs.

Correct: *Bruno's stomach **really** hurt after that big berry meal.*
            *The **real** story is that he ate his berries and Brixby's too.*

Incorrect: *It was a **real** bad idea to eat so many berries.*
            *Mom, is that bear the **really** thing?*

quick and quickly

Quick is an adjective. Use it before nouns and with linking verbs to modify a subject.
Quickly is an adverb. Use it to modify verbs.

Correct: *Could the vet find a **quick** cure for Bruno's ailment? How **quickly** will the medicine work?*
            *That remedy is **quick**!*

Incorrect: *Bruno got sick very **quick** after he ate the hiker's backpack.*
            *That's the **quickliest** I've ever seen a bear get sick.*

sure and surely

Sure is an adjective. Use it before nouns and with linking verbs to modify a subject.
Surely is an adverb. Use it to modify verbs, adjectives, and other adverbs.

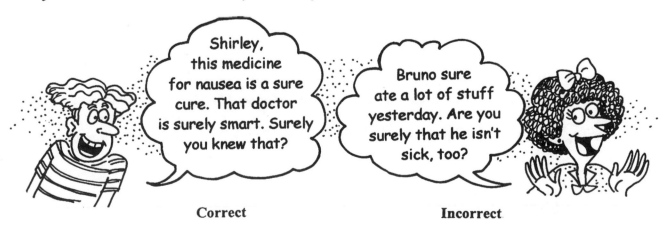

Correct   Incorrect

Get Sharp: Usage Guide

Capitalize

• • • all proper nouns and proper adjectives

A proper noun is the name of a particular person, place, thing, or idea.
Elmo, Omaha, Golden Gate Bridge, Independence Day

A proper adjective is an adjective formed from a proper noun.
Spanish dances, French fries, American flag

• • • the names of people and also the initials or abbreviations that stand for those names
Angela Algae, Homer S. Heartbreak, Aunt Blabby, Mr. Ragoo, Sir Munchalot

---

Dear Prim Ann Proper · *the last word in grammatical etiquette*

wednesday, 12th
dear miss prim,
    i have a Big problem. i think i'm using proper nouns Improperly. i am so Frustrated and confused. can you help me? i have 200 invitations to write for my bar mitzvah by thursday.
    thank You,
marvin q. From kalamazoo

Dear Marvin,
    You do have a problem. I think if you brush up on your capitalization techniques, you will be happy with the results.

    Good luck,
    Miss Prim Ann Proper

• • • names of countries, cities, counties, and towns
Malaysia, Jackson County, Los Angeles, Cairo, Little Rock, Argentina

• • • geographical names
Hudson River, Grand Canyon, Lake Ontario, Gopher Gulch, Rio Grande River

• • • words which indicate particular sections of a country or area
Southwestern U.S., Northern Italy, Western Europe, Middle East, South Pacific

• • • the names of languages, races, and nationalities *(and proper adjectives formed from them)*
Turkish, Caucasian, Russian, Columbian, Africans, Latin, Arabian

• • • the names of religions *(and proper adjectives formed from them)*
Islam, Judaism, Christianity, Buddhism, Buddhist, Catholic

- • • titles used with names of persons and abbreviations standing for those titles
  Mrs. Adams, Sir Francis Femur, Corporal Clang, Prince Charming, Lee Lang, Jr.

- • • words such as mother, father, aunt, and uncle when these words are used as names
  Aunt Suzy, Uncle Snoozy, Father Time, Mother Nature

- • • the first and last words of a title, and every word in between except articles (*a, an, the*), short prepositions, and short conjunctions

  The Legend of the Green-Footed Gorilla and Her Hidden Treasure
  What You Don't Know About the Bermuda Triangle
  Never Believe News from a Plastic Radio
  Everyone but Sara
  One Short Step from Firm Ground to Quicksand

- • • abbreviations of titles
  Mrs., Dr., Pvt., Mr. Sgt., Pres.

- • • abbreviations of organizations
  FBI, NASA, N.Y.P.D., NATO

- • • the names of days of the week and months of the year
  February, Monday, Wednesday

- • • the names of holidays and special days
  Valentine's Day, Easter, Fourth of July, Bastille Day

- • • names of historical events and documents
  Civil War, Declaration of Independence

Professor Skittle discusses his new book, a biography of three presidents, JFK, FDR, and LBJ, on the radio show, BOOK TALK.

KGAB ...the best in radio chat.

- • • names of periods of time
  Pleistocene Era, Middle Ages, Renaissance

- • • the names of organizations, associations, or a team and its members
  Olympians, Chamber of Commerce, Black Hawks, Justice Department

- • • names of businesses
  Terrific Toys, Inc., Popcorn Co., Old Typewriters, Inc., J.C. Penney Co.

- • • official names of products
  Kleenex, Coca-Cola, Pampers, Windex

- • • names of subjects taught in school when they name courses
  Geometry, Physics, Geography, Physical Education

- • • the first word of every sentence and of a direct quotation
  Never put worms in pancakes! She asked, "Why not?"

Punctuate with a comma,

On August 3, Mortimer took bug spray, jelly beans, beef jerky, extra socks and jalapeno peppers on his camping trip.

Five hours later, lost and weary, rain-soaked and foot-sore, Mortimer stumbled into camp.

As he blew on a pile of twigs, oh, how he wished that he'd come better prepared.

• • • between words, phrases, or clauses in a series (at least three items)
  Mortimer saw goblins, gorillas, geckos, and Gila monsters.

• • • to separate digits in a number to distinguish hundreds, thousands, etc.
  200,000,000 or 17,041,107 or 55,555

• • • to distinguish items in an address or date
  August 15, 1532

• • • to set off the exact words of a speaker from the rest of the sentence
  "If you hear a rumbling, be sure to run," shouted the guide.

• • • to separate a noun of direct address from the rest of the sentence
  Stay away from that pool of quicksand, Mortimer.

• • • between two independent clauses joined by such words as: but, or, nor, for, yet, and so.
  He brought no hiking boots, nor did he bring a sleeping bag.

• • • to separate an adverb clause or long modifying phrase from the independent clause following it
  Besides being hot and grumpy, Mortimer was quite sure he was lost.

• • • to separate an interjection or weak exclamation from the rest of the sentence
  Oh, how he wished he had stayed home for the weekend!

• • • to set off a word, phrase, or clause that interrupts the main thought of a sentence
  The last person to see Mortimer, other than the lizard, was Emily.

• • • to separate an explanatory phrase from the rest of the sentence
  His greatest weakness, a non-existent sense of direction, led to the mistaken wrong turn.

• • • to separate an appositive
  Jacob B. Shure, a high school friend, went searching after dark for Mortimer.

• • • to enclose a title, name, or initials which follow a person's last name
  The last person to join the trip was Dr. Ed Venturer, M.D.

• • • to separate two or more adjectives which equally modify the same noun
  A weary, frightened Mortimer finally stumbled into camp.

• • • to set off nonessential phrases (phrases or clauses which are not necessary to the basic meaning of the sentence)
  The fire, which had been blazing warmly, died just when Mortimer needed it most.

Punctuate with a period.

• • • to end a sentence which makes a statement or gives a command that is not an exclamation

I need to warn you that J.J.'s pet elephant is particularly fond of milkshakes.

Keep an eye on your milkshake when that elephant comes around.

• • • after each part of an abbreviation – unless the abbreviation is an acronym   *Mr., Dr., Co., Sept.*

• • • as a decimal point and to separate dollars and cents   *$666.66*

• • • after an initial   *J.R. Trubble, Lucy B. Fancy, C. I. A.*

Punctuate with a question mark?

STOP!

• • • at the end of a direct question (an interrogative sentence)
Didn't I tell you the elephant would go after your milkshake?

Punctuate with an exclamation point!

• • • to express strong feeling
(May be placed after a word, phrase,
or exclamatory sentence.)
Stop! My milkshake! Somebody stop that elephant!

*(Note: Never use more than one exclamation point
at the end of a word, phrase, or sentence.)*

TAKE ONE
MORE STEP
AND
YOU'LL
FALL OFF
A CLIFF!

Punctuate with an ellipsis . . . (three periods)

• • • to show that one or more words are left out of a quotation
"You should have known . . . I tried to warn you about it," Sam reminded her.

• • • when the final words are left out of a sentence (Place the ellipsis after the period.)
It was not her last encounter with an elephant. . . .

Punctuate with (parentheses)

• • • around words that are included in a sentence to add information or help make an idea clearer.
After that incident (the one with the milkshake), Lucy was more wary of elephants.

Punctuate with a semicolon;

• • • to join two independent clauses which are not connected with a coordinate conjunction.
He could never believe in something like Bigfoot; that changed last night.

• • • to join two independent clauses when the clauses are connected only by a conjunctive adverb (also, as a result, for example, however, therefore)
It could be an ordinary animal; but no ordinary animal has footprints like this.

• • • to separate groups of words or phrases which already contain commas
He heard grunts, screams, and moans; then a rumble, a crash, an ear-splitting shriek.

Punctuate with a colon:

• • • after the salutation of a business letter
Dear Ms. Sasquatch:

• • • between the parts of a number which indicate time
11:13 p.m.

• • • to formally introduce a sentence, question, or quotation.
So my question is this: What did you really see out there in the woods last night?

• • • to introduce a list.
You'd believe me if I said I saw any of these: a cougar, a bear, a moose, or an elk.

Dear Mrs. Sasquatch:

This letter is to inform you that your son, Harry, was seen at 10:47 in my huckleberry patch, again! So, tell me this: What are you going to do about it? Remember: I know the truant officer, I know where you live, and I've reached my wit's end!

Signed,
A Disgruntled Neighbor

Punctuate with a dash ——

• • • to indicate a sudden break or change in the sentence.
I really did come face to face with Bigfoot— not that I could ever convince you.

• • • to emphasize a word, series of words, phrase, or clause
The smell—a powerful, acrid odor like none other I've ever encountered—was overwhelming.

News Flash!
N o r t h w e s t   N e w s
Bigfoot, the well-known, but seldom-seen, legendary creature was spotted this morning in Mr. Griper's huckleberry patch. Update on K-LOG News at eleven p.m.

Punctuate with a hyphen –

• • • to make some compound words   *brother-in-law, passer-by, forget-me-not*
• • • to join the words in compound numbers from 21-99   *sixty-two, twenty-nine*
• • • between the numbers in a fraction expressed in words   *three-fourths, one-half*
• • • to join a capital letter to a noun or participle   *V-shaped, U-turn*
• • • to form new words beginning with the prefixes *self, ex, all,* and *great*   *self-taught, great-aunt*
• • • to join two or more words in a compound modifier   *well-groomed, highly-skilled*

Punctuate with *italics* (or underlining)

• • • titles of magazines, newspapers, pamphlets, books, plays, films, radio and television programs, book-length poems, record albums, and the names of ships and aircraft

Did you borrow my copy of *Three Dogs on a Surfboard*?

I read about lice in *The Journal of Yucky Ailments*.

Who sailed on the *S. S. Pinafore*?

Harry Potter and the Sorcerer's Stone was as good as you promised!

• • • foreign words not commonly used in everyday English   Let's eat some *petit fours*.

• • • scientific names   I've been bitten by a *Crocodylus acutus*.

• • • any word, number, or letter which is being discussed or used in a special way

The meaning of the word *maelstrom* is a whirlpool or swirling chaos.

Punctuate with an apostrophe '

• • • to replace letters that are omitted in a contraction
we're, it's, I'll, you've, can't

• • • to form the plural of a letter, number, or sign   *3's, z's, #'s*

• • • form the possessive form of a singular noun
Sam's surfboard, mosquito's bite, man's sunburn

• • • to form the possessive form of a plural noun
mosquitoes' bites, mice's tails

• • • with an expression indicating time   *three o'clock*

Get Sharp Tip # 6
Don't put apostrophes in words that don't need them.

I'll have one of those burgers, but hold the apostrophe!

ALL OUR HAMBURGER'S HAVE ONIONS!

Punctuate with "quotation marks"

• • • to punctuate titles of songs, poems, short stories, lectures, courses, episodes of radio or television programs, chapters of books, and articles found in magazines, newspapers, or encyclopedias

"Natural World" aired a whole episode about the Abominable Snowman.

Our whole class was mesmerized by Annie's poem, "The Legend of the Yeti Comes Alive."

• • • to set apart a word which is being discussed, to indicate that a word is slang, or to point out that a word is being used in a special way

This gives a new meaning to the word "monster."

Toni went "ballistic" when she heard the low growl behind her.

It was a really "smart" idea to explore the Abominable Snowman's cave.

• • • before and after direct quotations (See examples on page 113.)

AN ABOMINABLE TALE

A CLIMBER'S NOTEBOOK
by Jen Klymer

Friday, 13th, Somewhere in Nepal

Most of my fellow climbers were skeptical about the existence of the Yeti in this area.

1   "There's nothing to worry about, since there is no such thing as a Yeti," said Ben, my climbing partner.

2   I answered: "I'm not so sure."

3   "Many people tell stories about seeing an abominable snowman," I added.

4   "That's all they are is stories," Ben shouted back, "just fairy tales!"

5   "Anyway, let's get out of here," I begged.

6   Then I added, "Don't you sense something eerie?"

7   Ben was unshakable; "No stupid legend will scare me away!" he insisted.

8   I heard him mumble under his breath, "The Yeti is a foolish superstition!"

9   "Heeeeellllpppppppp!" he screamed as he ran away, terrified.

10 "So," I thought, "it's just a stupid legend, huh?"

11 What would Ben say now about the "foolish superstition"?

Punctuating Quotations

• • • Place quotation marks around **exact words** quoted *(all examples above)*.

• • • Periods and commas are **always** placed **inside** quotation marks *(1-5)*.

• • • An exclamation point or question mark is placed:
   inside the quotation marks when it punctuates the quotation *(4, 6-10)*
   outside when it punctuates the main sentence *(11)*.

• • • Semicolons or colons are placed **outside** quotation marks *(2, 7)*.

Get Sharp: Mechanics Guide

14 SPELLING RULES TO REMEMBER

1 Write *i* before *e* except after *c*, or when sounded like **long a** (as in **neighbor** or **weigh**).

Examples: *achieve, quotient, piece, believe, grief, convenient, shriek, hygiene, receive, deceive, conceit, freight, sleigh, neighbor, reign, weigh, sheik*

Rule breakers: *their, conscience, science, weird, neither, leisure, foreign, heir, height, seize, counterfeit, either, sovereign, financier*

2 The spelling of a base word does not change when you add a prefix.

Examples: *misunderstood, disregard, extraordinary, transatlantic, reinvestigate*

3 When a one-syllable word ends in a consonant preceded by one vowel, double the final consonant before adding a suffix that begins with a vowel.

Examples: *napping, hitting, shopped, reddish, fretted, muddy, robber, beggar*

4 When a multi-syllable word ends in a consonant preceded by one vowel, and the accent is on the last syllable, double the final consonant before adding a suffix that begins with a vowel.

Examples: *forgettable, beginning, regretted*

5 When a word ends in silent *e*, drop the *e* before adding a suffix which begins with a vowel.
Examples: *usable, vacation, rated, stating, liking, roper, hoping*

Do not drop the *e* when the suffix begins with a consonant.

Examples: *useful, statement, likeness, hopeless, spiteful, noiseless, lonely*

Rule breakers: *truly, argument, ninth*

6 If the letter before a final *y* is a vowel, do not change the *y* when adding a suffix.
Examples: *keyless, payable, joyous, playful, prayed, boyish*

7 If the letter before a final *y* is a consonant, change the *y* to *i* before adding any suffix except *ing*. The *y* never changes when adding **ing**.

Examples: *carried, laziness, pliers, fried, pitiless, business, fanciful, worrying, frying*

8 The ending pronounced *shun* is generally spelled *tion*.

Examples: *equation, conversation, motion, ration, vacation, education*

Rule breakers: *confusion, musician, cushion, decision, transfusion*

9 If the letter before a final *y* is a vowel, do not change the *y* when adding a suffix.

Examples: *sprayed, keys, joyful, rays, monkeying, boyhood*

10 When a prefix ends with the same letter that begins the main word, include both letters. When a suffix begins with the same letter that ends the main word, include both letters.

Examples: *misstep, illogical, illegal, immobile, accidentally, meanness, tailless*

11 When the letters *c* and *g* have a soft sound they are followed by *i, e,* or *y*.

Examples: *pencil, circus, celery, certain, cereal, cycle, saucy, gigantic, rigid, gesture, legend, gently, gyrate, edgy*

12 When the letters *c* and *g* have a hard sound they are followed by *a, o,* or *u*.

Examples: *cannot, cactus, organize, cougar, cupcake, cuckoo, copper, gallop, gastronomical, gorilla, ego, legume, gulp, gusto*

13 Suffixes that follow the ***soft c or g*** always begin with *i* or *e*.
Examples: *magician, contagious, negligence*

14 The letter *q* is always followed by the letter *u* in the English language.
Examples:

Unique Critiques
by Quentin Q. Quizzmore

★ ★ ★ ★

I want to ac**qu**aint the movie-going public with the **qu**irky movie, "**Qu**een Ra**qu**el, the Se**qu**el," released **qu**ite recently. It is the tale of a **qu**arrelsome **qu**een re**qu**ired to be**qu**eath a uni**que** pla**que** to a **qu**asi-heroic **qu**artet of mos**qu**ito-net salesmen who saved her from death in a **qu**agmire of **qu**icksand in the Kingdom of **Qu**ark. This **qu**ixotic tale, filmed in the e**qu**atorial jungles, **qu**ickened my desire to see se**qu**el number three. I be**qu**eath four stars to this movie for its **qu**aintness.

Words with Tricky Sounds

Here's a quick guide to those confusing letters that make different sounds in different places. To be a good speller, you need to get these straight!

Meet *FANTASTIC PHIL*
the Legendary Prestidigitator
of Magical Manipulation

It's Magic!

F The *f* sound can be spelled with *f* (*funny, fantastic, friend, gift, bereft*) or with *ph* (*phone, physical, phrase, graph*), or with *gh* (*laughter*).

G The **hard g** sound can be spelled with *g* (*gutter, gumball, leg, aggravate*) or with *gh* (*ghost, ghetto, ghastly*).

J The *j* sound can be spelled with *j* (*jelly, jolly, jester, eject*) or with *g* (*giant, gym, edge, legend*).

K The *k* sound can be spelled with *k* (*kickball, kitchen, liking, okay*), with *c* (*catalog, clever, Eric, Cancun*), or with *ch* (*chorus, chemist*).

N The *n* sound can be spelled with *n* (*nifty, ninety, blend, banana*), with *kn* (*knee, knot, knob*), with *gn* (*gnat, gnome*), or with *pn* (*pneumonia*).

R The *r* sound can be spelled with *r* (*riddle, rascal, argue, thrill, eager*), with *rh* (*rhinoceros, rhyme*), or with *wr* (*write, wriggle, wrong*).

S The *s* sound can be spelled with *s* (*sassy, sassafras, Sacramento*), with *c* (*celery, city, sincere*), with *sc* (*scissors, scene, scintillating*), or with *psy* (*psychiatry, psychic*).

T The *t* sound can be spelled with *t* (*tickle, tackle, tattoo, snippet*) or with *pt* (*pterodactyl*).

W The *w* sound can be spelled with *w* (*witch, wizard, wish, away*) or with *wh* (*whine, whistle*).

Z The *z* sound can be spelled with *z* (*zero, zoo, kazoo, sap*) or with *x* (*xylophone*).

KR The *kr* sound can be spelled with *kr* (*krypton*), with *cr* (*cranky, creepy, excruciating*), or with *chr* (*Christmas*).

SH The *sh* sound can be spelled with *sh* (*wash, shallow, shiver, shirk*), with *ch* (*chef, chateau*), or with *s* (*sugar, sure*).

SK The *sk* sound can be spelled with *sk* (*skinny, skate, whisk*), with *sc* (*scrape, scared*), with *sch* (*scheme, school*), or with *squ* (*squirt, squall, squeeze*).

Words with Missing Sounds

Some letters don't make any sound at all!
Pay attention to these words with silent letters. Learn their spelling well.

ache	gourmet	light	sword
answer	heir	muscle	talk
badge	heiress	pledge	thyme
ballet	heirloom	pneumonia	tomb
balmy	herb	psalm	wedge
bomb	honest	pseudonym	whimper
bridge	hymn	psychic	whistle
budge	judge	psychiatrist	whole
calm	knack	psychologist	wrangle
castle	knave	ptarmigan	wrap
chalk	knead	ptomaine	wrath
character	knee	raspberries	wreath
chlorine	kneel	reign	wreck
chord	knew	resign	wreckage
chorus	knickers	rheumatic	wren
cough	knife	rheumatism	wrench
crumb	knight	rhinoceros	wrestle
czar	knives	Rhode Island	wrestler
dough	knit	rhododendron	wretch
dumb	knock	rhombus	wretched
edge	knoll	rhubarb	wriggle
fudge	knot	rhyme	wring
ghetto	know	rhythm	wrinkle
ghastly	knowledge	scene	wrist
ghost	known	scepter	write
gnarled	knuckle	schedule	written
gnash	lamb	scheme	wrong
gnat	laugh	scissors	wrote
gnaw	ledge	sorbet	wrung
gnome	llama	stalk	wry

The gnome in knickers whistled and laughed as he knocked a whole pile of water bombs off the ledge.

Ha ha ha.

POP! SPLASH!

Get Sharp: Spelling Guide

Words with Tricky Endings

The English language has endings galore! And so many of them sound or look very much alike. These different endings can wreak havoc on your spelling, unless you know which ending is which for use on what word! Here are some of the tricky ones.

. . . end with *ant*

applicant	mutant
assistant	observant
attendant	occupant
defiant	participant
distant	pheasant
elegant	pleasant
elephant	redundant
hydrant	restaurant
ignorant	significant
important	vigilant
migrant	vacant

. . . end with *ent*

absorbent
adolescent
accident
ambivalent
apparent
belligerent
benevolent
fluent
negligent
president
resident
superintendent
temperament

. . . end with *ate*

accumulate	graduate
calculate	hesitate
candidate	hibernate
celebrate	imitate
chocolate	incubate
devastate	irrigate
decorate	liberate
delegate	operate
duplicate	rotate
educate	saturate
estimate	separate

. . . end with *al*

brutal
classical
commercial
electrical
fatal
frugal
hysterical
legal
practical
oral
recital
residential
rural
spiral
technical
theatrical
tropical
typical

. . . end with *el*

cancel	model
channel	shrivel
level	unravel
	vessel

. . . end with *le*

bundle	icicle
candle	terrible
clavicle	visible
gargle	wrestle

. . . end with *ile*

fragile	infantile
fertile	juvenile
futile	reptile
hostile	senile

. . . end with *ize*

apologize
criticize
equalize
familiarize
fantasize
hypothesize
optimize
realize
utilize

. . . end with *ise*

exercise
promise
supervise
surprise
televise

The End
(this space for rent)

Better Grades & Higher Test Scores / READING & LANGUAGE
Copyright ©2003 by Incentive Publications, Inc., Nashville, TN.

. . . end with *tion*
addition
dictation
portion
prevention
revolution
tradition

. . . end with *sion*
confusion
decision
erosion
explosion
invasion
transfusion

. . . end with *ion*
cushion
fashion

. . . end with *cian*
magician
musician

. . . end with *uous*
arduous
conspicuous

Elephants never forget **spelling rule #13!** Suffixes that follow the soft *c* or soft *g* always begin with *i* or *e*.

. . . end with *ious*
contagious
malicious

. . . end with *eous*
advantageous
courteous
gorgeous
igneous
outrageous

. . . end with *ius*
genius

Gorgeous Gertie

. . . end with *ous*
adventurous
anonymous
dangerous
frivolous
glamorous
jealous
marvelous
tremendous
wondrous

. . . end with *ence*
absence
abstinence
affluence
influence
consequence
dependence
evidence
independence
negligence
occurrence
sequence

. . . end with *ance*
abundance
acceptance
acquaintance
allowance
appearance
assurance
attendance
elegance
importance
insurance
nuisance
reliance

. . . end with *able*
abominable
admirable
allowable
commendable
conquerable
enjoyable
lovable
payable
perishable
reliable
understandable
washable

. . . end with *ible*
edible
eligible
accessible
admissible
gullible
impossible
invisible
legible
reversible
sensible
tangible
terrible

Better Grades & Higher Test Scores / READING & LANGUAGE
Copyright ©2003 by Incentive Publications, Inc., Nashville, TN.

Get Sharp: Spelling Guide

Confusing Words

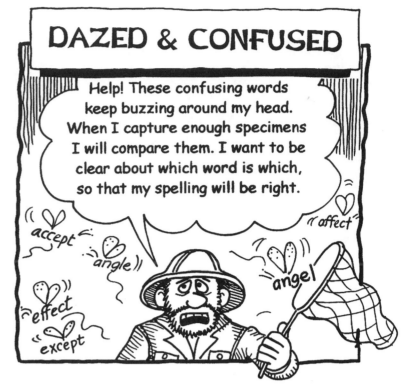

DAZED & CONFUSED

Help! These confusing words keep buzzing around my head. When I capture enough specimens I will compare them. I want to be clear about which word is which, so that my spelling will be right.

accept
angle
effect
except
affect
angel

accept? or except?

accept *(receive)*; except *(excluding)*

> *That ice cream shop doesn't **accept** checks.*

> *They sell all my favorite flavors **except** artichoke ripple.*

adopt? or adept?

adopt *(take on or take in)*; adept *(skilled)*

> *Mario just **adopted** twelve rattlesnakes.*

> *It's good he's so **adept** at handling snakes.*

advice? or advise?

advice *(recommendation)*; advise *(to give advice)*

> *When you were **advised** to stay away from that cliff, why didn't you take the **advice**?*

affect? or effect?

affect *(to influence)*; effect *(a result)*

> *Her mother's warnings did not **affect** her in the least.*

> *Even the sign saying, "Piranhas are Deadly" had no **effect** on her behavior.*

angle? or angel?

angle *(geometric figure)*; angel *(heavenly being)*

> *Do you think **angels** have to do geometry—things like measuring **angles** and naming triangles?*

attitude? or altitude?

attitude *(demeanor)*; altitude *(height)*

> *You have a sour **attitude** about mountain climbing! Is it because you get sick at high **altitudes**?*

carton? or cartoon?

carton *(container)*; cartoon *(funny picture)*

> *I heard you got a good job drawing **cartoons** on **cartons** of caramel corn.*

celery? or salary?

celery *(chewy, stringy vegetable)*; salary *(money paid for work)*
  Don't eat **celery** just before you ask your boss for a raise in your **salary**.

college? or collage?

college *(school of higher education)*; collage *(many items combined into a work of art)*
  A **collage** of baby pictures will not replace an essay on your **college** application.

coma? or comma?

comma *(mark of punctuation)*; coma *(state of unconsciousness)*
  After a month in a **coma**, Sal couldn't tell a **comma** from a semicolon.

desert? or dessert?

desert *(a very dry place)*; dessert *(a tasty, after-dinner food)*
  When I was lost in the **desert**, I had repeated dreams about cold, creamy **desserts**.

dairy? or diary?

dairy *(a place where milk products are processed)*; diary *(a written record of one's life)*
  We stumbled upon a secret **diary** hidden in a bottle in the **dairy**.

incredible? or inedible?

incredible *(unbelievable)*; inedible *(not fit for eating)*
  Wasn't it **incredible** how B. J. lunched on such **inedible** things as shoelaces?

lose? or loose?

lose *(be without something you had)*; loose *(not tight)*
  If you wear your pants so **loose**, you just might **lose** them!

though? through? thorough? or trough?

though *(however)*; through *(within something*; thorough *(complete)*; and trough *(feeding box)*
  Joe was **thoroughly** clean even **though** he rode his bike right **through** the pig's **trough**.

which? or witch?

which *(a question pronoun used to identify what one)*; witch *(a character with magical powers)*
  One witch wandered through poison ivy. One did not. **Which witch** has the itch?

Better Grades & Higher Test Scores / READING & LANGUAGE
Copyright ©2003 by Incentive Publications, Inc., Nashville, TN.

Get Sharp: Spelling Guide

Other Troublesome Words

Some of the most troublesome words for spellers
are borrowed from different languages. Other words that often
stump spellers are very short words or very long words.
Here's the correct spelling for some of the most common
of those tricky words—all at one quick glance.

French words taste the best!

Borrowed Words

acrobat	eureka	piano
algebra	fiancée	pirate
antique	juvenile	résumé
blitz	guru	sarong
bourgeois	ink	shampoo
buoy	khaki	status quo
carousel	kindergarten	tambourine
chauffeur	lasso	tornado
comet	magazine	tourniquet
cul-de-sac	mosquito	tsar
diamond	mandarin	tycoon
dynamite	octopus	veranda
elite	pajama	yacht

MENU
Borrowed Food Words

banana
crepe
tortilla
barbecue
omelet
petit fours
spaghetti
doughnut
macaroni
molasses
vanilla

lasagna
enchilada
crepes
bologna
sauerkraut
éclair
fricassee
paella
enchilada
soufflé
crème caramel
onion
hors d'oeuvres
gourmet
chef

LITTLE Words

about	enough	island	safety
all	enter	just	should
almost	entry	knives	since
already	ever	laugh	though
any	every	length	thought
awful	fifth	listen	toward
busy	first	many	truly
buy	fought	mine	tough
candle	forget	might	used
circle	four	much	very
color	forty	must	week
cough	friend	often	when
could	gym	open	which
does	half	people	while
drawer	here	please	whole
early	hope	really	won't
easy	hurried	refer	would

BIG Words

abominable

abracadabra   *ambidextrous*   arteriosclerosis

biodegradable   brontosaurus

circumstantial   delicatessen   ELECTROMAGNETIC

EXAGGERATION   hieroglyphics

hippopotamus

MAGNANIMOUS   **obstreperous**   ORTHODONTIST

(parenthetical)   PARLIAMENTARIAN

Pennsylvania   **perpendicular**   pharmaceutical

philanthropic   **phosphorescence**   plagiarism

polysyllabic   precipitation   **sarsaparilla**

simultaneously   *unambiguous*   VETERINARIAN

xenophobia   **xylophone**

WHAAAAA!

I do not exaggerate the degree of discomfort precipitated by the biodegradable deposit in my pantaloons. Yet, simultaneously, I remain philosophical about an eventual, satisfactory remedy.

Commonly Misspelled Words *(Spelled correctly!)*

Tom Foolery cautions you:
"Learn these words. They are often spelled wrong."

absence
about
accident
acre
account
accurate
accuse
ache
achieve
address
adolescent
advertise
again
aisle
allowance
almost
already
always
amateur
ambulance
among
amuse

ancient
angel
angle
anniversary
anonymous
answer
Antarctica
anxious
any
apologize
architect
argument
arithmetic
attendance
attention
August
balloon
banana
beauty
beautiful
because
been
beginning
believe
benefit
bicycle
biscuit
blizzard
blue
bookkeeper
brake
break
breakfast
breath (n.)
breathe (v.)
brief
broccoli
built
bureau

burglar
business
busy
cafeteria
calendar
canal
cancel
candle
cannot
canoe
capacity
carburetor
carton
cashier
caught
cauliflower
cemetery
certain
character
chief
chocolate
choose
chorus
cinnamon
citizen
climb
cocoa
collar
college
color
Columbus
coming
committee
cough
could
counterfeit
country
courage
courtesy

damage
dangerous
dear
deceive
defense
deficient
definitely
delicious
dependence
desert
desperate
diamond
dictionary
difference
dinosaur
doctor
dollar
easy
education
efficiency
elegant
elephant
embarrass
emergency
empty
enough
escape
esophagus
every
exaggerate
exciting
excuse
exercise
exhaust
explain
extraordinary
familiar
fatigue
February

fifth
foreign
forget
forty
fountain
fourth
fragile
frequent
friend
frighten
frugal

gauge
genius
ghost
gnaw
gorgeous
graduate
grammar
grief
guarantee
guess

half
Halloween
having
heaven
heard
height
here
hippopotamus
history
hoarse
honest
hour
hypothesis

icicle
ignorance
immature
immediately
improvement
incident
independence
infection
influence
initial

busness?
busyness?
business?
busness?
buisiness?

innocent
interrupt
interview
irregular
island
instead

jealous
jeopardy
journal
journey
juice
just
justice

kitchen
knead
knew
knife
knives
knock
know

laboratory
laid
language
laundry
laugh
lawyer
league
legislature
library
librarian
license
lieutenant
lightning
likable
likeness
limousine

Lincoln
literature
location
lonely
loose
lose
lovely

machinery
magic
magnify
making
manageable
many
marriage
maneuver
marshmallow
Mediterranean
meant
measurement
medal
medium
memorize
miscellaneous
minute
mischief
molecule
mortgage
mosquito
movement
much

national
naughty
necessary
negligence
neighbor
neither
nervous
niece
noodle
noticeable
nuclear
nuisance
numb

obey
occasionally
occur
occurrence
odor
official
often
once
opaque
opportunity
opposite
ordinary
original
ought
outrageous

Pacific
pajamas
paradise
particle
paid
parallel

surprize?
suprize?
suprise?
surprise?
supprise?

parliament
peculiar
people
perform
physician
picnic
piece
pilot
pleasant

Get Sharp: Spelling Guide

pleasure
pledge
police
politics
potatoes
practice
presence
privilege
promise
protein
quantity
quaint
quarrel
quarter
question
quiet
quite
quotient
raise
realize
really
receive
recent
recognize
rehearse
reign
remedy
require
reservoir
resign
restaurant
rhythm
ridiculous
said
Saturday
scared
schedule
scene
seems
seize
separate
sheik
shoes
shriek

similar
since
sincere
sleigh
society
sophomore
spaghetti
stalk
straight
stomach
success
sugar
sure
sword
tattoo
taught
technique
terrible
terrific
thorough
though
through
tired
tomorrow
tonight
tongue
trespassing
triangle
trouble
truly
Tuesday
toward
twelfth
typical
uncomplicated
unconscious
uniform
unique
united
universe
unusual
useable
used
usually

vacuum
vegetable
vacation
vehicle
very
villain
virtue
virus
visible
voice
waist
waste
weather
Wednesday
week
weigh
weird
where
whether
which
whoever
whole
women
won't
would
wreath
write
writhe
writing
wrote
xenogenesis
xenolith
xylophone
yellow
yacht
yesterday
yacht
your
you're
zealous
zephyr
zinnia
zoology

Don't be fooled!

These may look right, but they are not!

nesessary

freind   hieght   doller

bananna

beleive   lonly

Febuary   apologise

chocalate   calender

beautaful   attendence

wierd   lovly

seperate   exercize

tommorrow   lisence

resturant   excape

cafateria   literture

paralell

GET SHARP →

in

WRITING & SPEAKING

What to Write?

There are so many possibilities for writing. Think beyond paragraphs, stories, and essays. Here are some of the many genres (forms) that writing can take. Try them all!

I am not just fooling around when I talk about all the writing possibilities!

A-B-C books
adventures
advertisements
advice columns
allegories
analogies
anecdotes
announcements
answers
anthems
appeals
apologies
arguments
assumptions
autobiographies
awards

ballads
beauty tips
bedtime stories
beginnings
billboards
biographies
blurbs
books
book jackets
book reviews
brochures
bulletins
bumper stickers

calendar quips
campaign speeches
captions
cartoons
CD covers
cereal boxes
certificates
characterizations
children's books
cinquains
clichés
clues

codes
colloquialisms
comedies
comic strips
commercials
comparisons
complaints
consumer reports
contracts
contrasts
conundrums
conversations
couplets
critiques
crossword puzzles
cumulative stories

debates
definitions
descriptions
dialogues
diamantes
diaries
diets
directions
directories
documents
doubletalk
dramas
dream scripts

editorials
e-mails
encyclopedia entries
epics
epigrams
epilogues
epitaphs
endings
essays
evaluations
exaggerations
exclamations
excuses
explanations

fables
fairy tales
fantasies
feature articles
folklore
free verse

gags
game rules
good news/bad news
gossip
graffiti
greeting cards
grocery lists

haiku
headlines
health tips
horoscopes
how-to booklets
how-NOT-to booklets
hymns

improvisations
indexes
inquiries
interviews
introductions
invitations

jingles
job applications
job descriptions
jokes
journals
jump rope rhymes

lectures
legends
letters
limericks
lists
love notes
luscious words
lyrics

magazines
malapropisms
marquee notices
memories
memos
menus
metaphors
minutes
monologues
movie reviews
mysteries
myths

narrations
news articles
news flashes
newspapers
nonsense
notes
novels
nursery rhymes

obituaries
observations
odes
opinions

palindromes
pamphlets
parables
paraphrases
parodies
party tips
persuasive letters
petitions
phrases
plays
poems
post cards
post scripts
posters
prayers
predictions
problems
problem solutions
product descriptions
programs
profound sayings

prologues
propaganda
proposals
protest letters
proverbs
puns
puzzle clues
puzzle answers

quatrains
questions
questionnaires
quips
quizzes
quotations

raps
reactions
real estate notices
rebuttals
recipes
remedies
reports
requests
requiems
restaurant reviews
resumes
reviews
rhymes
riddles

sale notices
sales pitches
satires
sayings
schedules
science fiction
secrets
self-portraits
sentences
sequels
serialized stories
sermons
signs
silly sayings

skywriting messages
slogans
soliloquies
songs
sonnets
speeches
spoofs
spooky stories
spoonerisms
sports accounts
stories
summaries
superstitions

tall tales
telegrams
telephone directory
test items
textbooks
thank you notes
theater programs
travel posters
titles
tongue twisters
travel brochures
tributes
trivia
TV commercials
TV guides
TV scripts

understatements

vignettes
vitas

want ads
wanted posters
warnings
weather forecasts
weather reports
Web pages
wills
wise sayings
wishes
words

yarns
yellow pages

Well, maybe I am fooling around just a little bit.

Get Sharp Tip # 7

Choose a genre that fits the purpose of the writing.

Writing Modes

There are countless forms for writing (as you've seen on pages 128-129). In general, these fall into a few larger categories, or approaches to writing—called **modes.** Different modes of writing are used for different purposes.

Here are the different modes of writing. When you want to accomplish one of these purposes, it is your choice what form (genre) to use!

Get Sharp Tip # 8

A piece of writing (such as a poem) can fit into more than one category. It might be narrative, as well as descriptive and imaginary!

Expository – writing which explains or informs

Narrative – writing which tells a story about events that happened (real or imaginary or some of each)

Imaginary – writing which includes made-up details (not real)

Persuasive – writing which tries to convince a reader of something

Descriptive – writing which gives details about how something (or person or place) looks, acts, smells, tastes, sounds, or feels

Personal-Expressive – writing which shares the writer's personal reflection or perspective on a topic

The **genre (form)** you choose will depend somewhat on the purpose of the writing. However, there is no one form that must be used for a particular mode or purpose.
For example: To convince someone of something (persuasive), you might write an essay. Or you might write a letter or poem. But you could also use these same forms—essay, letter, or poem—to inform about something (expository).

I'll write an essay that persuades everyone to vote for me.

a recipe for peanut butter-salami ice cream *expository, imaginative, descriptive*

a poster advertising battery-operated tennis shoes *persuasive, descriptive*

safety rules on a ski slope *expository*

directions for taking a bicycle on the subway *expository*

a reflection by a leukemia patient *personal-expressive, narrative*

an editorial denouncing the new city taxes *persuasive, expository*

the diary of a space-dweller *personal-expressive, descriptive, narrative*

a science fiction story about a 25th century high school *imaginative, descriptive*

a news article about a shark attack *expository, descriptive, narrative*

an encyclopedia entry explaining sonic boom *expository*

a tall tale about a infant who founded a diaper company *imaginative, descriptive*

an opinion about the attractiveness of tattoos *persuasive, descriptive*

a short story about French-speaking frogs *imaginative, descriptive, narrative*

a travel brochure for a South Pacific island *persuasive, descriptive*

the autobiography of an Olympic skier *personal-expressive, narrative, descriptive*

In my essay, I'm trying to persuade
my father to let me go to Clown College.

— 131 —

WHAT'S THE DIFFERENCE?

Hey, Mindy! Hey, Mandy! What is **prose**? And what is **poetry**? What's the difference between the two, anyway?

Well, Digby, **prose** is writing or speaking that is done in an ordinary form using sentences and paragraphs.

Poetry is written in lines or stanzas (groups of lines). These may or may not contain complete sentences.

Poetry is usually shorter than prose.

The words and lines in poetry are usually arranged to have more rhythm than prose lines.

Sometimes there is rhyme in a poem.

poetry

The baseball has broken your dining room window.
And I know you're expecting company for dinner shortly.
I'm sorry.
It was a fine hit.
And I got a home run.

prose

Dear Aunt Landra,

This afternoon when I was playing baseball, I got one incredible hit. Actually, it was a home run. Unfortunately, I hit the ball so far that it sailed over the fence and crashed right through your dining room window. I am sorry for the mess it caused when you were getting dinner ready. I will pay for the window to be replaced.
Your apologetic niece,
Sandra

More About Poetry

These are some special characteristics often found in poetry. Many (except for rhyme) are found in prose, too. But poetry makes consistent use of these.

Poetry takes an especially imaginative look at something.

Poetry adds life to an idea, or makes something extraordinary out of an ordinary event.

Poetry has a strong appeal to the senses and the emotions.

The sounds of poetry are pleasing to hear. Poetry makes use of rhyme, rhythm, repetition, alliteration, assonance, and onomatopoeia.

Poetry makes special use of figurative language (techniques such as similes, metaphors, puns, imagery, idioms, personification).

Some Poetry Forms

ballad – a poem which tells a story, usually written in quatrains (4-line stanzas)

blank verse – unrhymed poetry with a meter (repetition of accented and unaccented syllables) The lines are generally 10 syllables in length, with an accent on every other syllable, beginning with the second syllable.

The music tugs my arms and pulls my toes.
It drags me to my feet and begs me, "Move!"
I cannot sit. I cannot walk away.
And soon enough, I'm dancing 'round the room.

cinquain - 5-line poem usually following this form:
Line 1 one word (a title)
Line 2 two words (descriptions of the title)
Line 3 three words (actions about the title)
Line 4 four words (a feeling about the title)
Line 5 one word (a repeat of title, or a synonym)

couplet – two lines of verse that rhyme

Teacher said, "John, write a better verse."
I wrote another; alas, it turned out worse.

elegy – a poem that expresses sadness about someone's death

Oh, no! I think I gave my **cinquain** to the wrong twin!

Crush
Private, delicious
Hiding, blushing, hoping
Sparkles up my life
Secret

Get Sharp: Writing Guide

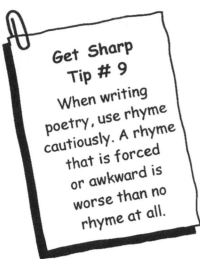

Get Sharp
Tip # 9

When writing poetry, use rhyme cautiously. A rhyme that is forced or awkward is worse than no rhyme at all.

epic – a long story poem, usually telling the adventures of a hero. Probably the most famous epic poem is The Odyssey, a book-length poem by Homer. It follows the adventures of Odysseus, a Greek hero, over a period of many years.

free verse – unrhymed poetry that has no meter

I dreamed the clouds were dragons.
Billows of fluff, not fire,
Came toward me.
I needed not my sword.

haiku – a kind of Japanese poetry which gives an impression of something in nature. It has three lines. The first line has 5 syllables; the second has 7 syllables, the third line has 5 syllables.

Fiercely churning seas
Carving, clawing ancient rocks
Leave striking arches.

limerick – a 5-line humorous poem with a particular rhyme and rhythm scheme

A school cook named Mojo McClure
Thought the health of the students was poor.
He said, "No junk food!
Get stuff that is good—
Like broccoli and cabbage, for sure."

Lines 1,2, and 5 rhyme with each other, and each have three accented syllables. Lines 3 and 4 rhyme, and each has two accented syllables.

lyric – a short poem giving a personal feeling or perspective

ode – a long lyric poem

quatrain – 4-line poem, usually with *aabb, abab,* or *abcb* rhyme

Mix an onion milkshake,
Take a hearty drink,
You'll wind up with a headache
Quicker than you think.

sonnet – a 14-line poem that gives a poet's personal feelings. A sonnet has a very specific line length, meter, and rhyme scheme.

What Makes Writing Effective?
When in Doubt - Phone Your Friends

Read a lot of stuff.[1]

Check out how other writers write.[2]

Study up on writing devices.[3]

Know what you're doing.[4]

Translation: Read a lot of good writing of many different forms. Notice what the writer **does** to accomplish the things shown in the "effective writing" list.

Translation: Carefully review the list of writing skills. (See pages 136-137 and 146-147.) Notice how other writers use them. As you write, practice using them.

Translation: Review the list of devices writers use to make their writing more interesting and effective. (See pages 138-141.) Include these in your writing.

Translation: Follow a process when you write. Include all the steps. (See pages 142-143.)

You're constantly reading what other people write. As part of your life as a student, you are repeatedly asked to write something. In school, your writing is often evaluated in some way. Even if it isn't, you want to write something that is good, makes sense, or has some effect. So, how can you tell if writing is "good?" Here are some characteristics of writing that *works.*

Effective writing. . .

. . . makes sense.

. . . reads smoothly.

. . . keeps the reader's attention all the way through.

. . . says what the writer wants to say.

. . . accomplishes the purpose the writer intends.

. . . speaks to the audience the writer intends.

. . . uses words that are interesting and powerful.

. . . pleases, satisfies, informs, or challenges the reader.

. . . arranges ideas and details in a way that gets the point across.

. . . has, says, or does something unique to that piece of writing.

. . . is not cluttered with irrelevant words or ideas.

. . . is not cluttered with repetitive words or ideas.

. . . does not rely on over-used words or clichés.

. . . is not confused by errors in spelling and mechanics.

Get Sharp: Writing Guide

Writing Skills

Use this as a checklist as you write. Put the skills to use in your own writing.

I. WORD USE

_____Choose precise words for accurate meaning and interest.

_____Choose fresh, original, and varied words and phrases.

_____Recognize and avoid over-used words or clichés.

_____Recognize and choose active rather than inactive words and phrases.

_____Select words that help to create the mood you want to set.

_____Include figurative language; use it in fresh, appropriate ways.

_____Choose appropriate words for the purpose and audience.

_____Arrange words within sentences to make the meaning clear.

_____Arrange words in sentences to give an interesting rhythm and smooth flow.

_____Avoid repetitive or unnecessary words or phrases.

_____Recognize and choose words and phrases that produce strong sensory images.

II. SENTENCE CONSTRUCTION

_____Create sentences that have a sensible and natural flow.

_____Include sentences with varied length, structure, sound, and rhythm.

_____Write sentences that communicate meaning clearly.

_____Structure sentences to focus attention on main ideas and important details.

_____Write sentences that sound pleasing when read aloud.

_____Only include sentences that contribute to the meaning and purpose.

_____Provide smooth transitions between sentences.

_____Use dialogue correctly and appropriately in written pieces.

III. CONTENT & ORGANIZATION

_____Create written pieces that show clear understanding of the particular writing task.

_____Create written pieces that show completeness and clear organization.

_____State main ideas and purposes clearly.

_____Use sufficient and relevant details and examples to support a main idea.

_____Combine ideas and details in a way that flows smoothly.

_____Combine ideas and details in a way that develops meaning clearly.

_____Combine ideas and details in a sensible sequence.

_____Contribute ideas that have freshness.

_____Create strong titles for written pieces.

_____Create strong, attention-getting beginnings.

_____Create strong, effective endings or conclusions.

IV. USE OF FORMS & TECHNIQUES

_____Produce a variety of kinds of writing: expository, descriptive, persuasive, narrative, imaginative, and personal-expressive writing.

_____Develop experience writing a variety of forms and genres.

_____Effectively use a variety of writing techniques and literary devices. *(See pages 138-141.)*

_____Develop a consistent and appropriate point of view for the passage.

_____Adapt form, style, and content appropriately for appeal to a specific audience.

_____Adapt form, style, and content appropriately for the purpose of the writing.

_____Include dialogue in the text, where effective and appropriate.

_____Engage the audience and convey personal commitment (voice) to the writing.

V. EDITING & REVISING

_____Recognize and replace overused, ordinary, or inactive words and phrases.

_____Revise sentences for clarity, rhythm, and flow.

_____Rearrange ideas or lines for proper sequence, better meaning, or better flow.

_____Eliminate excess or repetitive words or ideas in sentences.

_____Eliminate repetitive or unrelated ideas in passages.

_____Replace awkward transitions.

_____Vary lengths of sentences for smoothness or effectiveness in conveying meaning.

_____Strengthen a passage by adding dialogue, or by changing existing text to dialogue.

_____Revise writing for accuracy in capitalization and punctuation (including quotations).

_____Revise writing for correct use of grammatical construction.

_____Improve weak beginnings and/or endings.

_____Replace weak or imprecise titles.

_____Revise writing for spelling accuracy.

VI. USE OF THE WRITING PROCESS

_____Show ability to participate in each part of the writing process.

_____Take part in motivational activities that stimulate ideas.

_____Actively and fluently collect ideas, words, and phrases for writing.

_____Organize a rough draft using collected ideas.

_____Examine own writing for technique, effectiveness, and organization.

_____Examine and respond to others' writing appropriately and constructively.

_____Use responses and observations to make revisions in own writing.

_____Review your own writing carefully for correct conventions.

_____Prepare a polished, finished piece after reviewing for revision needs.

_____Take part in sharing, presenting, or publishing of finished products.

Get Sharp Tip # 10
Don't try to polish all your writing skills at once! Work on one (or a few) at a time.

Writing Techniques & Devices

Here are some of the things writers use or do to make writing effective. They can make your own writing better. Include them when they fit the form and purpose.

assonance - **repeated vowel sounds in a line, phrase, or sentence**

Assonance occurs within words. It gives rhythm to the phrases and is pleasing to hear.

Example: *Stay away from that hay today. Don't play in the hay today!*

alliteration - **repeated consonant sounds in a line, phrase, or sentence**

Alliteration usually appears at the beginning of words. It sets a rhythm or mood to sentences or phrases. It is fun and pleasing to the ear.

Example: *Harried and hassled, Hannah hurried home.*

characterization – **the way the writer explains the characters in the story**

Characterization tells readers about a character's personality, appearance, motivations, or behaviors.

consonance - **repeated consonant sounds in a line, phrase, or sentence**

Consonance is different from alliteration in that consonance is the repetition of a consonant sound anywhere in the words of a line, not just at the beginning. Like alliteration, it adds to the mood and rhythm of the line. It is fun and pleasing to the ear.

Example: *Cute Katie can't kick her chronic hiccups.*

figurative language – **a way of using language that expands the literal meaning of the words and gives them a new or more interesting twist**

Metaphors, similes, puns, and idioms are examples of figurative language.

foreshadowing - some suggestions within the text or story that give the reader hints about something that may happen later in the story

This technique increases suspense and leads the reader to anticipate events to come.

hyperbole - extreme exaggeration used to increase the effect of a statement

This serves to add humor and imagination to particular types of writing, such as tall tales. It also adds emphasis to a point a speaker or writer is trying to make strongly.
Example: *It was so cold that my words froze before they reached her ears.*

imagery - details that appeal to the senses

Imagery makes the experience more real!

Example: *Sweet, slow drops of deep purple juice drip from the corners of my mouth and flow in little blueberry rivers down to my chin.*

irony - a discrepancy between what is said and what is meant, or between what appears to be true and what is really true

Example: *The man dressed in rags was the richest man in the country.*

metaphor - a comparison between two things that are not ordinarily alike

Like other figurative language, metaphors make writing fresh, interesting, moving, humorous, or touching.

Examples: *Her eyes were deep, purple pools.*
Writing a poem is opening a can of yourself.
Your bedroom is a black hole.

mood - the feeling in a piece of writing

Mood is set by a combination of the words and sounds used, the setting, the imagery, and the details. Mood may give a feeling of mystery, rush, softness, cold, fear, darkness, etc.

onomatopoeia – use of a word whose sound makes you think of its meaning

The use of onomatopoeia adds auditory appeal to the writing.

Example: Hissing, sputtering, and crackling, the fireworks split the night sky.

personification - giving human characteristics to a nonliving object

Personification compares two dissimilar things by attributing human thoughts, feelings, appearances, actions, or attitudes to an object or animal.

Examples: That toaster reached out its fiery fingers and gobbled up my toast.

Sneaky fog slinks around corners, using its gray paintbrush to cover the city.

point of view - lets the reader know who is telling the story

The story may be told by a character in the story, a narrator who is in the story, or a narrator who is not in the story. Within the story, a character may tell the story about himself or herself (first person). Some stories have a series of narrators, speaking in first or second person.

pun – a play on words

A pun is a word or a phrase used in a way that gives a funny twist to the words.

Example: Going to the dentist is a fulfilling experience.

rhyme - repeating of sounds

Rhymes may occur at the ends of lines, or within the lines.

Example of ending rhyme: There once was a guy from Belize
Who built racing cars out of cheese.

Example of internal rhyme: Wearing galoshes, they sloshed through mushy, gushy mud.

satire - writing that makes fun of the shortcomings of people, systems, or institutions for the purpose of enlightening readers and/or bringing about a change

Satires are often written about governmental systems of persons of power and influence. They can range from light fun-making to harsh, bitter mockery.

simile - a comparison between two unlike things, using the word *like* or *as* to connect them

Like other figures of speech, similes make writing fresh, interesting, moving, humorous, or touching. They surprise and delight the reader, and make the description more real.

Examples: *My big brother demolishes his food as fast as a garbage disposal.*
Homework is like hiccups—hard to get rid of.

theme - the main meaning or idea of a piece of writing

It includes the topic and a viewpoint or opinion about the topic.

tone - the approach a writer takes toward the topic

The tone may be playful, hostile, humorous, serious, argumentative, suspicious, etc.

Get Sharp: Writing Guide

The Writing Process

Stage 1 ROMANCING

This is the reason for writing! It is the spark that gets ideas brewing.
It can be

... a group experience   ... a thought
... an individual experience   ... a feeling
... a piece of literature   ... a question
... an unexpected happening   ... a memory
... a life event   ... a discussion

Many things can romance you into writing. Whatever it is, the romance
stage serves to inspire ideas, fancies, impressions, emotions, opinions,
questions, beliefs, explorations, or mysteries. It brings to the surface
those possibilities and imaginings which are tucked away in your mind,
and gets you ready to write. Don't skip this stage. When writers can't
write, or can't think of anything to say—they haven't spent enough time
on this!

Stage 2 COLLECTING

This is a wonderfully creative stage of the writing process. It's the time you gather
words, phrases, fragments, thoughts, ideas, facts, questions, and observations—the
process of brainstorming about and broadening of the original idea. Allow plenty of
time for collecting. Write down everything.

Stage 3 ORGANIZING

This is the time when you take a close look at all those impressions you have collected and
start thinking about what fits together. This is the time to ask yourself . . .

- *What goes with this idea?*
- *Which ideas should be grouped together?*
- *Where would this fit into the whole picture?*
- *What do these ideas or phrases have in common?*

Then, use some method to visually connect the pieces together. Your organizational
tool may be a chart, or a web, or a storyboard, or an outline, or a series of boxes, or a
diagram, or a list, or series of note cards. It can be anything that groups your usable
ideas together in a way that will help you connect them in your writing.

Stage 4 DRAFTING

Okay, now it's time to write! Start putting those words together into phrases, those
phrases together into lines or sentences, those sentences together into paragraphs.

Stage 5 REVIEWING

This is the author's chance to get the writing out into the light and see how it looks
and hear how it sounds–before sharing it with anyone else.
Ask questions yourself such as . . .

- *Does it make sense?*
- *Do I like it?*
- *Are the ideas in the right order?*
- *Will the beginning attract readers?*

- *Does it say what I intended?*
- *Is it smooth and clear?*
- *Are any words or pieces missing?*
- *Is the ending memorable?*

Stage 6 SHARING for PRAISES and QUESTIONS

Ask someone else to review and respond to your writing. The response can be in the form
of praise, compliments, questions, or suggestions. Ask someone who will take time to
read it seriously, and who will give you responses that can actually help you improve
your writing.

Stage 7 REVISING

In this stage, you get to make use of the response from another reader and from your
own review (Stage 5). Revise, replace, add, delete, rearrange, and otherwise strengthen
your writing.

Stage 8 CHECKING MECHANICS

Now it's time to inspect your latest draft for spelling, correct grammar, mechanical and structural
errors or weaknesses—and to fix them! A teacher or parent may give you some help here.

Stage 9 POLISHING

All the changes have been made. Now is the time to create a final, accurate copy.
This might be typed, written, dictated, or recorded some other way.

Stage 10 SHOWING OFF

Now that the writing is polished, it is time to share it. There are dozens
and dozens of possibilities for this. Find some way to publish, display,
or otherwise showcase your final product.

Helping Students with Writing

Advice to Parents & Teachers

Saturate students with literature. Writing flourishes in an environment that's loaded with lots of literature (of all kinds). Hearing good writing motivates students to write. It sparks ideas and lets them see how many things there are to write about.

Sensitize students to everyday experiences. Let them know that they can write about anything—simple or earth-shattering, mundane or outrageous, sad or funny, serious or frivolous, public or private. Help them find words for telling about virtually any person, place, feeling, experience, or event.

Instigate meaningful writing activities. Ask students to write only about topics that are relevant to them and their lives. They'll have more to say and they'll write better if they feel a connection to the topic.

Think short! It is easier for the student to handle the writing process when working on short pieces of writing. Long stories are difficult to revise and polish. There are many short forms of writing that can be used to teach and practice the writing process.

Offer choice. Allow writers as much choice as possible. Writers are always more eager to write when they "own" the topic (when they've chosen a topic that is personally appealing).

Write together—often. When a student is introduced to a new form, when a writer seems stuck, when a topic is difficult, when a writer is reluctant or insecure—write together (as a group). Besides being fun and satisfying, collaborative writing refreshes and reinforces the process. It lets students experience immediate success with fewer struggles.

Emphasize the process. Dwell on the various stages. Talk a lot about each step. Do each step together. Discuss what makes each step important. Remember that the process is more important than a particular final product.

Avoid overworking every piece of writing. Don't pressure students to go through the entire writing process every time they write. If you do, they'll quit writing! Remember this: every stage of the writing process is important in itself. Students will have a real writing experience even if they only get through stage 1, 2, or 5.

Allow plenty of time for writing. Give students the time they really need to work through parts of all of the process. Good writing cannot and should not be rushed.

Top **10** Writing Tips
to Share with Young Writers

10. Collect more ideas than you need. Write down lots of thoughts, phrases, and words. The ones you don't need can be dropped later.

9. Use all your senses when you brainstorm ideas. Think about feelings, sights, sounds, smells, tastes, experiences, places, people.

8. Use interesting, strong action words.

7. Use fresh, original adjectives and adverbs. (But don't use too many.)

6. Use a variety of sentences—different structures, lengths, and beginnings.

5. Don't get bogged down trying to write everything correctly. You can fix spelling, punctuation, and grammar later.

4. Remember the reader. Would someone want to read or hear this all the way through?

3. Put yourself into your writing. Let your personality and passions show.

2. Read your written work aloud (if only to yourself). Does it sound smooth, sensible, and pleasing? Does it make sense?

1. Find a way to share what you write.

Note to Adults:
YOU WRITE, TOO!
When you write at the same time your child or student is writing, everything changes. Model the use of the process for students. Share what you write in its various stages. Ask for their input.

Let's see, Dad. Your beginning is a little weak. If you're going to get this job, your letter needs to sell yourself from the very start.

WRITING PROCESS SCORING GUIDE

TRAIT	SCORE OF 5	SCORE OF 3	SCORE OF 1
CONTENT	• The writing is very clear and focused. • The main ideas and purpose stand out clearly. • Main ideas are well-supported with details and examples. • All details are relevant to the main idea. • The ideas have some freshness and insight. • The ideas fit the purpose and audience well. • The paper is interesting and holds the reader's attention.	• The writing is mostly clear and focused. • The main ideas and purpose are mostly clear. • Details and examples are used but may be somewhat limited or repetitive. • Most details are relevant to the main idea. • Some details may be off the topic. • Some ideas and details are fresh; others are ordinary. • The paper is interesting to some degree. • The ideas and content are less than precisely right for the audience and purpose.	• The writing lacks clarity and focus. • It is hard to identify the main idea. • The purpose of the writing is not evident. • Details are few, not relevant, or repetitive. • Ideas or details have little sparkle or appeal to hold the reader's attention. • The paper has not developed an idea well.
WORD CHOICE	• Writer has used strong, specific, colorful, effective, and varied words. • Words are used well to convey the ideas. • Words are well chosen to fit the content, audience, and purpose. • Writer has chosen fresh, unusual words, and/or has used words/phrases in an unusual way. • Writer has made use of figurative language, and words/phrases that create images.	• Writer has used some specific and effective words. • A good use of colorful, unusual words is attempted, but limited or overdone. • The words succeed at conveying main ideas. • The writer uses words in fresh ways sometimes, but not consistently. • The word choice is mostly suited to the content, audience, and purpose.	• There is a limited use of specific, effective, or colorful words. • Some words chosen are imprecise, misused, or repetitive. • The words do not suit the content, purpose, or audience well. • The words do not succeed at conveying the main ideas.
SENTENCES	• Sentences have a pleasing and natural flow. • When read aloud, sentences and ideas flow along smoothly from one to another. • Transitions between sentences are smooth and natural. • Sentences have varied length, structure, sound, and rhythm. • The structure of sentences focuses reader's attention on the main idea and key details. • The sentence sound and variety make the reading enjoyable. • If the writer uses dialogue, it is used correctly and effectively.	• Most of the sentences have a natural flow. • When read aloud, some sentences have a "less than fluid" sound. • Some or all transitions are awkward or repetitive. • There is some variety in sentence length, structure, sound, and rhythm; but some patterns are repetitive. • The sentences convey the main idea and details, but without much craftsmanship. • If the writer uses dialogue, it is somewhat less than fluid or effective.	• Most sentences are not fluid. • When read aloud, the writing sounds awkward or uneven. Some of the paper is confusing to read. • Transitions are not effective. • There is little variety in sentence length, structure, sound, or rhythm. • There may be incomplete or run-on sentences. • The sentence structure gets in the way of conveying content, purpose, and meaning.

A score of 4 may be given for papers that fall between 3 and 5 on a trait. A score of 2 may be given for papers that fall between 1 and 3.

WRITING PROCESS SCORING GUIDE

TRAIT	SCORE OF 5	SCORE OF 3	SCORE OF 1
ORGANIZATION	• The organization of the piece allows the main ideas and key details to be conveyed well. • The piece has a compelling beginning that catches the attention of the reader. • Ideas are developed in a clear, interesting sequence. • The piece moves along from one idea, sentence, or paragraph to another in a manner that is smooth and useful to develop the meaning. • The piece has a compelling ending that ties up the idea well and leaves the reader feeling pleased.	• Organization is recognizable, but weak or inconsistent in some places. • For the most part, the organization of the piece allows the main ideas and key details to be conveyed. • The structure seems somewhat ordinary, lacking flavor or originality. • The piece has a beginning that is not particularly inviting to the reader or not well-developed. • Some of the sequencing is confusing. • The piece does not always move along smoothly or clearly from one idea, sentence, or paragraph to another. • The piece has clear ending, but it is somewhat dull or underdeveloped, or does not adequately tie up the piece.	• The piece lacks clear organization. • For the most part, the lack of good organization gets in the way of the conveyance of the main ideas and key details. • The piece does not have a clear beginning or ending. • Ideas are not developed in any clear sequence, or the sequence is distracting. • The piece does not move along smoothly from one sentence or paragraph to another. • Important ideas or details seem to be missing or out of place. • The piece leaves the reader feeling confused.
VOICE	• The writer has left a personal stamp on piece. A reader knows there is a person behind the writing. • It is clear that the writer knows what audience and purpose he/she is reaching. • The writer engages the audience. • The writer shows passion, commitment, originality, and honesty in conveying the message. • The voice used (level of personal closeness) is appropriate for the purpose of the piece.	• The writer has left a personal stamp on the piece, but this is not as strong or consistent as it might be. The reader is not always sure of the writer's presence. • It is not always clear that the writer knows his/her audience and purpose. • The writer engages the audience some, but not all of the time. • The writer shows some passion, commitment, originality, and honesty in conveying the message, but this is inconsistent.	• The writer has not left any personal stamp on the piece. The writing feels detached. • There is little sense that the writer is speaking to the audience or clearly knows the purpose of the writing. • There is little or no engagement of the audience. • The writer shows little or no passion, commitment, originality, and honesty in conveying the message.
CONVENTIONS	• There is clear control of capitalization, punctuation, spelling, and paragraphing. • There is consistent use of correct grammar and language usage. • The strong use of conventions strengthens the communication of the work's meaning. • The piece needs little editing/revision.	• There is some control of capitalization, punctuation, spelling, and paragraphing. • There is inconsistent use of correct grammar and language usage. • The uneven use of conventions sometimes interferes with the meaning. • The piece needs much editing/revision.	• There is poor control of capitalization, punctuation, spelling, and paragraphing. • There is a lack of correct grammar and language usage. • Poor use of conventions obscures meaning. • There are multiple errors; the piece needs extensive editing/revision.

A score of 4 may be given for papers that fall between 3 and 5 on a trait. A score of 2 may be given for papers that fall between 1 and 3.

Get Sharp: Writing Guide

Collecting

Once you have your topic for writing, get busy collecting. This step in the writing process is very important to creative thinking. It is also a step that's critical to gathering enough content to cover your topic.

- Get as much raw material as possible that pertains to your topic.
- Keep collecting until you get past the ordinary stuff to the fresh and unusual.
- Don't quit this stage too soon! Too many ideas are better than too few.

Gather:
facts
fragments
ideas
observations
phrases
words
sentences
questions
facts
memories

Ways to collect:
brainstorm
research
interview
search
read
ask questions

City Sounds

engines humming and choking

screeching brakes, rattling trains

horns honking

screaming sirens

buses strain and moan with their loads

clink, clink of coins tumbling down the throat
    of the bus's hungry money grabber

music pouring out doors of restaurants, clubs, theaters

impatient passengers shout, "Taxi!"

ATMs whir as they suck in cards and spit out cash

swish of tires on wet pavement

clunking of wheels through potholes

pavement groaning under the weight of trucks

panting breath from rushing commuters

click-click of heels hurrying down stairs to the subway

shopping bags brush and crinkle on crowded trains

purses and wallets zipping and unzipping for change

collective pedestrian sighs of weariness

cool guy saunters rhythmically along while boom-
    boom- boom throbs from speakers on his shoulder

Places I'd Rather Not Visit

the dentist's chair
an emergency room
a sinking boat
a sewage treatment plant
a war zone
my sister's piano recital
a piranha pool
the bottom of a bird cage
inside a bee hive
a lion's mouth
an opera rehearsal
a burning building
the bottom of a crevasse
the principal's office
a cuckoo clock repair shop

Facts about crocodiles –

long body, cigar shape	powerful jaws	3 endangered species
webbed feet	bury eggs	females guard nests
long teeth	short legs	aggressive, may attack humans
pointed snout	eat small animals	live in swamps, marshes
powerful tail	4th tooth visible	most live in E. Hemisphere

In many countries, laws prohibit hunting.
Valve in throat keeps water out when underwater.
Eyes and nostrils stay above water.

Organizing

There is not one right or best way to organize your ideas for writing.
The only "rule" about organizing is that you should do it!

Find a method, tool, or process to organize each time you write.
It does help to connect and plan ideas in some visual way.

There are many possibilities for methods to organize.
The tool you choose will depend on the writing genre,
the time you have, and your personal preference.

Try these

clusters	webs	diagrams	lists
outlines	charts	note cards	
tables	story maps	time lines	

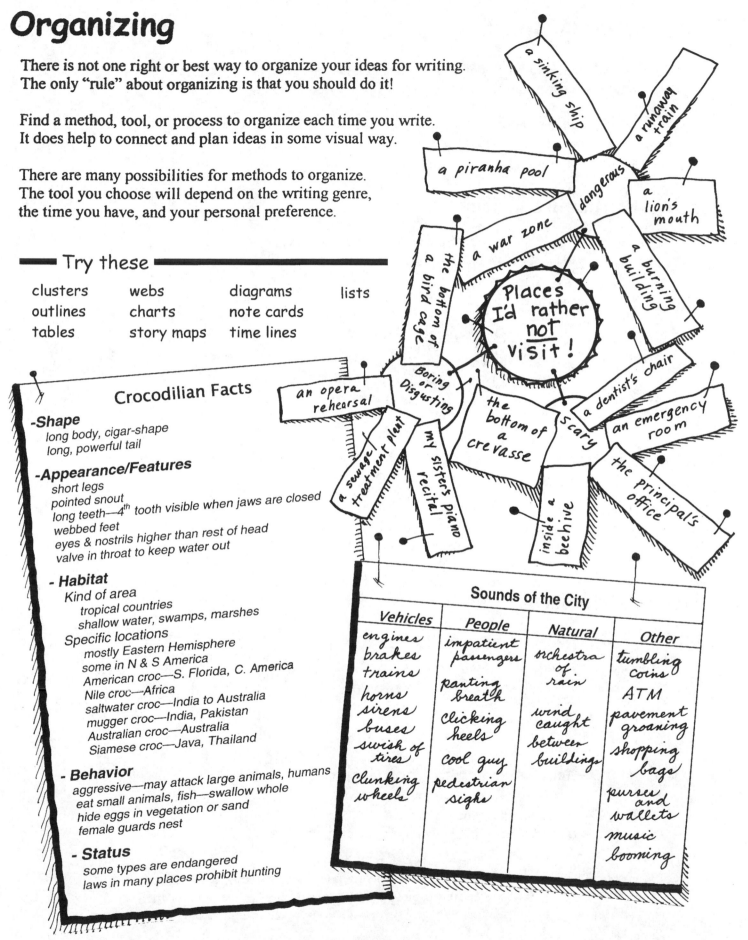

Crocodilian Facts

-Shape
- long body, cigar-shape
- long, powerful tail

-Appearance/Features
- short legs
- pointed snout
- long teeth—4th tooth visible when jaws are closed
- webbed feet
- eyes & nostrils higher than rest of head
- valve in throat to keep water out

- Habitat
- Kind of area
  - tropical countries
  - shallow water, swamps, marshes
- Specific locations
  - mostly Eastern Hemisphere
  - some in N & S America
  - American croc—S. Florida, C. America
  - Nile croc—Africa
  - saltwater croc—India to Australia
  - mugger croc—India, Pakistan
  - Australian croc—Australia
  - Siamese croc—Java, Thailand

- Behavior
- aggressive—may attack large animals, humans
- eat small animals, fish—swallow whole
- hide eggs in vegetation or sand
- female guards nest

- Status
- some types are endangered
- laws in many places prohibit hunting

Places I'd rather not visit!

dangerous: a sinking ship, a runaway train, a piranha pool, a lion's mouth, a war zone, a burning building, the bottom of a bird cage

Boring or Disgusting: an opera rehearsal, a sewage treatment plant, my sister's piano recital

scary: the bottom of a crevasse, a dentist's chair, an emergency room, the principal's office, inside a beehive

Sounds of the City

Vehicles	People	Natural	Other
engines	impatient passengers	orchestra of rain	tumbling coins
brakes	panting breath	wind caught between buildings	ATM
trains	clicking heels		pavement groaning
horns	cool guy		shopping bags
sirens	pedestrian sighs		purses and wallets
buses			music booming
swish of tires			
clunking wheels			

Better Grades & Higher Test Scores / READING & LANGUAGE
Copyright ©2003 by Incentive Publications, Inc., Nashville, TN.

Get Sharp: Writing Guide

Effective Words

Words are the building blocks of your writing. They need to be the right ones, and they need to work for your purposes in the writing. Choose your words carefully.

Here is some advice to help you polish your word choice. Note that each bit of advice on this page is followed with an ordinary example, followed by an example of better word choice.

Use words that are precise.

a **steep** 200-ft drop

a **precipitous** 200-ft drop

Terri's friends were **worried** when she teetered on the edge of the canyon.

Terri's friends were **terrified** when she teetered on the edge of the canyon.

a sleepwalker **walking** around the house

a sleepwalker **meandering** around the house

Use words that are interesting.

When the jewel thief held out his hand, it held a pretty diamond necklace.

The thief's **clenched fingers uncurled; in his palm** lay an **exquisite** diamond necklace.

Use active words.

The January wind **was** cold and icy.
A cold and icy January wind **bit** my nose.

The shark **seemed** to be smiling.
The shark **sneered** as he passed by.

Use words that are fresh and original.

That waiter has a **sour attitude**.
That waiter has a **peppermint personality**.

Dark clouds swirled, pouring out heavy drops of rain.
Petulant clouds **threw tantrums, sputtering** out wet torrents.

The examples on this page show effective use of words for each piece of writing.

Use words in unusual ways.

Bus # 27 groaned when twelve Sumo wrestlers climbed on board.

A cream-cheese moon oozed toward the midnight end of the city.

Use words that evoke images.

Every time my sister chews gum I hear cows walking through mud.
The traffic light winked its yellow eye at me.
Waves of warm, greasy popcorn-air caressed my nose.
How lucky the lilac bush is to spread its toes in the warm, velvet mud.

Use figurative language.

Snow peaks on the fencepost like sugary meringue-drop swirls.
That pesky wave chased me all the way down the beach, grasping at my heels.
My mailbox mocks me with its empty, careless yawn.
Living with Maxie is as dangerous as living near an active volcano.

——— Avoid these over-used words. ———

amazing	dark	fly	kill	right
angry	delicious	funny	little	run
ask	destroy	get	look	say
awful	difference	go	love	scared
bad	do	good	make	show
beautiful	dull	great	move	slow
begin	end	gross	neat	stop
big	enjoy	happy	new	story
brave	explain	hate	old	take
break	fair	have	part	tell
come	fall	help	place	think
cool	false	hide	plan	true
cry	fast	hurry	pretty	ugly
cut	fat	important	put	unhappy
dangerous	fear	interesting	quiet	wrong

Get Sharp Tip # 11
A few well-chosen words are better than a whole string of adjectives and adverbs.
Last night's moon
A single silver sliver
A lone light in a slate sky

Better Grades & Higher Test Scores / READING & LANGUAGE
Copyright ©2003 by Incentive Publications, Inc., Nashville, TN.

Get Sharp: Writing Guide

Clear, Interesting Sentences

Smooth, clear, interesting sentences are the heart of your writing. You can choose all sorts of wonderful, fresh words and phrases, but if you aren't able to combine them into clear sentences, your writing won't be very effective. Here are some hints to help you strengthen your writing style with sentences that are meaningful, clear, natural-sounding, and interesting to read.

Use each sentence to express a complete idea.

Make sure each sentence has a reason for being included. Each sentence should state a main idea or add something to support the main idea. Watch out for sentence fragments, run-on sentences, or sentences that just ramble on.

Make sentences interesting.

Interesting sentences add more meaning to the writing. They also hold the reader's attention.

> I am terminally disgusted by the condition of our city streets! My elegant new shoes are now frosted with sun-sautéed grape bubblegum of an indeterminate vintage.

You can make sentences interesting . . .

. . . by including colorful adverbs and adjectives.

Less interesting: *An avalanche chased the skiers.*

More interesting: *A sudden avalanche, fiercely roaring, chased the terrified skiers.*

. . . by including phrases.

Less interesting: *Agatha Abernathy decided to sue the town of Middleburg.*

More interesting: *With great reluctance, Agatha Abernathy decided to sue the town of Middleburg for failing to protect her from deadly scorpions.*

Less interesting: *We met Tom Twister while he was working.*

More interesting: *We met Tom Twister, the famous contortionist, while he was working on a new position called "The Pretzel."*

. . . by varying the sentence structure.

Less interesting: *Claude loved cream puffs, and he was angry because the bakery used artificial cream.*

More interesting: *Claude, a great lover of cream puffs, was angry to find that the bakery used artificial cream in their desserts.*

Write sentences that flow smoothly.

Sentences that are short and choppy don't read smoothly. Neither do sentences that are too long and tangled. Try to write sentences that sound natural. Use sentences of different lengths. Read your writing out loud. Listen to see if it sounds smooth. Combine choppy sentences into longer, smoother sentences. Break over-complicated sentences into simpler ones.

Not smooth: *After the lights went out, we saw that long shadows were lurking everywhere and nothing was moving, and it was silent except for scraping sounds.*

Smooth: *The lights went out, long shadows lurked everywhere, and nothing moved. Scraping sounds broke the silence.*

Not smooth: *The back door was locked. The front door was also locked, and the windows were undamaged and locked. Someone got in and took the whole cookie jar and left footprints. Nothing was broken. Someone must have had a key.*

Smooth: *Though all the doors and windows were locked and there was no sign of a break-in, the cookie jar was missing. The culprit, who must have had a key, left footprints.*

Write sentences that make the meaning clear.

Pay close attention to the meaning of each sentence. Can the reader get the meaning easily? The arrangement of words in a sentence can confuse the reader or make the meaning muddy. Watch out for misplaced phrases, subjects and verbs that don't agree, and pronouns without clear antecedents.

Unclear: *Simone enjoyed her corned beef sandwich listening to the radio.*
Clear: *While listening to the radio, Simone enjoyed her corned beef sandwich.*

Unclear: *We were harassed by a shark sailing our boat.*
Clear: *A shark harassed us when we were out sailing our boat.*

Unclear: *It was a relief when she and Tom met them and they climbed on their sailboat.*
Clear: *Tom and she were greatly relieved to climb on the sailboat of their friends.*

Write sentences that are concise.

A concise sentence gets to the point without a lot of extra detours or details. Examine your sentences to see that they are not cluttered with unnecessary words and details.

Not Concise: **Concise:**

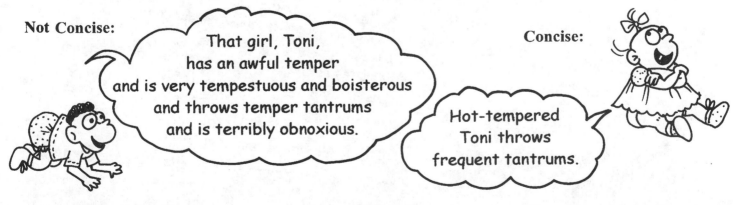

That girl, Toni, has an awful temper and is very tempestuous and boisterous and throws temper tantrums and is terribly obnoxious.

Hot-tempered Toni throws frequent tantrums.

Get Sharp: Writing Guide

Meaningful Paragraphs

A paragraph is a group of sentences that are related because they cover a specific subject or idea. Paragraphs are used for the many different modes of writing (see pages 130-131). This means a paragraph can explain, define, inform, persuade, or tell part of a story.

But all paragraphs have some things in common. All paragraphs need a beginning, middle, and end. Every paragraph has a main idea. The purpose of the paragraph is to communicate that main idea clearly. A well-written paragraph is carefully planned to state and support the main idea.

The Beginning ⟶

The beginning of the paragraph lets the reader know what the paragraph is about.

Each paragraph needs a topic sentence; usually this is at the beginning.

The topic sentence names the subject or main idea of the paragraph.

The topic sentence also gives some unique detail or impression about the subject.

The Middle ⟶

Most of the sentences in the paragraph make up the middle part.

These sentences add the details needed to support the main idea.

These sentences clarify the topic.

Every sentence must add something to explain or broaden the main idea.

These sentences should be put in a meaningful sequence.

The End ⟶

The final sentence wraps up the paragraph.

This sentence follows the sentences with the details or examples.

The final sentence restates or reminds the reader of the paragraph's main idea.

Some paragraphs may seem simple and easy, because they're short. Beware! Paragraphs are more complicated than they look.

Remember, a good paragraph . . .
. . . states the main idea clearly.
. . . includes enough details to support the idea.
. . . uses a variety of sentences.
. . . includes sentences which begin in different ways.
. . . has sentences in a clear, sensible order.
. . . uses well-chosen transitions to connect sentences.
. . . reads smoothly, connecting words or phrases.
. . . concludes with a reminder of the main idea.

Topic Sentence →

It was a bad idea to linger so close to the gorilla cage, but Chester couldn't help it. All the signs warned him not to feed the animals and not to go past the railing. Yet, he couldn't keep himself away.

Supporting Sentences →

What was it about those gorillas that fascinated him so? For one thing, they were having such fun, and Chester was sure they were doing it just to entertain him. Pounding their bristly chests rhythmically, they nimbly romped through games of tag and steal-the-banana, and delighted Chester with teasing gestures. Another lure was Gloria, the biggest and jolliest gorilla. Mischievously, Gloria beckoned him closer. "She likes me better than the other visitors," Chester thought foolishly.

Concluding Sentence →

And though he knew better, he inched dangerously, carelessly, nearer to Gloria's quick fingers.

Transitions Between Sentences
Some Useful Words & Phrases

about	as soon as	finally	inside	soon
above	as well as	first	lastly	that is to say
across	before	for example	later	therefore
additionally	behind	for instance	likewise	throughout
after	beneath	furthermore	meanwhile	to begin with
after a while	below	in addition	moreover	to conclude
afterward	beside	in comparison	next	to continue
against	between	in conclusion	next week	to elaborate
along with	beyond	in contrast	on the other hand	to emphasize
also	beyond that	in fact	on top of	to restate
although	down	in front of	otherwise	to repeat
among	during	in other words	outside	to summarize
around	even though	in summary	second	today
as a result	even so	in the same way	similarly	yesterday

Get Sharp: Writing Guide

Successful Compositions

Compositions (such as essays) have a main idea, a beginning, middle, and an end—just like paragraphs. However, a composition is different. A composition covers a longer topic. It is more complex and needs several paragraphs. Writing a good composition takes some skills beyond writing good paragraphs. It requires careful planning and skillful combining of paragraphs.

Some Tips for Good Compositions

The opening paragraph serves as the introduction to the written piece.

A well-written opening paragraph . . .
- grabs the reader's attention.
- states the main idea or topic of the whole composition (the thesis statement).
- sets the stage for the rest of the piece.

The body includes several paragraphs that develop and support the main topic.

In a well-written body . . .
- each paragraph states a sub-idea and provides details to illustrate or support it.
- a new paragraph begins when there is a change to a new subtopic.
- paragraphs flow naturally from one to another.
- paragraphs are arranged in a logical order.
- paragraphs and sub-ideas are organized so as to develop the main idea clearly.
- the point of the piece gains strength as paragraphs progress.
- information in the paragraphs is accurate.
- the language of the paragraphs is colorful and pleasing to the reader.

The closing paragraph ties the composition together.

A well-written concluding paragraph . . .
- restates or reviews the thesis.
- somehow summarizes the meaning of the composition.
- leaves the main point firmly in the mind of the reader.
- keeps the reader's attention right to the end!

Get Sharp Tip # 12
Don't fizzle on the conclusion. Resist the temptation to give in to weariness and settle for a hurried, bland closing. Remember, it is the LAST thing the reader hears from you about your topic. Make it memorable!

How to Write an Essay

Bobbie, I haven't got a clue how to write this essay!

Well, brother Bob, let me tell you. Begin with a good introduction. The introduction needs to grab the reader's attention. It should give a short explanation of what the paper is about. It should include the thesis.

Thesis? What is a thesis?

The thesis states the paper's main idea. It tells what you are trying to prove, support, describe, or explain. Make sure your thesis is clear.

Next, you need a strong body . . .

Are you hinting that I don't have a strong body?

No, silly. The body of an essay is the writing between the introduction and the conclusion. Each of these paragraphs needs a good topic sentence stating what the paragraph is about. Include details in each paragraph to support the topic sentence. And of course, all paragraphs should support the paper's main thesis.

I can do this!

Ouch!

Finish with a good conclusion. Summarize what the essay has said. Restate the thesis in different words. Write a conclusion with lots of punch— an ending that leaves an impression on the reader.

Better Grades & Higher Test Scores / READING & LANGUAGE
Copyright ©2003 by Incentive Publications, Inc., Nashville, TN.

Get Sharp: Writing Guide

Attention-Grabbing Beginnings

A good beginning catches the reader's attention right away. It gives a hint at what is going to happen or what is going to be argued. Yet, it doesn't give the whole story, explanation, or argument away. A good beginning makes the reader curious enough to continue on.

There are unlimited ways to begin. Of course, the way you start will depend on many things, such as the form, purpose and audience. Your effective beginning might include . . .

- a surprising statement
- a tantalizing or unexpected claim
- an unusual fact
- a fascinating quote

- a question or series of questions
- a brief quip about a famous character
- a strong opinion

ordinary beginning:

Dear Team Members,

Another month has passed and it is already time for the February newsletter. Spring is here and it's time to really get in shape for the new season. I'd like to remind you to do your drills and run regularly.

attention-grabbing beginning:

Dear Grizzlies,

How many times did you run this week? Are you really doing those drills, or just checking them off on the calendar? Is your soccer ball full of air and getting a regular workout? It's February already, and the first game is just 36 days away. Will you be ready to be a part of a winning team?

ordinary beginning:

At last night's school board meeting, high school students staged a protest.

attention-grabbing beginnings:

No one can remember a school board meeting like this one.

There were fireworks over food at last night's school board meeting.

Who dared to deliver rotten meat loaf and slimy pudding to the school board meeting?

"Down with lousy lunches!" was the cry heard at last night's school board meeting.

Protesting high school students "treated" board members to samples of cafeteria food at last night's meeting.

ordinary beginning:

There is a new policy at our school that is a mistake. I disagree with it and most students don't like it.

attention-grabbing beginnings:

We're all over fourteen years old, and somebody is still telling us how to dress.

There are groans, complaints, and unrepeatable words being said today as Turlow High students about the new School Dress Code.

T-shirts are nixed. Jeans are out. Shirt-tails are (tucked) in. Turlow High School administrators have spoken on the dress code, and students are not happy about it.

Memorable Endings

A strong ending is as important as a good beginning. Like the opening, your conclusion will depend on the topic, form, and purpose of the writing. Yet for each piece of writing, there are many possible ways to wrap it up. That's what your ending must do; it must drive the point home, solidify your argument, or tie up the tale with gusto. However you end, try to write the sentence, paragraph, or line that will leave the reader satisfied with the writing.

Your effective ending might include . . .
- a fresh way to restate the thesis
- a short summary of the main points
- a mystery that leaves the reader wondering
- a surprise turn of events
- an unexpected solution
- a lesson or moral taught
- one more great argument

- a question to the reader
- a final wrap-up quote

ordinary ending:

You see that there is quite a difference between black holes and wormholes.

memorable ending:

So if you do get pulled into a black hole, don't give up hope (though they say nothing can escape from one). Take heart, the black hole just might be linked to a wormhole, and you could escape after all.

ordinary ending:

Learn about what you can do to protect these three species of crocodiles from extinction.

memorable ending:

If you're a crocodile hunter, find another sport. If not, do your part by passing up those crocodile shoes.

ordinary ending:

That's the end of the tale about a lively field trip.

memorable ending:

Yes, this was a lively field trip. But wait until you hear about what happened on the next one!

ordinary ending:

At last, Wilbur Worthington was found. After a mysterious disappearance and a three-year absence, he had returned to his family. Everything was back to normal for the Worthingtons. His daughter snuggled in next to her dad in front of the fire, both of them writing in their diaries their own tales of this amazing day.

memorable ending:

At last, Wilbur Worthington was found. After a mysterious disappearance and a three-year absence, he had returned to his family. Everything was back to normal for the Worthingtons. Only his young daughter still wondered. As she watched him write in his journal at the end of that amazing day, she wrote in her own journal, "I was so sure my dad was left-handed like me."

Get Sharp: Writing Guide

Strong Voice

Voice is the way a writer uses language to show his or her unique personality and feeling about the topic. Your voice is expressed in your writing through many of the techniques and devices you use: word choice, choice of form and format, structure of sentences, tone, topics you choose, sequence and organization of the writing, and use of dialogue.

To find your voice . . .

- be yourself.
- choose topics that interest you.
- know your audience.
- care about saying something to your audience.
- show your passion for the idea or message.
- be original—use your own ideas.
- show your commitment to expressing the ideas.
- keep your writing honest. (*Write what you really feel.*)
- write in the style and voice you use in your own diary.
- write as if you were talking honestly to your best friend.
- let readers know something about your values and opinions.

Voice can be . . .
- casual or formal
- down-to-earth or snooty
- fresh or traditional
- intimate or distant
- light-hearted or serious
- earthy or pristine
- somber or cheery

This writer described some guests at a fancy ball. Her voice shows that she has a good sense of humor. She seems to be having fun with the writing. Her writing is down-to-earth with a touch of pretend haughtiness fitting for the subject. She speaks directly to the reader.

Lady Columbine brashly shows off her beauty and grace. She just knows that you're gazing at her, and have eyes for no one else. But if you are not a young, handsome, and wealthy prince, she won't waste her time on you.

Little Prince Mischief is so small that the guests hardly notice him. He lurks under tables and behind curtains, eavesdropping and spying. Occasionally he slips a gooey cream puff inside a lady's shawl or tucks a crudité into a tall hairdo.

Judge d'Éclair is a terribly important man. He hovers close to the plentiful food at these lavish parties. Oh, how he loves to eat! If you stop to chat with him, do bring along a pastry or two.

Look quickly! There's Dowager La-de-da! How honored you should be to come into the presence of this rich grande dame. Be sure you say nothing rowdy or risqué in her presence. She has no time for foolishness.

Count Pompous is strutting about the great hall with a frilly hat and silver-bowed high-heeled boots. He will probably keep his nose in the air the entire evening.

Countess Dainty dances blithely across the ballroom floor. She needs no partner. I swear she floats just above the surface with her light step. Everything about her seems silky soft, sweet, and sincere. Is she for real?

Editing & Revising

Here's an easy-to-use plan to guide you through the response and revision stages of the writing process. The first P and the Q are response tactics: Praise and Question. The last P is the revision tactic: Polish. Writers of all ages can make improvements in their writing by remembering these three steps.

The **P-Q-P** Plan for Editing and Revision

P = Praise

Writers tell each other...
...what's strong.
...what's good.
...what's effective.
...what works.
...what caught their ear or eye.
...what's pleasing.
...what sparked a thought.
...what taught them something.
...what surprised or delighted them.

Ask someone to read what you have written and give you clear, specific "praises" for the parts you've written well.

Some examples of helpful praise:

- *Crash! was a great choice for the opening sentence! It grabbed my attention right away.*

- *It was a good idea to string all those short words together in this part. It made the girl seem very much in a hurry.*

- *I liked the way you repeated the **t** sound over and over in this poem. That gave a marching rhythm to the poem.*

- *I like the wet words for your rain poem. My favorites were **slosh...slurpy...slush...drizzle... slop...**and **splatter**.*

- *The ending was a great surprise. It really caught me off guard.*

- *The part about the alligator swallowing the umbrella was my favorite! It was so unexpected.*

- *I like the part about the **squirmy, squishy, soft** and **mushy** worm. The internal rhyme is pleasing.*

- *Tom, your title, "The Food No Kid Should Eat," made me want to listen to your paragraph.*

- *It was such a good idea to end the argument with a question. That really made me question the safety of skateboards too.*

- *These two sentences right here-really show your sense of humor.*

- *I like the way you started the argument by telling all the good things about fast foods before you switched to your pitch against them. That gave an unusual twist, and caught my attention.*

Get Sharp: Writing Guide

Q = QUESTION

Writers ask questions that will help the author review and think about the writing to . . .

. . . realize where things may not be clear.

. . . hear where something is missing.

. . . notice where something could be stronger, funnier, more suspenseful, more informative, etc.

. . . consider what could be changed or added or removed.

This is not harsh criticism. No outside opinion is forced on the writer. That's the reason for using the question form. A question is stated and left for the author to answer and decide the answer. Find someone you trust to read your writing and ask you specific questions—questions that will inspire you to clarify and improve your writing.

Some examples of helpful questions:

- *Could you add a few sentences in your autobiography to tell about your preschool years?*
- *I'm confused about the difference between a white hole and a wormhole. Are they the same?*
- *It can't be too easy to lose a tuba. How did your tuba get lost anyway?*
- *I felt as if you gave away the ending too soon. Could you add something to prolong the suspense?*
- *Could you replace the word **neat** with a different word in two of the three places you used it?*
- *What is your opinion about this topic? I'd like to get more of a feel for your voice.*
- *How did the girls get into the volcano in the first place? That's unclear.*
- *What was your relationship with this friend? How did you feel when she moved away suddenly?*
- *Are all the crocodile species you mentioned endangered? I can't tell from your essay.*
- *Didn't the gorilla have to escape from the zoo before he sat on the mayor? Shouldn't this sentence come before this one?*
- *What is your feeling about this earthquake? I can't tell much about your involvement in this.*

P = POLISH

After gaining some responses from others, the author decides what input to use

. . . what suggestions to discard or include.

. . . what changes to make.

. . . which feedback is important.

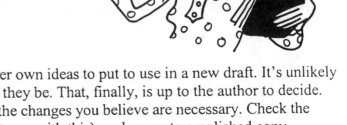

Then the author adds this information to his or her own ideas to put to use in a new draft. It's unlikely that all of the responses can be used. Nor should they be. That, finally, is up to the author to decide. When you are ready to write a final draft, make the changes you believe are necessary. Check the spelling and mechanics (or ask someone to assist you with this), and go on to a polished copy.

Editor's Guide

_____ Substitute stronger words *(more colorful, more specific)*.

_____ Replace inactive verbs with more active, lively ones.

_____ Eliminate repetitive or unnecessary words.

_____ Add more interesting words *(fresh, rich, original, energizing)*.

_____ Add words or phrases that create or add to a certain mood.

_____ Rearrange words within a sentence for clarity of meaning.

_____ Rearrange words or sentences for smoother flow.

_____ Rearrange words or sentences for more interesting sound.

_____ Expand sentences to include more detail.

_____ Make sure main ideas are well-developed and relevant.

_____ Make sure each sub-idea is developed in its own paragraph.

_____ If needed, include more details that are relevant and rich.

_____ Expand or rearrange paragraphs to improve clarity and focus.

_____ Make sure each paragraph has clear organization.

_____ Rearrange sentences for different or clearer meaning.

_____ Rearrange sentences or paragraphs for better sequence.

_____ Vary sentence length, structure, and rhythm within paragraphs.

_____ Vary transitions; make sure they are smooth.

_____ Eliminate repetitive or unnecessary ideas.

_____ Break up excessively long sentences.

_____ Add dialogue where it would be effective.

_____ Examine beginning; revise to make it more inviting.

_____ Examine ending; make sure it is memorable and gives clear closure.

_____ Decide if the written piece accomplishes the purpose.

_____ Adapt content and form to fit the audience.

_____ Include literary techniques that make the writing more interesting
   or appealing *(i.e: personification, onomatopoeia, hyperbole,
   understatement, exaggeration, foreshadowing, or irony)*.

_____ Include figures of speech *(metaphors, similes, idioms, puns)*.

_____ Replace ordinary titles with strong, "catchy" titles.

_____ Remove bias from piece *(unless called for)*.

_____ Revise to strengthen voice *(liveliness, originality, personality, conviction, author
   involvement, good communication with audience)*; make sure a personal flavor is evident.

_____ Examine pieces for correct conventions *(punctuation, spelling, capitalization, paragraphing,
   grammar and usage)*.

Get Sharp Tip # 13

Don't think of editing as a chore. Instead, think of it as a gift—a second chance for you, the writer. It's a chance for you to make your writing say what you **really want** it to say. Also, it's a chance to spark your originality, unique flavor that will make people glad they read it!

Steps for Writing a Report

1. Choose a topic.

I plan to do a report on quasars.

- Think about what you want to learn on that topic.
- Write a list of sub-topics or categories you need to explore.
- Write a list of questions you'd like to answer on the topic.

Do . . . Don't . . .

- Choose a topic that is manageable.

- Choose a topic that has enough information available to develop it.

- Choose a topic that is too broad. *(War)* or *(Animal Diseases)*
- Choose a topic that is too narrow. *(Stomach Ailments of Pintos)*
- Choose a topic that is too vague. *(People Who Travel)*
- Choose a topic that is too obscure. *(Mosquito Psychology)*

2. Find resources.

- Look for sources that will provide the information you need.
- Head for the library. Look for books, magazine articles, newspapers, and encyclopedias.
- Search for information on CDs, videos, and the Internet.
- Don't forget to consult people, too. Some good information can be gained from interviews.

3. Take notes.

- Write down bits of information. Write phrases, sentences, facts, or quotes.
- Write each piece of information on a separate card.
- At the top of the card, write a key word or phrase title to show the subtopic or subcategory.
- Write the source on each card (the complete name of the author, article, book or magazine, dates, and page numbers).
- Keep researching until you find enough details, examples, or information for each of the categories you chose.

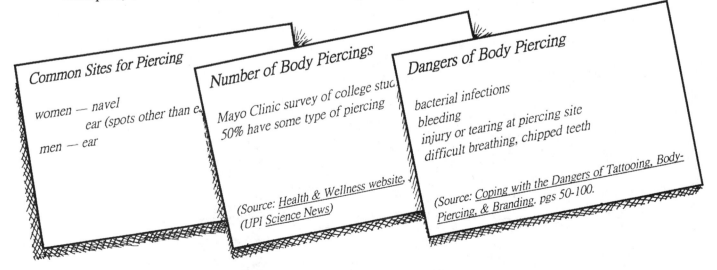

Common Sites for Piercing

women — navel
     ear (spots other than e
men — ear

Number of Body Piercings

Mayo Clinic survey of college stud
50% have some type of piercing

(Source: Health & Wellness website,
(UPI Science News)

Dangers of Body Piercing

bacterial infections
bleeding
injury or tearing at piercing site
difficult breathing, chipped teeth

(Source: Coping with the Dangers of Tattooing, Body-Piercing, & Branding. pgs 50-100.

4. Sort & organize the note cards.

- Group together the cards with the same key word titles.
- Make a pile for each category.
- Organize the cards in a sensible sequence within each category.
- Place the category piles into a sensible order.

5. Make an outline.

- Write each category as a main idea in outline.
- Under each category, write the supporting details or examples (or subcategories).
- If necessary, list sub-subcategories under the subcategories.
- Do your outline carefully. A complete, organized outline will make the writing easier.

6. Write an introductory paragraph.

- Start the report with something catchy that will get the reader interested in your topic. Include a thesis statement if your paper is going to make a particular main point.
- Make sure your introductory paragraph lets the reader know the general idea of the report.

7. Write the body of the report.

- Write carefully from your outline, referring to your notes as needed.
- Build a paragraph on each subtopic topic.
- Include a topic sentence for each paragraph.
- Add details to support each main idea.
- Make smooth transitions between the sentences and paragraphs.

8. Write a concluding paragraph.

- Use this to repeat the main point of the paper, summarize the main points, or conclude with a generalization.
- Finish with a sentence that has punch— one that readers will remember.

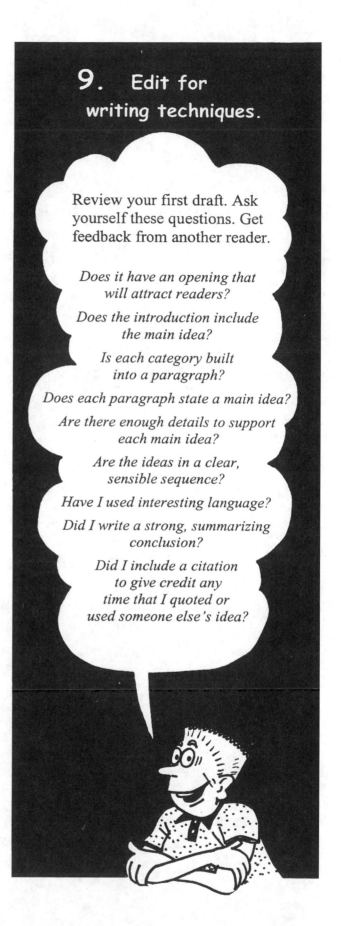

9. Edit for writing techniques.

Review your first draft. Ask yourself these questions. Get feedback from another reader.

Does it have an opening that will attract readers?

Does the introduction include the main idea?

Is each category built into a paragraph?

Does each paragraph state a main idea?

Are there enough details to support each main idea?

Are the ideas in a clear, sensible sequence?

Have I used interesting language?

Did I write a strong, summarizing conclusion?

Did I include a citation to give credit any time that I quoted or used someone else's idea?

10. Proofread for conventions.

- Check for sense, fluency, and completeness of the sentences.
- Check for correct grammatical construction.
- Check for correct spelling, capitalization, and punctuation.

11. Revise to write the final draft.

- Make use of the information you gained from steps 9 and 10.
- Make the changes and corrections you feel are necessary.
- Decide on a format (handwritten, typed, etc.) and write the final copy.

12. Add extra materials to text.

- Decide what you might add to make your report more instructive or interesting.
- Add drawings, diagrams, lists, charts, maps, graphs, time lines, and surveys.

13. Choose and write a good title.

- Make sure your report has an accurate and inviting title.

14. Add a list of sources used (bibliography).

- Make a list of the sources you used for information in your report.
- Write these in alphabetical order
  (by last name of author, or by title if there is no author).
- Attach this to your report.

Follow this form for bibliography entries:

Book: Author last name, first name. <u>Title</u>. Place: Publisher, Date.

Encyclopedia Article: "Title." <u>Encyclopedia</u>. Volume, pages. Date.

Magazine Article: Author last name, first name. "Article Title." <u>Magazine</u> (Date of Publication): page numbers.

Newspaper Article: Author last name, first name. "Title," <u>Newspaper</u>, day, month, year.

CD: "Title." CD-ROM. <u>Title of CD</u>. Publisher, Date.

Video: <u>Title.</u> Videotape. Production Company, Date.

Internet Article: —Author last name, first name. "Title." (Date) Name of Web Site. URL.

15. Share.

- Find a way to show off, share, publish, or display your finished report.

Writing a News Article

A news article is a short non-fiction form that presents a factual account of a current event.

How to Write a Good News Story

1. Get the facts.
Answer the questions **who, what, when, where,** and **how.** Gather information by interviewing people who were involved in the event or situation. Try to interview other people knowledgeable on the subject. Always write down the precise words that are said to you.

2. Write an opening sentence.
This is called a **lead.** This gives the story's main idea and grabs the interest of the reader.

3. Write the body of the story.
Include all the details needed to tell the known facts about the story.

4. Create a headline.
A headline needs to be short and attention getting. It is not always a complete sentence. Make sure your headline gives some clue about the story.

Corinna Clack – Cub Reporter

Tsk, tsk, another wolf accosts another grandma! It's a dangerous world, isn't it? You did a great job of getting all the facts, Corinna.

WOODLAND TIMES

Volume 137

Tuesday, August 19

Woodcutter Praised for Daring Rescue

(Red Bluffs, California; UPI) Quick thinking and bold action by a woodcutter saved the life of a local girl yesterday. Woody Axle was awarded a medal of honor today for rescuing Ms. Red R. Hood from the jaws of a hungry wolf. Mr. Axle reported that he was chopping east of town when he heard cries at about 3 p.m. He entered the 286 Apple Lane house, found the girl trapped by a wolf, and overpowered the wolf with his axe.

According to Mrs. Agatha R. Hood, grandmother of the girl and owner of the home, she was alone when the wolf forcibly entered the house around mid-day Monday. The wolf allegedly snatched her bonnet and gown, tied her up, and locked her in the closet. It appears the wolf then donned her clothing, climbed

According to authorities, the wolf wore grandma's clothes to deceive Ms. Hood.

into her bed, and awaited the granddaughter's arrival.

Young Ms. Hood was treated for a broken arm, abrasions, and bruises. The grandmother was unharmed.

The SPCA has issued a complaint about the cruel treatment of the wolf, a member of an endangered

(continued, page 5, column 2)

Writing a Short Story

- A short story is a form of fiction that can be read in a relatively short amount of time.
- The action and setting of a short story is far more limited than in longer pieces, such as novels.
- The tale told in the story can be real, or it can be imaginary (fantasy).
- Some short stories are science fiction.
- A short story has a conflict, a problem, or complication that is the center of the story. The statement of this conflict, and its development and resolution are part of the story plot.

Short Story Elements

ASK

PROFESSOR KNOW-IT-ALL

She knows a lot!

How does a writer create a character?

ANSWERS:

. . . by describing the character's appearance or personality

. . . by describing the character's behavior, actions, thoughts, and feelings

. . . by writing what the character says

. . . by showing what other characters say, think, or feel about him or her

point of view

The point of view of the story is the angle or perspective from which the story is told. The point of view changes depending upon who is telling the story.

first person point of view – The narrator telling the story is one of the characters in the story (uses the pronouns *I* and *we*).

third person point of view – The narrator is an observer, standing outside the action of the story (uses the pronouns *they*, *she*, *he*, and *it*).

characters

A short story develops through the actions of one or more characters. A short story has just a few characters. Characters are brought to life in the story through characterization (the creating of a character).

setting

The setting is the time and place (or times and places) where the story's action happens.

theme

The theme is the central idea or message of the story (i.e. jealousy can poison a person's life; sometimes losing is better than winning; courage is not a lack of fear).

mood

Mood is the atmosphere or feeling the writer creates in the story. The writer uses language skillfully to cause a particular emotional response in the reader (*i.e.: annoyance, fear, impatience, anticipation, suspense, empathy*).

plot

The plot is a series of events or situations related to the action of the story, usually involving some sort of a problem or conflict.

Plot Structure:

exposition—the introduction to the characters and setting

rising action—introduces and develops the conflict of the story to a point of high intensity

climax—the highest point (most intense point) of action in the story

falling action—the events that follow the climax, usually started by some turning point

resolution—the ending of the conflict or solving of the problem

dénouement—any details or parts of the story that occur after the resolution

Tips for Writing a Good Short Story

Get Sharp Tip # 14
Start a new paragraph each time you begin a quotation from a new speaker.

- Make reading a constant part of your life. Read good stories written by a variety of authors. This will give you ideas for your own writing. More important, it will give you models for good story writing.

- Review the elements of short stories. Include them all in your story.

- Find an idea for your story. Look nearby—in your own life. Think about people you know who are interesting characters; review your journal for things that have interested you; watch for ordinary or extraordinary events that you could describe; notice things you feel strongly; notice things that have changed.

- When you have a general idea for a story, think about the theme— the message or idea you want readers to get from your story. Settle on this before you begin writing.

- Stay with just a few characters. A story can get complicated with too many characters. Choose a few to develop well. Include some dialogue in your story to show who your characters are.

- Allow yourself plenty of time to develop your story. After you write it, let it sit for a few days. Then come back to it with a fresh look.

Better Grades & Higher Test Scores / READING & LANGUAGE
Copyright ©2003 by Incentive Publications, Inc., Nashville, TN.

Get Sharp: Writing Guide

Writing a Letter

Basic Parts of a Letter

The heading includes your address and the date. In a business or formal letter, the heading has a second part, called the inside address. This is the name and address of the person to whom you are writing. Skip at least one line after the heading. (In a business letter, skip four or more lines.)

The greeting or salutation speaks to the person you are writing. It begins with the word Dear (capitalized), and is followed by the name of the person receiving the letter. In a personal letter, a comma follows the name. In a business letter, a colon follows the person's name. Skip one line after the greeting.

The body is the main part of the letter. Often the first line of the body is indented. If this is indented, all paragraphs must also be indented. Keep the paragraphs in a letter fairly short. Skip one line after the body and between paragraphs.

The closing has a capital beginning its first word. A comma always follows the closing. In a friendly letter, the closing can be personal (*Love, Your friend, Sincerely, With love, Affectionately, Your buddy*). In a business letter, the closing should be formal (*Yours truly or Sincerely*).

Signature — Always sign your letter. In a business letter, your name is also typed or printed below your signature.

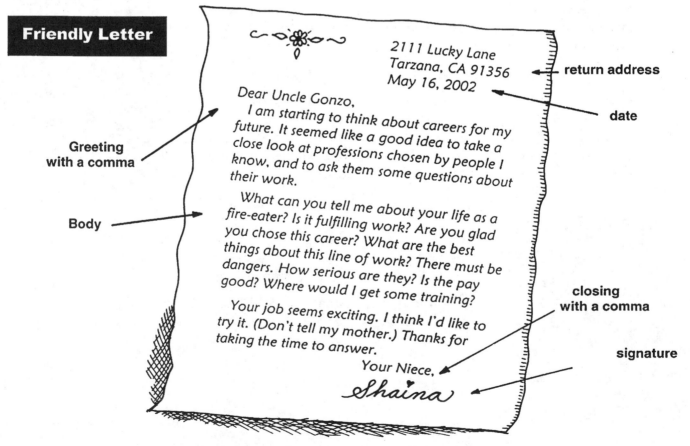

Friendly Letter

2111 Lucky Lane
Tarzana, CA 91356
May 16, 2002 ← **return address**

← **date**

Dear Uncle Gonzo,
   I am starting to think about careers for my future. It seemed like a good idea to take a close look at professions chosen by people I know, and to ask them some questions about their work.

   What can you tell me about your life as a fire-eater? Is it fulfilling work? Are you glad you chose this career? What are the best things about this line of work? There must be dangers. How serious are they? Is the pay good? Where would I get some training?

   Your job seems exciting. I think I'd like to try it. (Don't tell my mother.) Thanks for taking the time to answer.

Your Niece,
Shaina

Greeting with a comma

Body

closing with a comma

signature

Business Letter

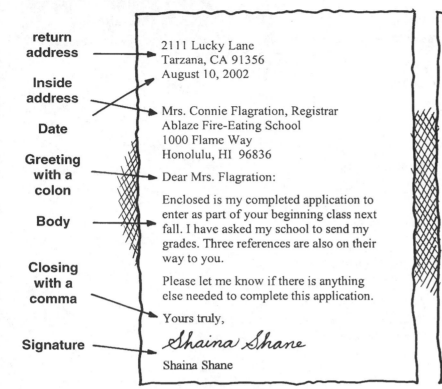

return address

Inside address

Date

Greeting with a colon

Body

Closing with a comma

Signature

2111 Lucky Lane
Tarzana, CA 91356
August 10, 2002

Mrs. Connie Flagration, Registrar
Ablaze Fire-Eating School
1000 Flame Way
Honolulu, HI 96836

Dear Mrs. Flagration:

Enclosed is my completed application to enter as part of your beginning class next fall. I have asked my school to send my grades. Three references are also on their way to you.

Please let me know if there is anything else needed to complete this application.

Yours truly,

Shaina Shane

Shaina Shane

Full Block Form

2111 Lucky Lane
Tarzana, CA 91356
August 10, 2002

Mrs. Connie Flagration, Registrar
Ablaze Fire-Eating School
1000 Flame Way
Honolulu, HI 96836

Dear Mrs. Flagration:

    Enclosed is my completed application to enter as part of your beginning class next fall. I have asked my school to send my grades. Three references are also on their way to you.

    Please let me know if there is anything else needed to complete this application.

Yours truly,

Shaina Shane

Shaina Shane

Semi-Block Form

Finally, all these applications are finished!

slurp

Return Address

Address

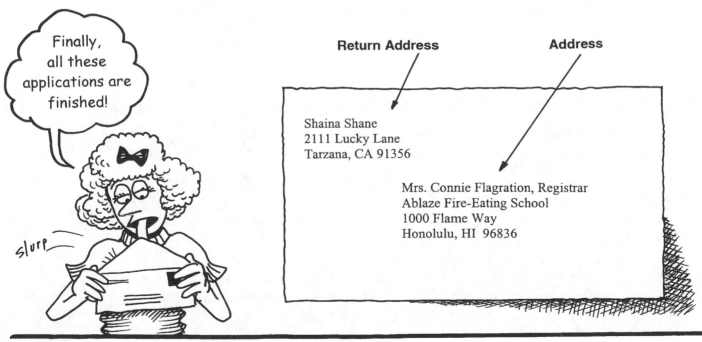

Shaina Shane
2111 Lucky Lane
Tarzana, CA 91356

Mrs. Connie Flagration, Registrar
Ablaze Fire-Eating School
1000 Flame Way
Honolulu, HI 96836

Expository Writing

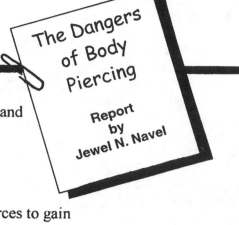

The purpose: to explain or inform

Examples: essay, book report, research paper, news article, and instructions

Tips for Your Expository Writing

- Choose a creative, fresh approach to explaining the topic.
- Investigate your topic before you write. Use a variety of resources to gain information.
- Use reliable, well-supported evidence for your explanation.
- Include fresh, unusual examples.
- Present your facts, examples, or opinions in an organized manner.
- Choose a particular approach for your organization. *(i.e.: how-to-do steps for the reader to follow, compare and contrast similarities and differences, identify and explain the causes and effects, give a detailed and broad explanation of an idea, analyze idea – break down into its parts and show how the parts work together as a whole.)*

Narrative Writing

The purpose: to recount an event or series of events

Examples: short story, poem, biography, and anecdote

Tips for Your Narrative Writing

- Use time as your way of organization. Usually narration is told in chronological order, unless you specifically choose to jump back and forth in time.
- Choose a fresh, creative approach to telling your story.
- Keep the focus on a particular event; don't wander off too far on minor events.
- Pay attention to characterization. Make your characters come alive for the reader.
- Be aware of your audience as you write. Make sure the approach and language are appropriate and appealing for the audience.
- Use vivid anecdotes and details to keep the story alive for the reader.
- Include some interpretation or analysis of the events, so the reader understands their importance to the story.

Persuasive Writing

The purpose: to convince readers to respond in some way (to agree with something, change attitude or behavior about something, desire something)

Examples: advertisement, editorial, petition, argument

IN THE DARK?

Tips for Your Persuasive Writing

- Choose a topic that is of interest currently to many people, at least to many people in the group that will be your readers or listeners.

- Choose a topic about which you have strong opinions and feelings.

- Know and state clearly what your viewpoint is.

- Choose a creative, fresh approach to arguing your viewpoint.

- Gather reliable, sensible arguments to back up your position.

- Do research, if necessary, to have credible sources behind your arguments.

- State the alternative view or views. Show that you know the other side.

- Carefully "combat" each opposing argument, showing the flaws or weaknesses in each.

- Use words and phrases that are authoritative and convincing.

- Give good examples and illustrations to show why your viewpoint works.

- Make the examples specific and interesting. Use real-life stories.

- Present at least one strong example or story to back up each point in your argument.

- Present your arguments in an organized manner.

- Carefully build your argument so that it gains strength as the writing moves along.

- Use your two strongest arguments first and last.

- Write a strong conclusion that wraps up all the arguments.

Get Sharp: Writing Guide

Descriptive Writing

The purpose: to "paint a picture" of a person, place, thing, or idea

Examples: travel brochure, character study, catalog entry

"The neighborhood kids thought that old Mrs. Wiggins was a witch. Her hair looked like twelve generations of spiders had lived their lives in it . . ."

Tips for Your Descriptive Writing

- Write about a person, place, thing, event, or idea that you know well.

- Spend time observing the subject of your description.

- Take notes, collecting details and observations.

- Pay attention to the physical characteristics of the person, place, event, or thing.

- Use all your senses to observe the subject.

- Talk to others about the subject. Gather their feelings and reflections.

- Notice the way other people respond to the person, place, event, or thing.

- If you're describing a person, interview him or her. Write down some specific quotes the person says.

- Recall particular incidents involving the person, place, event, or thing.

- After you have collected observations and details, decide what the main impression is that this subject has made on you. Use this as your main idea or thesis.

- In your introduction, use an anecdote, quote, or vivid description that will immediately cause the reader to "picture" the person, place, or thing.

- Write sentences that add to an ever-broadening picture you're trying to show of the subject. Only include things that relate to the point you are making.

- Work to paint a colorful picture of the subject. Use specific, vivid adverbs and adjectives and specific, active verbs in your description.

- Include figurative language, especially metaphors which compare the subject imaginatively to something the reader will understand.

- End your description with a final feeling or bit of information that emphasizes the importance of this person, place, or thing to you or to others.

Imaginative Writing

The purpose: to entertain with make-believe events

Examples: fairy tale, science fiction story, myth, ghost story

The Ghost at Clawfoot Hall by Susan Specter

Tips for Your Imaginative Writing

- Choose a unique, fresh approach and form.
- Use language that surprises the reader and draws her/him in.
- Include figurative language to enrich the tale (alliteration, metaphor, personification, etc.)
- Develop interesting characters. Since the writing is imaginary, you can make them unusual, even outlandish!
- Include some dialogue, imagery, foreshadowing, and other literary elements.
- Choose words and phrases that spark the imagination. Avoid ordinary ways of describing events or characters.
- Make sure the beginning lets the reader know this will be no ordinary tale.

Personal Writing

The purpose: to express the writer's personal opinions, insights, questions, reflections, or perspectives

Examples: diary, journal, autobiography, reflection on a poem

Tips for Your Personal Writing

JEB'S PRIVATE JOURNAL

Keep Out!

- Focus on putting yourself honestly into the writing.
- Let your personal perspective shine through. Avoid being swayed by what someone else might think, or what you feel you're "supposed" to say.
- Reflect on the topic seriously. Connect it to your personal experiences and observations.
- Include concrete examples and anecdotes to support your thoughts and ideas.
- Write as if you are writing for yourself or a close friend. Use a natural style.
- Allow your passion and commitment for the topic to show.
- Make sure the opening and closing let the reader know this is a personal opinion or reflection.

Get Sharp: Writing Guide

Public Speaking

There are times in your life when you will need to speak
in front of an audience—even if that is a very small audience.
You might give a speech for any one of many purposes: to tell
a story, to share information, to convince someone about something,
to report on a book, to recite a poem, to interpret a poem,
to take part in a debate, or to narrate an event or a multimedia presentation.
In all these situations, there is one basic purpose for giving a speech:
you want to communicate some idea or feeling—and you want
your audience to hear, understand, and respond favorably.

Kinds of Speeches

Impromptu speech—a speech given without advance preparation

Usually there is very little or no warning that you'll need to give a speech. All of a sudden, in a school assignment, or in a real life situation, you need to say something on some topic or in response to some event. If you're lucky, you might get a few seconds to brainstorm or collect your thoughts, but don't count on it!

You might give an impromptu speech when . . .

- someone makes a statement and asks you to give your opinion (in front of a group).
- you get an award or honor you were not expecting.
- you walk into a surprise party (and it's for you)!

Memorized speech—a speech that you have written and memorized word for word

A memorized speech is carefully planned and written, then memorized precisely.

You might prepare and memorize a speech when . . .

- you are going to receive an award, and you know you'll have to respond.
- you want to run for an office, and you'll need to make a campaign speech.

Extemporaneous speech—a planned speech, given with the help of notes

An extemporaneous speech spares you the need to memorize every word, because you have help from your notes. However, it feels more spontaneous (like an impromptu speech) because your language doesn't have to stick to a memorized script.

You might give an extemporaneous speech when . . .

- you've been assigned to give a speech in school (and allowed to use notes).
- you want to share an opinion at a meeting.

Speaking Troubles

Students often have problems with speaking. Maybe you have some of the same troubles. It's quite common to be nervous about giving a speech. Follow these tips for better speaking.

Better Grades & Higher Test Scores / READING & LANGUAGE
Copyright ©2003 by Incentive Publications, Inc., Nashville, TN.

Get Sharp: Speaking Guide

Preparing for a Speech

Get prepared! It's the best way to feel more confident and have better success with public speaking.

Steps for Preparing a Speech

1. Choose the topic.

Select a topic that is important or interesting to you. It can be a new topic for you if you are going to do research. Otherwise, choose something with which you are very familiar.

2. Decide the purpose and the audience.

Be sure about the reason for giving the speech and who the listeners will be. Ask yourself these questions:

- *What is the purpose for giving the speech?*
- *Will I share information, tell how to do something, compare some things, or try to convince someone about something?*
- *What do I want to accomplish?*
- *Who is the audience?*
- *What will be interesting to the audience?*
- *What questions will they have that I should try to answer?*
- *What objections will they have that I should consider?*

Get Sharp Tip # 15
Are you nervous about giving your speech? The best defenses against speech anxiety are good preparation and practice.

3. Find information and take notes.

First, write down what you already know about the topic. Write questions you would like to answer about the topic. Search a variety of references to answer your questions and learn about the topic. Interview people to get more information. Write down key ideas, questions, phrases, and facts about the topic. Write down direct quotes or specific statistics you might want to use in your speech. If you plan to quote someone or use an exact statistic, write down the source. Write a key word or subtopic label on each card.

4. Organize your material.

Gather all the notes together into subtopic or category groups. Organize the groups into a sensible sequence.

5. Plan the timing.

Know how much time you have for the speech. This will help you with the organization. You may need to drop some of the subtopics or points. If your material seems too skimpy to fill the time, you may have to do some more research.

Better Grades & Higher Test Scores / READING & LANGUAGE
Copyright ©2003 by Incentive Publications, Inc., Nashville, TN.

6. Write an introduction.

Create an attention-grabbing introduction—one that makes the audience eager to hear the whole speech. In the first few sentences, make the topic or purpose of the speech clear to the audience. You might start with

a startling fact.
a funny anecdote.
an explanation of your interest in the topic.
a questions or group of questions.
an interesting quote.
a demonstration or illustration of your topic.

7. Write the body of the speech.

Write the main points. Describe or explain each point clearly. Give interesting examples. Move the points along smoothly. Don't overwhelm the listeners with facts and dates and statistics. Use examples that make a point an capture the listeners' interest.

8. Write a conclusion.

End your speech by reminding the listeners of the main point. Be sure about what you will say at the end. Make your final sentences statements with a punch. Leave the listeners satisfied, amused, ready to act, or fascinated with the topic.

9. Memorize the speech OR Prepare your note cards.

Write the information on your cards that you will need in order to move the speech along smoothly. This might be in outline form. Write clear, specific introductory information— maybe even word-for-word. Write the ending clearly, too—maybe even word-for-word. Write neatly on your cards so you will be able to use them from quick glances at them.

10. Memorize your introduction and conclusion.

Know exactly what you will say to start and end the speech.
Don't leave either part up to chance.

11. Practice.

Rehearse your speech. Do this in private, to a tape recorder, in front of a mirror, in front of a video camera. If you wish, rehearse in front of a friend who will give you feedback.

12. Practice.

Review the tips on page 180. Use the advice while you practice.

13. Practice.   14. Practice.   15. Practice.

Giving a Speech

I think that I'm as well-prepared as I can be.

A well-prepared speech is just the beginning of your task! Now, you need to give the speech. Review the tips (below) for successful delivery of a speech. Then follow the advice as you practice giving your speech. Get to know these so well that they'll stay with you when you give your speech. Polishing your delivery skills will give you a huge boost as a speaker.

Top 10 Things to Remember
When Giving a Speech

1. Confidence — *Your planning **will** pay off! You **do** know more about the topic than the audience. Believe that the audience wants to hear what you have to say.*

2. Posture — *Stand straight, but not stiff. Relax. Don't slump, slouch, or bounce around. Don't sway. Do move a little. This will help to keep you relaxed.*

3. Hands — *Make a plan for your hands. Don't let them dangle awkwardly by your side, nervously pull at your hair, or absent-mindedly scratch your nose. Use your hands for gesturing or demonstrating, and to hold your note cards. Let your hands relax, and use them naturally.*

4. Language — *Talk as if you were speaking to someone. Use your own language. Don't use big words.*

5. Smoothness — *Think ahead about how you will move from one idea to the next.*

6. Tone — *Use a friendly, natural tone. You don't want to sound timid and hesitant. Nor do you want to sound arrogant or impersonal. Avoid a monotone sound.*

7. Volume — *Speak loudly enough so all listeners can hear you, but don't shout.*

8. Speed — *Don't rush. A common speaking problem is talking too fast. Practice brief pauses. This gives the listeners a chance to absorb your latest point.*

9. Contact — *Look at your audience. Keep eye contact and talk directly to the people as individuals. Look at different faces as you speak.*

10. Enthusiasm — *Show enthusiasm for your topic and keep that enthusiasm up— from the start to the very end.*

SPEAKING SCORING GUIDE

Peers, teachers, or parents in responding to a speech given by a student may use this. Students may also use this guide for self-evaluation after a speech. It can be used for preparation and practice, as well as for assessment.

TRAIT	Score of 5	Score of 3	Score of 1
CONTENT & IDEAS *(main ideas, supporting details, appropriateness to audience and purpose)*	• Main ideas are clear and focused. • Main ideas, purpose stand out clearly. • Main ideas are well-supported with details and examples relevant to topic. • Ideas fit the audience and purpose well. • Ideas are interesting and command audience attention. • Content is creatively presented. • Content includes a variety of sources, viewpoints, or examples. • Conclusions reached are based on strong evidence. • The speaker shows strong insight into the topic.	• Main ideas are mostly clear and focused. • Main ideas, purpose are mostly clear. • Details and examples are used but may be limited or repetitive. • Most details are relevant to the topic. • Ideas fit the audience and purpose somewhat. • Ideas are mostly interesting and command audience attention some of the time. • Some ideas are creatively presented. • Content includes different sources, viewpoints, or examples, but variety is limited. • Some, but not all conclusions reached are based on strong evidence. • The speaker shows insight into the topic. • All in all, the speech is a successful attempt to present coherent ideas and details effectively to the audience.	• The speech lacks clarity and focus. • Main ideas are hard to identify. • Ideas are not supported well with details and examples. • The purpose is not clear. • Details given are not relevant. • Ideas do not fit the audience or purpose. • Ideas have little sparkle and do not command audience attention. • Content is presented with no creativity. • Conclusions reached are not based on any evidence. • The speaker shows little insight into the topic.
ORGANIZATION *(system of organization including introduction, main body, transitions, and conclusion)*	• Organization allows the main ideas and details to be conveyed well. • A strong, creative introduction grabs the listeners' attention. • The speech moves along from one idea fluently, with smooth transitions. • Details and examples are well-placed in the speech so as to maintain interest and strengthen the main point. • The speech has a strong, creative conclusion that fits the purpose and strengthens the message.	• Organization is recognizable, but is weak or inconsistent in places. • For the most part, the organization allows the main ideas and details to be conveyed. • The introduction has a beginning that is recognizable but not compelling. • The speech moves along from one idea relatively well, but some parts are choppy or transitions awkward. • Details and examples are mostly well-placed in the speech so as to maintain interest and strengthen the main point. • Conclusion fits the purpose and strengthens the message, but may be uncreative or unmemorable.	• Little or no organization is evident. • Poor organization interferes with communication of message. • Introduction is missing or irrelevant. • Speech does not flow smoothly. There are no transitions between ideas. • Details and examples have little relevance or purpose. • The conclusion is missing or irrelevant.

A score of 4 may be given for speeches that fall between 3 and 5 on a trait. A score of 2 may be given for speeches that fall between 1 and 3 on a trait.

Get Sharp: Speaking Guide

SPEAKING SCORING GUIDE, continued

TRAIT	Score of 5	Score of 3	Score of 1
LANGUAGE USE *(language use which communicates main points; correctness of grammar/usage; use of language appropriate to the purpose and audience)*	• Language is fresh and colorful. • Language communicates with and interests the audience. • Proper English language is used, unless slang or jargon is chosen to fit the purpose well. • Speech uses language creatively. • Terms used are pronounced and explained clearly. • Grammar and usage are correct.	• Language is somewhat original, but does not always work well in the speech. • The language communicates the point but does not have a strong impact on the audience. • For the most part, proper English language is used; slang or jargon may interfere with the purpose at times. • There are attempts at creativity, but they are not always successful. • Terms used are sometimes, but not always, pronounced and explained clearly. • Grammar and usage are mostly correct.	• Language very ordinary • Language unclear. Some words are the wrong words. • Language does not work to communicate the main ideas. • Language, including slang and jargon, is used inappropriately or improperly. • Terms are not used or are not explained or are used improperly. • Grammar and usage are frequently incorrect. Poor grammar interferes with the meaning of the message.
DELIVERY *(pronunciation, enunciation, eye contact, fluency, rate, volume, tone, body movements, and gestures)*	• Speaker has very clear (and correct) pronunciation and enunciation. • Speaker maintains good eye contact with audience. • Rate, tone, and volume fit the purpose and lend to good communication of the message. • Speaker's delivery engages audience and keeps their attention. • Delivery is very smooth. • Interesting and appropriate use of gestures, facial expression. • Body movements do not detract from the effectiveness of the speech.	• Pronunciation and enunciation are sometimes less than clear. • Eye contact is minimal. • Rate, tone, and volume are inconsistent. • Speaker's delivery engages audience and keeps their attention only part of the time. • Delivery is choppy in some places. • Interesting and appropriate use of gestures, facial expression some of the time; at other times gestures and expressions are nonexistent or inappropriate. • Some body movements interfere with effectiveness of the speech.	• Speaker has very poor pronunciation and enunciation. • There is no eye contact with audience. • Rate is too fast or too slow, volume is too soft or too loud, tone is monotone. • Speaker is not able to command audience attention with delivery. • Delivery is halting and interferes with communication of the message. • Gestures and facial expressions are not used at all, or are distracting or inappropriate. • Body movements are distracting.

A score of 4 may be given for speeches that fall between 3 and 5 on a trait. A score of 2 may be given for speeches that fall between 1 and 3 on a trait.

GET SHARP ⟶

in

READING & WORD MEANING

Purposes for Reading

Just think of all the different things you read each day—signs, ads, news headlines, reminders on the refrigerator, phone numbers, calendars, maps, menus, textbooks, test questions, directions, puzzle clues, CD labels, movie reviews, email, stories, novels, your sister's diary, notes from friends, Internet website information. You are looking for different things in these different reading tasks, and you read them in different ways. To get the most out of your reading, it's good to understand your purpose for reading before you even begin.

In general, the reasons you read fall into these three categories:

Reading for Personal Enjoyment & Experience

You want to find out something about a person or group, a place, or an idea. You want to explore a different culture. You want to enjoy a good story. Much of your reading is for the purpose of pure enjoyment or expansion of your world and mind. Follow these suggestions for effective personal reading:

Notice the setting. Picture it in your mind.

Get to know the characters.

Identify the main idea or story conflict right away.

Watch for delicious words and phrases. Re-read them for enjoyment.

Read poems aloud to appreciate the special sounds and rhythms.

Relate the reading to what you know and how you feel.

Relate the reading to your personal experiences.

> **Get Sharp Tip # 16**
> Don't rush your personal reading. Slow down and notice all the words, sounds, and ideas.

Get involved in the material. Ask yourself questions like these:

How would I feel in this setting?
How would I solve this problem?
When have I been in a situation like this character is in?
Who do I know like this character?
What do I already know about this topic?
What will happen next? What would I like to see happen?

Reading to Find Information

You're looking for an answer to a specific question. Generally, when you're reading to find information, it is an immediate need. You are probably reading reference books, journals, newspapers, ads, or Internet sources. When you read for information, follow these suggestions:

Clearly identify beforehand what you need to find. That way you can keep from wasting time looking at things you don't need.

Skim each source. Ask these questions:

For what purpose was this material written?
What is the exact source of the fact or information?
Is this a reputable source?
Does the material or site name the author?
How current is the information?

Scan the material for references to the topic you are seeking.
Take notes on the information you find.
Review graphics that might expand your information.

Reading to Learn

Get Sharp Tip # 17
Before you start, have an idea what you're looking for.

You want to learn and remember something. Generally, when you read for this purpose, you are reading nonfiction—articles, newspapers, magazines, nonfiction books, textbooks. Follow these suggestions for reading to learn:

Plan plenty of time to do the reading well.

Don't rush through the assignment.

Start by skimming the material to get an overview of the structure and contents.

Think ahead of time about what you already know on this subject.

Determine your purpose for the reading. What do you need to learn?

Read all the titles, subtitles, and headings first.

Read the questions at the end, if there are any.

Read the vocabulary words, if any are introduced.

Read through one section at a time.

Stop after each section and think about what it said. Take notes.

Summarize each section in your mind or notes.

Re-read anything that was confusing.

Follow the SQ3R Strategy for an effective method to get more out of your reading.

Get Sharp Tip # 18
Allow plenty of time for reading to learn. You can't do it in a rush!

Get Sharp: Reading Purposes & Methods

Reading Methods

The way you read can change—according to the kind of material being read and the purpose for the reading. When you approach a written work, there is something you need to get from the material, or something you hope will happen when you read. You are constantly adjusting the method of reading, depending on those needs and hopes.

3 Different Reading Methods

Scanning– a quick look through written text to find specific facts or particular information

When you scan, run your eyes quickly over the material, watching for a key word or phrase. This helps you locate the part that will give you the information you need. When you find this, change to another reading method—slowing down to read this portion closely.

Example: *You scan through a flier describing electronic equipment on sale until you find the name or section of the device you want to buy. Then you switch to careful reading to get the details of the equipment, including the sale price.*

Skimming– a quick overview of the whole piece, to get a general idea of the content

When you skim, closely read headlines, titles, subtitles, headings, captions, and words in bold type. Closely read opening and closing paragraphs, and anything labeled "conclusion" or "summary" or "results." Don't forget to skim graphics to learn what they show.

Example: *You skim over a menu to see what kinds of things they serve and the general categories. Then you switch to careful reading, choosing some portions of the menu to examine carefully, and possibly ignoring other parts altogether.*

Close Reading– a slow, careful reading of all the material, taking time to enjoy or think about each sentence or paragraph or section

When you read closely, stop after each sentence, paragraph, or section, to think over what you have read. Be sure you appreciate or register the main idea before you go on. Look up any unfamiliar words to find their meanings. Take notes, underline key points, or write a brief summary of each section.

Examples: *You read closely when you are reading an assignment from your textbook, or when you read a book, story, or poem for enjoyment.*

The SQ3R Strategy

The SQ3R Reading Strategy is a method for helping you get the most out of your reading when you are reading to study or learn information. Use the SQ3R Strategy right now to learn about this method. Get to know all five steps—and practice them!

S = SURVEY

Survey (skim) the material to get a general understanding of what's in it. Notice these things:

- the organization of the material
- the title or heading and subheadings
- the introduction, conclusion, and summary
- review questions at end of chapter
- pictures, graphs, or other graphics
- words in boldface, color, or italics
- captions under pictures or graphics

Q = QUESTION

While you are surveying, and before you read, ask yourself:

- What do I already know about this subject?
- What is the point of this material?
- What is the author trying to say?
- What did the teacher say to look for when reading this?
- What point is made by each graphic aid?

Turn each title, heading, or subheading into a question. Write these questions down to use as you read.

R = READ

Read the material closely. Read one section at a time. As you read:

- Look for answers to the questions you wrote.
- Pay close attention to the main ideas.
- Study the graphic aids and their captions.
- Go back and read any unclear or confusing sections.
- Take notes. Write down main points and key ideas.

R = RECITE

Stop after each section, and:

- Talk to yourself. Re-state what you just read.
- Try to summarize it succinctly.
- Take notes on the part you read.
- Write down main points and key ideas.
- Write down important definitions.
- Underline important points.

R = REVIEW

When you finish your reading:

- Try to say the answers to the questions you wrote.
- Re-read the main headings and re-state the main ideas you now know.
- Review your notes, definitions, and summaries.
- Re-read the questions at the end of the material. Recite the answers.

Finding Main Ideas

One of the most basic and important reading comprehension skills is the ability to find the main idea in any written work. Often the main idea is stated in the first sentence or paragraph (or in a poem, in the first few lines).

Sometimes the main idea is literal—stated clearly and obviously. Sometimes the main idea is implied—stated less directly. Be alert for both ways of presenting the main point.

Notice the literal and implied main ideas from the following passages.

Atlantis, a great mythical empire on an island in the Atlantic Ocean, was created by a Greek writer, Plato. Supposedly, great storms and earthquakes shook the whole island and caused it to sink. For centuries, people have been fascinated with Plato's tales about the island. Many wondered if it was a real place or just another Greek myth. Over the years, many stories and fantasies have been told about a great city that lies beneath the ocean. Some think it is still inhabited by sea creatures such as mermaids and mermen. Some scientists think a real island in the Aegean Sea inspired the tales. This island, Thira, was destroyed in 1500 B.C. by a volcanic eruption.

Main Idea: There is much fascination and mystery surrounding the existence and fate of Atlantis.

Main Idea: Though most records are set with people doing an activity, some are set by non-activity. ↓

Most records are set with active feats
Of speed or strength or skill.
But did you know that prizes go
To folks who just stay still?

To win renown, some dive from planes
Or juggle two-edged swords.
Some walk on ropes, or wrestle snakes,
Or surf through air on boards.

But records, too, are broken
For doing nothing at all.
For standing still, sitting in trees,
Or relaxing on a wall.

The Main Event: Wally Bumpkin vs. Dead-eye Dan

You can imagine that walking on water is a rather tough thing to do. Yet, it seems that walking on your hands may be even harder. The world records for the two events hint at this. A water-walker covered 3502 miles on skis to set the record. The person who walked on his hands, however, could cover only 970 miles.

Main Idea: It is probably harder to walk on hands than on water.

Main Idea: A judge sampled cream puffs to decide a case about a bakery falsely advertising its use of genuine cream in its pastries.

Circuit Court Case # 215

The *Cream Puff Heaven Patisserie* was charged with false advertising in Judge Leslie D'Law's courtroom. Mr. Charles E. Claire, who buys four dozen cream puffs each day from the patisserie, brought the suit. According to Mr. Claire, the bakery is using artificial cream in its puffs. Mr. Claire brought the bakery's newspaper ad, which claims that genuine cream is used in all their pastries. Judge D'Law ordered the bailiff to run right over to the bakery and purchase a dozen cream puffs. The judge ate all twelve. She decided that the cream was indeed artificial. Mr. Claire was awarded $1000 to compensate for the cost of the 1200 cream puffs he had purchased during the past year.

COUPLE SUFFERS PAIR OF STRANGE DISEASES

City Center Hospital admitted a man and his wife today. Each suffers from a rare eating disorder. The husband, Mr. Jack Sprat, of 1616 Hambone Lane, has a condition that makes it impossible for him to eat anything that contains fat of any kind. His wife, Maryanne Sprat, can eat nothing but fat. Each has suffered the respective ailments his or her entire life. Medical experts who are looking for the cause of their ailments are testing both of them. The doctors are baffled about how to treat the couple. Mr. Sprat had a positive spin on the situation. "One good thing," he said, "is that no food is wasted in our household!"

Main Idea: Medical experts are seeking explanations as to why a man can eat no fat, and why his wife can eat no lean foods.

189

Identifying Details

To understand the meaning of a written passage, the reader needs to be able to find the examples or details that support the main idea. Keep your eye sharp for those details, and you'll get more out of your reading.

Find details in passages...

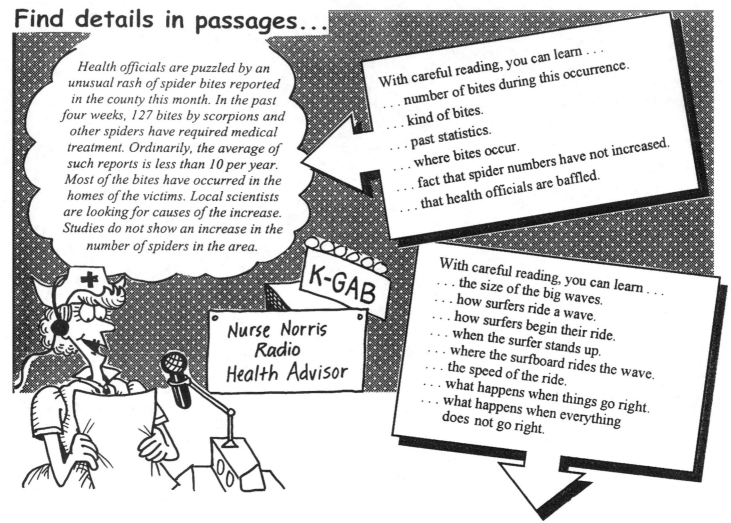

Health officials are puzzled by an unusual rash of spider bites reported in the county this month. In the past four weeks, 127 bites by scorpions and other spiders have required medical treatment. Ordinarily, the average of such reports is less than 10 per year. Most of the bites have occurred in the homes of the victims. Local scientists are looking for causes of the increase. Studies do not show an increase in the number of spiders in the area.

K-GAB

Nurse Norris
Radio
Health Advisor

With careful reading, you can learn . . .
. . . number of bites during this occurrence.
. . . kind of bites.
. . . past statistics.
. . . where bites occur.
. . . fact that spider numbers have not increased.
. . . that health officials are baffled.

With careful reading, you can learn . . .
. . . the size of the big waves.
. . . how surfers ride a wave.
. . . how surfers begin their ride.
. . . when the surfer stands up.
. . . where the surfboard rides the wave.
. . . the speed of the ride.
. . . what happens when things go right.
. . . what happens when everything does not go right.

A "wall" of water: it's the big wave that surfers wait for and thrill to ride. Thousands of surfers all over the world rush into wild surf day after day, looking for that perfect big wave. Sometimes these perfect waves are higher than 30 feet!

When they find the perfect wave, how do surfers ride it? The idea is to ride along the vertical face of the wave, just ahead of the wave's crest (the place where it is breaking). Of course, the surfer needs to stay ahead of the crest and not get crushed under it.

Surfers start by kneeling or lying on the surfboard and paddling out to the area beyond where the waves are breaking. Here they wait for the right wave. When a surfer sees a good wave coming, she turns and paddles furiously toward shore, trying to move as fast as the wave. If she times it right, the wave will pick up her surfboard and carry it along. At this point she will stand up on the board at the top of the wave and ride it down the wall (vertical face) of the wave. She actually gets going faster than the wave is moving. She must keep an eye on the wave's crest and turn the board to stay ahead of the crest.

If she gets it right, the surfer can enjoy a nice ride for several minutes, moving at a good speed—up to 10 miles an hour. Or, if she doesn't get it right, she can wipe out (be sent smashing beneath the water by the tremendous weight and force of a monstrous wave).

Find details in graphics . . .

Pay close attention to illustrations, ads, charts, graphs, tables, diagrams, and maps. There are plenty of details to be read in these and other graphic presentations.

With careful reading you can learn . . .
. . . the date, time, place of the music festival.
. . . the name of the event.
. . . the titles of all the songs.
. . . the names of all the performers.
. . . the order of the program.

With careful reading you can learn . . .
. . . the names of the unusual journeys.
. . . the lengths in miles.
. . . the time each journey took.

GRANITEVILLE MUSIC FEST

Place: Hard Rock Arena
Date: Full Moon Evening Time: After Dark

PROGRAM

I Dhino If You Love Me Anymore
Mick Jagged & the Rolling Boulders

I Feel Like a T-Rex Stomped on My Heart
The Petro Cliff Trio

Your Love is Like a Saber-Tooth Tiger
Teri Dactyl & the Hot Rocks

Sha-boom, Sha-boom, Sha-Rock
The Lava-Ettes

You're as Cuddly as a Wooly Mammoth
The Smashing Marbles

INTERMISSION

Be a Little Boulder, Honey
Curt McCave

The Gravel Pit Rock
The Cro-Magnan Crooners

Don't Take Me for Granite, Baby
The Standing Stones

My Cave's on Fire
The Paleo-Lyths

Your Heart's Made of Stone
Bronto & the Cave Dudes

Dancin' at the Quarry
Tommy Shale

I've Cried Pebbles Over You
The Limestone Lovers

I'll Lava You Till the Volcano Blows
The Square Wheels

STRANGE & AMAZING JOURNEYS

walking on stilts
3008 miles in 107 days

leapfrog trip
996 miles in 245 hours

backwards run
2100 miles in 107 days

unicycle trip
3261 miles in 44 days

walking on hands
870 miles in 55 days

lawnmower journey
3366 miles in 42 days

Get Sharp: Reading Comprehension

Find details in titles and captions . . .

Don't miss the good information that's given in titles and captions. Read them closely. Often, you can pick up a main idea for a whole article, essay, or other written work.

With careful reading you can learn . . .

. . . the name of the skier.

. . . an idea of what aerial skiing includes.

. . . how skiers launch the air flight.

. . . the basis for scoring.

Aerial skier Andy Agile performs flips and twists after jumping off a 66-yard long ramp. Judges gave him a score based 20% on the takeoff, 50% on the flight, and 30% on the landing.

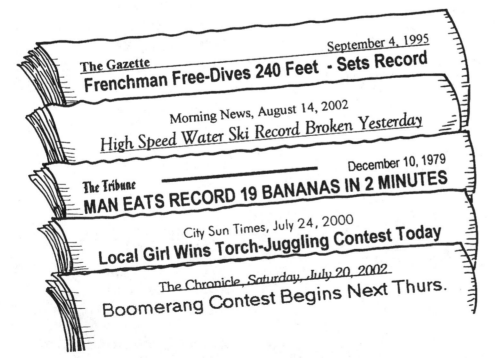

September 4, 1995

The Gazette

Frenchman Free-Dives 240 Feet - Sets Record

Morning News, August 14, 2002

High Speed Water Ski Record Broken Yesterday

December 10, 1979

The Tribune

MAN EATS RECORD 19 BANANAS IN 2 MINUTES

City Sun Times, July 24, 2000

Local Girl Wins Torch-Juggling Contest Today

The Chronicle, Saturday, July 20, 2002

Boomerang Contest Begins Next Thurs.

With careful reading you can learn . . .

. . . the names of records set or broken.

. . . the dates of the records.

. . . exact details of some records.

. . . who set or broke some of the records.

Identifying Fact & Opinion

A sharp reader will be skilled at separating fact from opinion in written material. There is nothing wrong with an author writing his or her opinions. The problem with opinions develops when they are stated as if they are factual information.

Interview With an ACW Climber

Interviewer: What in the world is an ACW, anyway?

Climber: It's the key feature in a great new sport. ACW is an artificial climbing wall.

Interviewer: Describe these ACWs.

Climber: These walls are not the rock walls climbed in natural outdoor settings. They are created artificially with materials other than rock. Usually the ACW is used indoors.

Interviewer: Why climb an ACW instead of a real rock or cliff?

Climber: They are easy to get to without long hikes. The climber doesn't have to worry about weather. Climbers can learn or practice climbing skills in a safer setting that is not extremely high.

Interviewer: Which is more appealing to climbers: real rocks or an ACW?

Climber: Everybody is happier climbing an ACW because it is safer.

Interviewer: I hear this is a fast-growing sport. Why?

Climber: Everyone should do this. ACW climbing is safer and more accessible to beginners. People are too afraid to climb real cliffs. They like this better.

In this interview, most of the climber's statements are factual description of ACWs. Notice the circled statements. These are stated as fact, but are, in fact, the climber's personal opinions.

Identifying Cause & Effect

A sharp reader will also be alert to passages that describe causes and effects. Understanding cause and effect involves two skills: seeing what specific happening caused or sparked an event (or response), and recognizing what specific results came about because of a certain event or action.

Look for the causes and effects in the cures described here.

If your ears are ringing, check to see if the doorbell or phone is ringing. If not, your ears are telling you that someone is talking about you. Stick a finger in your ear. When you do this, the person who is gossiping will bite his or her tongue, and the ringing will stop!

If nosebleeds trouble you, one of these remedies will help. Have a gorilla pinch your nose, and the bleeding will stop in 10 minutes. Stand on your head and sing "Yankee Doodle". The bleeding will stop by the time you get to the chorus. If none of these work, fry some onions and hold your head over the pan. Sniffing the fumes will make the blood clot immediately.

Better Grades & Higher Test Scores / READING & LANGUAGE
Copyright ©2003 by Incentive Publications, Inc., Nashville, TN.

Get Sharp: Reading Comprehension

Generalizing

The skill of **generalizing** is using specific details you have read to arrive at a general understanding about the topic. When you make a generalization about something you've read, make sure that the written material provides enough examples or details to support your generalization.

On Sale Now! All Equipment   thru Friday
Mountain Store, 3910 A St, Ashville

USED EQUIPMENT

- picks
- sleeping bags
- tents
- maps
- camping stoves

GREAT DEALS!

Mountain Supply
166 Main, Ashville

THE
ULTIMATE TENT

See it! Try it out!
100% waterproof,
lightweight shelter

All Tents, Sleeping Bags & Equipment

ON SALE, NOW

**Climber's Shop
1000 Broad St. Ashville**

ZOOM

Headlamp
Best one on the market!

$39

SATURDAY ONLY

Come in and see our wide selection of camping goods.

*Camping, Ltd.
201 1st St. Ashville*

SLEEPING BAGS
for cold places
100% fine goose down

Good to – 60°F

All bags
30% off
**Camp Central
1 N. Green St
Ashville**

International Dog Sled Race—Weather Report

Day 1: Skies will be clear today, with temperatures at 0° F. Light snow covers the ground.

Day 2: Temperatures warming. Expect a light rain, turning to freezing rain by afternoon.

Day 3: Heavy fog will bring moist air to hover over the snow; harsh winds this evening.

Day 4: Extreme blizzard conditions reported. Warnings issued for complete white-out conditions. Winds blowing up to 60 mph with drifts up to 6 feet.

Day 5: Temperatures will climb to 20° F with light snow showers and light winds.

Day 6: Temperatures plunge. At noon, -15° F recorded with a –40° F wind chill factor. Race postponed.

Which of the following generalizations are appropriate to make from the ads and the weather reports above?

A shopper could buy some camping equipment on sale at several of the shops.

In Ashville, a camper has a good variety of camping stores for buying equipment.

Just about all of the camping supply stores sell sleeping bags.

A shopper could buy camping equipment in Ashville any day of the week.

The weather during the dog sled races was similar all six days.

The weather varied widely over the six days of the International Dog Sled Race.

There were more wet days than dry days during the International Dog Sled Race.

Inferring

To **infer** is to make a logical guess based on information. When you make an inference about something you have read, make sure that inference is based on examples, details, and information actually provided in the text.

HA! My sister's diary is the best.

THINGS I'VE READ THIS WEEK

A. a recipe for asparagus-salami cheesecake

B. the diaries of all four of my sisters

C. a poster advertising my favorite word: "sludge"

D. an argument promoting tattoos for dogs

E. five poems about mummification

F. a report on the eyeballs of Gila monsters

G. a tall tale about a race of giant toenails

H. several Internet studies about the uses of saliva

I. directions for getting to the city dump

J. 30 obituaries in the newspaper

K. the ingredients in all the frozen dinners at the grocery store

L. definitions for all the words in my dictionary that begin with *s*

M. a poster promoting a day to wear your clothes backwards to school

Which inferences are sensible guesses based on the list of Axel's reading?

Axel has unusual interests.

Axel had a boring week.

Axel's parents are unhappy with his choice of reading material.

Axel has a good sense of humor.

Axel is the weirdest kid in his class.

Axel does a lot of reading.

Axel has the ability to make use of many sources of written information.

Get Sharp: Reading Comprehension

Predicting

To predict is to make a statement about what will happen. When you make a prediction about something you've read, make sure that the written material provides some basis on which to make your prediction.

Each of the selections below is just right for making predictions. As a reader, you will probably be anxious to know what would happen next. See the predictions that another reader has made.

> This book is a treasure trove!

For a whole year, Spike had looked forward to his trip to the amusement park near his cousin's home on the West Coast. The main attraction was the colossal new roller coaster, *Goliath*. Spike has ridden eighty-four different coasters. This new one would be the steepest drop of his coaster-riding career.

He got to the park early. Much to his disappointment, the line for *Goliath* had a 3-hour wait. If he waited that long, he knew he would miss out on using his ticket for other rides. But the line for Goliath would probably just get longer as the day went along.

> *Spike will get in line and wait for Goliath. He traveled all this way for this ride. To him, it's more important than the other rides—after all, it's the steepest!*

The third skater in a line of twenty skaters hit a huge crack in the path. She tumbled head over heels, smashing her knee into a tree. There was a deep gash. She dragged herself back to the path so someone might find her. As she waited, her head began to spin and her vision got fuzzy.

> *Someone will find her and help her soon since there were 17 skaters behind her.*

Judge Law opened the proceedings in his courtroom to settle the will of multi-millionaire Alfred B. Lodad. Judah P. Lodad, the deceased's grandson, was the heir to the fortune. Things did not go smoothly. Seven young men sat in the courtroom. All seven claimed to be Judah P. Lodad. All seven brought birth certificates to verify their identities.

> *Judge Law will probably delay the settlement until the birth certificates can be examined and verified. Obviously six of them are fakes.*

196

Drawing Conclusions

A **conclusion** is a general statement made after analyzing examples, details, or facts. It involves an explanation that you develop through reasoning. When you draw a conclusion about something you have read, make sure that the text has enough evidence to support your conclusion. Different readers may draw different conclusions from the same material.

A Teacher's Field Trip Blues

I am never taking this class on a field trip again! I mean it! Never!

The trouble started, as it always does, with the bus ride to the marine park. Jason somehow sneaked a salami sandwich on the bus, even though I had collected all the lunches before we boarded the bus. Very soon, the sandwich ended up under Rosa Benson. By the time we left the school parking lot, the mustard was all over her white shorts, the bus seat, Ramon's new jacket, and Jennifer's hair. And it was only minutes later that Melanie sprayed hairspray on the bus driver and Louis threw up his breakfast.

I won't even try to describe the noise level on the bus, or the other bus disasters. I will only mention that fish in one marine tank are now enjoying chocolate milk, twenty-six 7th graders have wet clothes, the $50 bill that Kim's mother let her bring is in the belly of a large shark, two of my students thought they could ride the killer whale, and the aquarium manager banned me from bringing a class next year.

And while I'm complaining, I'll add my annoyance at the parent chaperones who managed to avoid having any impact on the field trip chaos. Mrs. Vincent spent most of her time in the bathroom doing her makeup and hair after getting drenched at the dolphin show. Mr. Hornsby said something like this every three minutes: "I don't allow my children to be this disrespectful." (His children were spraying drinking fountain water down the collars of the kindergartners from St. Mary's School.) Mrs. Flannery kept wringing her hands and saying, "Can't you DO something about this?"

"Oh yes!" I said to myself. "What I can do, is never, ever, set foot in an aquarium, zoo, planetarium, museum, or marine park with anyone under 25 years of age—ever again!"

Here are some conclusions different readers drew after reading this:

The adults had little control over the students on this field trip.

This teacher has experienced chaotic bus rides on other field trips.

The students were wild from the very beginning of the trip.

Some of the students were quite disrespectful of the animals' health.

The parent chaperones were not much help to the teacher.

The teacher is a clever writer, and wrote this to poke fun at field trips.

Get Sharp: Reading Comprehension

Evaluating

When you **evaluate** a piece of writing, you make a judgment about something in it. Evaluations should be based on evidence. Evaluations do include opinions, but these opinions should be supported or explained by examples from the written text. When you evaluate writing, ask such questions as:

How well does the writer make the point or accomplish the purpose?
Are the conclusions reached based on good examples and facts?
Is this believable? Does it make sense? Is it realistic? Is the writer biased?

Dear Leroy,

    Congratulations on your graduation! I hear you plan to celebrate with a big adventure—learning to sky dive. I'm sure that is a most interesting sport. I wonder what made you decide to choose that treacherous activity.

    I remember how cute and clumsy you were with your new scuba diving equipment. I almost had a heart attack when I heard of your near-fatal hang gliding accident. You've had so many close calls and mistakes with extreme sports!

    Well, have fun with your adventure. I do hope I see you alive again.

       Lovingly,

       Aunt Rita

Aunt Rita is being deceitful here. She does not really want him to enjoy his adventure.

This writer did a good job of "selling" his product. The words are delicious. I want one of these burgers right now!

She really does hate oysters. She is willing to withstand so many terrible fates to avoid oysters. The writer gave enough examples to convince me she is serious about this!

Try the mouthwatering burger, dripping with charbroiled flavors! It's draped in creamy melted cheddar and crisp fresh bacon. Then it's drenched with your choice of buttery fried onions, crisp and tangy dill pickles, plump tomato slices, or crunchy green lettuce—all nestled inside a soft home-made bun, fresh from the oven.

Don't ask me to eat oysters, 'cause
The taste I could not stand.
I'd rather swallow goldfish live,
Or gulp a cup of sand.
I'd eat my cell phone, chew CDs,
Munch my earphones any day—
But put an oyster on my tongue?
Are you kidding? No way!
You can torture me with scorpions,
Hang snakes from all my walls,
Fill my bathtub with piranhas,
Push me over Niagara Falls.
You can swear to light my underwear,
Feed me motor oil in steady drips.
No matter what you threaten—
Oysters will never touch my lips!

Identifying the Purpose

Every piece of literature is written for a purpose. As a reader, you should try to determine the purpose when you begin to read. That way you'll get more out of the reading. Also, you can then judge if the writer accomplished the purpose.

CHEESE SOUFFLE

Warm your oven to 425°
Shred 1 pound of sharp cheddar cheese. Set aside.
Whip 5 egg whites until stiff peaks form. Set aside.
Beat 5 egg yolks with ½ cup of milk.
Add ½ tsp. salt and ½ tsp pepper to the yolks.
Gently fold the yolk mixture into the egg whites.
Gently fold in the shredded cheese.
Pour into a buttered 9 x 9 inch glass baking dish.
Bake for 35 minutes until puffy and golden.
Serve immediately.

Purpose: to give instructions

Karin: What do you call the towel that a snake uses after his bath?

Darren: A viper wiper.

Purpose: to entertain

Learn the Art of Snake-Sitting
You too can safely sit in a tub with a dozen rattlesnakes!
No bites! No danger!
Lessons by Jake
State Champion Snake-Sitter
Call 552-0098
or email www.jakesnake@viper.com

Purpose: to advertise, to get customers

You Should Know Better
Don't ever put watermelon seeds
In your nose or in your ears,
Or you'll have a melon patch
On your head in a few years.
Your hair will turn green
And get stripes like a rind.
And sweet, pink juice
Will drip from your mind!

Purpose: to warn

SNAKE-SITTER SETS RECORD

Twenty competitors from 12 counties took part in the state's 30th annual snake-sitting competition, held last week. Jake Abernathy, a local favorite, took home the top honors. He sat in a bathtub with 29 rattlesnakes for several hours over a week-long period. This is Jake's 28th win in this strange sport. The second place prize went to 25-year old Sarabeth Samson of Tallahassee, Florida, who sat with 22 snakes.

Purpose: to inform

Get Sharp: Literature Skills

Identifying the Audience

Usually, when a writer works on a piece of literature, she or he has an audience in mind. There is someone whom the author hopes will read the writing and appreciate it, learn from it, act on it, or respond in some way. The audience is closely tied to the purpose of the piece, of course. Often, a reader decides that he or she is not a part of the intended audience—and skips reading it altogether.

EXTREME SPORTS, INC.

Lessons in Radical Outdoor Enterprises

Learn to command a speeding ice yacht!

Probe the depths of the underwater world!

Take your courage and skill to the air: try hang gliding!

Relish the thrills of riding the biggest waves!

Succumb to the desire for a free fall!

Take a precarious walk across a high wire!

Soak in the joy of free fall.

Pursue your wildest dreams today!
Call 609-8574

Audience: risk-taking adults

WARNING!

If you cross your eyes,
They'll probably stick.
If you eat with dirt under
your fingernails,
You'll wind up sick!

Audience: little kids

Audience: people needing house-sitters or anyone wanting a good laugh

WANTED: Responsible young rat is looking for house-sitting jobs. Available to take good care of your house and yard any evening or weekend. Experienced. References provided. Houses with good supply of cheese preferred. No homes with cats, please.
    Contact Raymond at 665-8787
    or e-mail: raymond@rodent.com

MEETING NOTICE

The Blackburn School Board will hold its regular monthly meeting on Monday night at 7:00 p.m. in the district boardroom at 415 Grand Ave. Agenda items include a high school dress code, complaints about the transportation system, changing the school lunch program, and funding shortages.
The public is welcome.

Audience: parents, school staff, interested community members

Your eyes make me weak.
Your smile melts my heart.
The shine of your hair tingles my fingers.
I can't stop watching and hoping.

Audience: a secret crush of the writer

Identifying Author's Tone

The tone in a piece of literature is the approach a writer takes toward the topic, or the attitude the writer has toward the topic. It's a good idea for a reader to pay attention to the tone. This will give you clues about the author's biases, as well as his or her purpose for the writing.

This letter to the editor really steams me!

Dear Editor:

It's about time your paper had something in it besides country music news. Thousands of people in this city are interested in sports, theater, dance, and other kinds of music. But we are constantly bombarded with the life stories, gossip, awards, accomplishments, finances, and troubles of personalities and companies in the country music business. Get a life outside this narrow box for your paper. You're about to lose my subscription if you can't appeal to an audience beyond those who want to hear about broken hearts and miserable lives!

Yours truly,
Iydou Rapp

Tone: angry, accusative

Identifying Point of View

Someone tells each story. When you look for the point of view, you find who is telling the story, and whether or not they, themselves, are inside the story or an outsider looking in.

How exciting to see Talula's name is in lights where it belongs. She's been a'singin' her heart out since she was just an itsy, bitsy girl. I watched her make a pretend microphone from her mama's egg-beater when she was just knee-high to a dinner table. She just stood there and belted out the tune, "Your Cheatin' Heart," at the top of her little lungs. If anyone deserves to be a big star—it's Talula.

Point of View: Narrator in the story

I headed for Nashville at age 16 with my guitar over my shoulder and a song in my head. I planned to be a star. Ten years later, without a dollar to my name and no hit songs, I headed out of town. Everyone in Nashville wants to be a star. I heard, "You're not quite what we're looking for," a thousand times. No one wanted my singin', my song-writin', or my guitar playin'. It's a town that'll break your heart and your bank account.

Point of View: First person, narrator writing about self

Rising Star James T. Twang has a new hit. His song, "You've Broken My Fax, My Computer, and My Heart," leaped to the top of the country music charts last week. The previous six weeks, this song had been lingering at number two or three. There are rumors of a coveted Country Music Award nomination for Twang as best new artist of the year. This is good news for a hometown boy.

Point of View: Narrator outside the story

Better Grades & Higher Test Scores / READING & LANGUAGE
Copyright ©2003 by Incentive Publications, Inc., Nashville, TN.

Get Sharp: Literature Skills

Identifying Author's Bias

Watch for clues to the author's bias in each written piece. **Bias** is the writer's personal opinion about the topic. If the author lets his or her bias show, that bias can influence the way the subject is presented to the reader. This can be interesting to the reader, but it can also twist information or leave out important facts—specially in a piece that pretends to be neutral.

Have you ever really looked at a sausage?
A slick brown sausage, a hot blunt stinky sausage
With little pieces of grainy fat stuck in on the sides?
A slinky slippery slimy serpentine sausage?
A gushy fuzzy with mold reeking sausage?
A wrinkly crinkly scabby sausage?
Have you ever really looked at a sausage?

You need to have a stomach strong
To eat my sister's cooking,
Or else, bring a dog along
To feed when she's not looking.

Author has a bias against sister's cooking. You can tell this because writer suggests feeding the food to the dog.

Author has a bias against sausage—thinks it's disgusting and unsightly. The choice of greasy words shows this bias.

Identifying Stereotype

A **stereotype** is a false idea (usually uninformed or unexamined) that someone has about a person or a group of people. Be alert for stereotyping in written pieces—particularly in works that are intended to present facts or information. Usually bias can be found right alongside stereotype in passages.

Restaurant Review
by Food Critic, Cecil B. Gourmand

Dinner at *Lagoni's Fifth Street Tratorria* was a disappointing culinary experience. Even before we were seated, my appetite was dampened by a survey of the overweight clients, plates piled high with starchy pasta. But then, such a sight is expected when you're around Italians. What an unhealthy culture—constantly dining on offerings like the *Trattoria's* Parmesan Caesar Salad, and Three-Cheese Artichoke Ravioli. It's no wonder the waiters with names like Giovanni move so slowly. They can't help it, given their ethnic and culinary heritage.

All the items we sampled—entrées and salads, and especially the hearty minestrone and dessert tiramisu, were tasty and prepared exquisitely. But to enjoy this food, you have to forget about your cholesterol levels and join a less-than-desirable dining crowd.

Pretty obvious stereotyping of Italian people and their food—what a snobbish writer!

Analyzing Characters

Characterization is a writer's way of explaining the people in a story or other piece of writing. As a reader, you observe the characters, think about them, and respond in some way.

My sister, Latitia, is the most entertaining person I know. Every weekend and summer day, she turns our backyard into a regular theater of excitement. She has made a habit of trying out weird and wacky antics. Each one seems more unique and wild than the last.

One weekend, she'll be balancing glasses on her chin. The next, she'll be making a sandwich that reaches around the whole yard. She has eaten record numbers of pickled eggs, raced pet mice inside roller-skates up and down the driveway, climbed ladders upside down while holding a flaming torch in her teeth, built a scarecrow taller than our house, and invited the whole town to a paperclip chain-making party.

Often she will involve all the neighborhood kids in the fun. They have joined her for bathtub races, backwards lawn-mower pushing, cricket-spitting contests, grass-picking tricks, bubble-blowing competitions, and sausage-eating marathons.

Last weekend, her whole soccer team was here to balance eggs on spoons. Next week, her eighth grade class is coming for an onion-peeling race. There is never a dull moment living with Latitia!

I kid you, not!

To analyze a character, you can ask questions about the person and the way the author presents the character. For practice, ask yourself these questions about the character in the example above.

- *Is the character believable?*
- *Is the character colorful?*
- *What is likable (unlikable, annoying, disturbing, etc.) about him/her?*
- *Does the character evoke a strong response from me?*
- *What is my response to this character?*
- *Why do I respond this way?*
- *Would I like to know this character?*
- *Am I like this character in any way?*
- *Have I had any similar problems or been been in the same situation?*

- *Does this character remind me of anyone I know?*
- *Would I respond to this situation in the same way the character did?*
- *What specific things about the character led her/him to do what he did?*
- *Does this person do things in the story that are true to the character?*
- *What are the author's feelings about this character?*
- *Has the author done a good job of making the character "come alive?"*

Get Sharp: Literature Skills

Identifying Literary Devices

These are techniques authors use to make writing effective. Look for them, and appreciate the color, interest, and power they add to the writing.

Literary Terms and Devices

alliteration - the repetition of consonant sounds at the beginnings of words
flimsy flippers flailing and flopping

allusion - a reference in one piece of literature to something else that is well known (It may be part of another piece of literature, an object, a person, or an event.)

anecdote - a short tale of an incident, generally highly interesting or comical

antagonist - the character in a story who struggles against the main character

assonance - similar vowel sounds repeated in successive or nearby words containing different consonants
a slick city hill
Ouch! I've been knocked out by downed boughs!

bias - the writer's personal opinion about the topic (usually a stubbornly-held opinion)

central conflict - the main problem in the plot of a story, play, or story-poem

character - a person (or animal) who takes part in a story

characterization - the act of creating or describing a character in a written work

cliché - an overused expression

climax - the highest point of suspense in a written work

conflict - a problem or struggle between two people, things, or ideas in a piece of literature

consonance - is the repetition of a pattern of consonants within words which have different vowel sounds between the consonants; or the repetition of consonant sounds anywhere within words

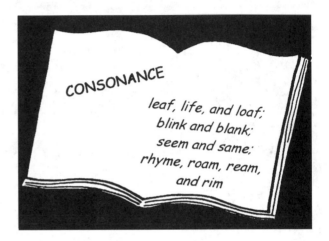

CONSONANCE
leaf, life, and loaf;
blink and blank;
seem and same;
rhyme, roam, ream,
and rim

crisis - turning point in the plot of the story

dénouement - the part of a fiction plot that follows the resolution of the conflict

dialogue - conversation of two or more characters in a literary work

drama - story told by actors taking the parts of characters

dramatic irony - the situation in some dramas where the audience knows something that the characters do not

exposition - the introduction to a story; the part that tells readers about the setting and characters of the story

fiction - prose writing that tells a story

figure of speech - words, phrases, or sentences that are meant to be taken imaginatively rather than literally (pun, idiom, proverb, metaphor, oxymoron, hyperbole, personification, simile *(For more examples, see pages 138-141, 227-230.)*

flashback - part of a story, play, or story-poem that tells about events which happened earlier than the current setting of the story

foreshadowing - the author's way of giving readers hints about something that might happen later in a story, play, or poem-story

genre - the form or type of *literature (such as poem, joke, essay, novel, epitaph)*

hyperbole - an extreme exaggeration used for a particular purpose in a written piece

(For more examples, see page 139)

It was so hot you could fry eggs on the sidewalk.

idioms - a phrase or expression whose meaning is different from what the words say literally

He put his foot in his mouth

(For more examples, see pages 229-230.)

image - a mental picture created in the mind of the reader by the words the writer uses

a slice of silver-slivered moon
in a plum-purple sky

Imagery - the use of images in a passage

inciting incident - in a story plot, the event which triggers or introduces the central conflict

irony - a situation in literature in which something is different than it appears; or when there is a difference between what is spoken and what is meant or a difference between what readers or characters think about a situation and what is truly the case

metaphor - a figure of speech in which something is compared to an unlike thing; one thing is written about as if it were another

Life is a can of spaghetti surprises.

(For more examples, see pages 139, 228.)

meter - the pattern of beats in a poem

mood - the feeling or atmosphere created by the writer

moral - the lesson taught by a piece of literature

narrator - the person telling the story

novel - a long work of prose fiction

novella - a work of fiction that is shorter than a novel but longer than a short story

onomatopoeia - the use of words that sound like the thing or noise they name

bang, pop, hiss, splat, sizzle, bark

oxymoron - an expression made up of two words which seem to contradict each other

(For more examples, see page 231.)

Tori speaks in a loud whisper.

?

paradox - a statement that is actually true, though it seems to go against common sense

parody - a work that makes fun of another work by imitating some aspect of the other writer's style

205

personification - a figure of speech in which human characteristics are given to non-living things
> *Midnight grabbed me and dragged me into its shadows.*
> *(For more examples, see page 140.)*

plot - series of events that make up a story
A plot involves a central conflict, or problem. The problem is introduced, builds to a climax, and is eventually resolved in some way.

poetry - a kind of writing or language which is written in lines, and has more emphasis on sounds and rhythms than ordinary (prose) writing *(See pages 132-134.)*

point of view - the angle or perspective from which a story is told

prose – writing that is not drama or poetry. Prose is generally written in complete sentences and paragraphs, and can be either fiction or nonfiction

protagonist –the main character in a story, usually one which faces a problem or conflict

proverb - a saying that gives some wisdom in a sneaky way; often the meaning is something other than what the words say literally
> *A rolling stone gathers no moss.*
> *(For more examples, see page 230.)*

pun - a figure of speech which uses double meaning to make a play on words
> *Teachers have a lot of class.*
> *(For more examples, see pages 140, 230.)*

resolution - the ending or solving of the conflict in a story, play, or poem-story

rhyme - repetition of similar sounds at the ends of words

rhyme scheme - the pattern of the rhyming lines in a poem

rhythm - the pattern of beats in a line of poetry or prose

satire - writing that makes fun of the shortcomings of people, systems, or institutions for the purpose of enlightening readers or bringing about a change

setting - the time and place of a story

simile - a metaphor where two things are compared using *like* or *as*
> *She was as prickly as an artichoke.*
> *(For more examples, see page 141.)*

stereotype - a false idea (usually uninformed or unexamined) that someone has about a person or a group of people

style - the way an author chooses and arranges words in getting a message across or telling a story

symbolism - the use of symbols (concrete objects) to stand for ideas in a written work

theme – the main idea or message of a text

tone - the writer's attitude or approach toward the subject or toward the writing

understatement - the opposite of exaggeration; bringing attention to a subject by treating it as if it is less important or less powerful than it really is

Going over Niagara Falls in a barrel— now that's a dull way to spend an afternoon!

voice - the way a writer's personality shows through in the writing

Identifying Figurative Language

Figurative language is a way of using language that expands the literal meaning of the words and gives them a new meaning or twist. When authors use *figures of speech*, it makes the language more colorful and vivid. It sparks the reader's imagination and brings the subject to life. Watch for the way good writers use figures of speech, such as hyperbole, idioms, puns, metaphors, personification, oxymorons, proverbs, similes.
(For definitions of the specific figures of speech, see pages 138-141 and 204-206.)

Look for figurative language in the examples below.

YELLOW

Yellow never wants help
But steps right out on its own
Throwing bright flashes everywhere,
Yellow dashes through flower gardens,
Splashes on fried eggs,
Drips on traffic lights,
And wraps itself around bananas.
Yellow is bigger than the sun,
Brighter than day.
It reaches out from spotlights
Like lemon-streaked fingers
Grabbing attention.
Yellow never gives up.
Yellow is BOLD.

A poster invites me to hear "a rollicking blues band"—and sets me to wondering about the elusive identity of blue. Which are you, mysterious blue? Are you rollicking or are you somber? Are you rich and smooth like blue velvet, or as tainted as blue blood? Are you the croon of woes to the soulful muted plea of a sad saxophone? Are you the icy cold embrace of blue arctic air? Or are you sassy and sizzling —the hottest part of a flame?

I've ached from the blue-black slap of a broken heart. I've tasted danger in the wild blue whipping water racing through rapids. I've heard you call excitely from blue chaos in the whirlpool at the bottom of the waterfall. I've put my life in your blue arms, thrilling and balancing atop a 20-foot wave, and I've cursed your ocean-blue temper when you push me to bruising crashes against my surfboard.

Are you blue-black, ice blue, or calm cobalt? Are you ecstasy, melancholy, serenity, terror, or despair? Who are you, blue? Who are you, blue?

Get Sharp: Literature Skills

Personal Response to Reading

There are dozens of times when you respond in a personal way to the material you read. Actually, it is unlikely that you ever read anything without some personal response. But, at particular times, you might be asked to write or tell a personal response. Get in the habit of paying attention to your own reactions and feelings about something you have read.

Read the passages on this page and the next.
Ask yourself questions such as these:

> *How do I feel about this passage?*
> *How do I identify with this?*
> *What experiences, memories, emotions are stirred up by this?*
> *What words, phrases, lines or ideas appeal to me? Why?*
> *What writing techniques seem most effective?*

Ode to September

I've dreaded your arrival,
Looked forward to you, too.
Oh, month of new beginnings,
I'm glad, yet scared, of you.

I hate the loss of summer.
Though I love the things in store.
The year will bring mixed outcomes:
Hard tests and fun galore.

New classes, new teachers
New chances, new shoes
Old worries, old habits
Old friends with new news.

You bring each one back.
I'm nervous you're here,
And excited, September.
You start the new year.

OFF HER ROCKER

Mom has lost her marbles! By 10 o'clock this morning, she had blown her top several times. When the baby dumped his cereal on his head, she lost her cool. When Jenny put the cat in the washing machine, she was fit to be tied. And when Tommy ate her lipstick, she just screamed her head off.

I think it was the toilet paper fort in the living room that was the last straw. She ran around the room yelling about how we were driving her up the wall. She just went totally bananas. After that, she just wandered around the house in a fog. I tried to keep a lid on the little kids and keep them out of her hair.

When dad got home, he was out in the cold about her bad day. So when he shouted, "Happy birthday, dear. How does it feel to be over the hill?" he did not understand why she crowned him with the frying pan.

Get Sharp: Literature Skills

Better Grades & Higher Test Scores / READING & LANGUAGE
Copyright ©2003 by Incentive Publications, Inc., Nashville, TN.

To Tattoo or Not to Tattoo?

Tattoos have been used for many purposes over a period of hundreds of years. They have been a mark of membership in a group or a sign of rank in a group. Some tattoos were worn as protection against evil or ill fortune. Others showed courage. Tattoos were used to brand criminals, or to serve as disguises. But mostly, through history, tattoos have been used for decoration. Today, tattoos are becoming popular as a fashion item of body decoration. Since the 1980s, the tattoo process is even being used to add permanent eyeliner or lip color. With the popularity of this practice on the rise, many people are considering getting a tattoo.

What, exactly, is a tattoo? It is a permanent design decorating the human body. Tattoos are made by cutting or pricking the skin and inserting a colored dye or pigment under the skin. The modern tattoo process uses electric needles. In the past, instruments such as knives, thorns, and sharpened bones were used.

Is it a good idea to slice your skin and put color under it permanently? Many doctors don't think so. Serious side effects often accompany tattoos. Besides plaguing infections and eye damage from the permanent eyeliner, cancers have been linked to tattoos. Contaminated needles and equipment can also spread diseases, including AIDS. Many parents are irate that a child can get a tattoo without their permission. A parent's signature is required for ear piercing for minors in most states; yet kids can often get tattoos without parental permission. One of the major concerns about tattooing is that there are few controls or restrictions on the process. No training or licensing is required in many places. As a customer seeking a tattoo, you cannot be sure of the person's ability or experience. Neither can you be sure of the safety or cleanliness of their equipment.

So think about this: **when you get a tattoo, what else are you getting?**

Get Sharp: Literature Skills

Creative Book Reports

Do you need to do a book report? Unless you have a particular form to follow, think about doing something different. There are many ways to show that you have read a book, explain what you have learned from it, or share your response to it.

Try one (or several) of these ideas for your book reports.

Advertisement - Make a poster, banner, T-shirt, or magazine ad that advertises your book.

Book in Costume - Dress up as one of the characters and tell the story from a first-person point of view. *(Or make a mask of a character, and do the same.)*

Book Review - Write a book review to be printed in the school newspaper.

Changed Parts - Create a different beginning, middle, or ending for the story.

Changed Sequence - Retell the story in a different sequence. Make sure it makes sense!

Character Portrait - Write a description of one of the main characters. Paint a portrait or caricature to accompany the description.

Complaints - Write a letter to the main character of the book. Ask a question, protest some situation, make a complaint or suggestion, etc.

Comic Book - Rewrite the book as a comic book.

Compare Illustrations - Compare the illustrations of two books. Tell how the illustrations influence the reader.

Crossword Puzzle - Make a crossword puzzle using ideas, new words, or names from a book. Give the puzzle to someone who has read the book. Make enough copies to keep on hand for others who read the book.

Diary - Write a diary from the main character's viewpoint to explain the events of the story.

Drama - Turn the book (fiction or nonfiction) into a drama. Perform it.

Email - Email the author, asking questions about his/her writing process, asking questions about purposes or themes in the book, or suggesting some changes that might improve the book.

Interview - Make a list of questions you would ask one of the characters in the book if you could interview him/her.

Joke Book - After reading a joke and riddle book, make a scrapbook of original jokes and riddles.

Letter - Write a letter recommending (or not recommending) the book to a friend or relative in another city. Or, write a letter to the school librarian telling why she or he should recommend the book to other classes.

Missing Facts - For a non-fiction book, write a list of 10-20 questions or facts that are NOT covered in the book.

Movie Comparison - Read a book that has been made into a movie. Write an essay comparing the movie to the book.

New Point of View - Rewrite the story from the point of view of a different character (or an animal or inanimate object in the story).

New Genre - Rewrite the story as a poem, advertisement, essay, TV script, myth, tall tale, fable, or other form of literature.

News Article - Change the story into a feature news article with a headline that tells the story as it might be found on the front page of a newspaper in the town where the story takes place.

On-Line Review - Log onto an Internet book-selling site that has a place for readers' reviews of books. Add your own review to the collection.

Picture Book - Rewrite the story as a picture book. Use simple vocabulary so that the book may be enjoyed by younger students.

Poetry Scrapbook - If your book is a poetry book, make a scrapbook containing 15 or 20 of your favorite poems.

Puppet Show - Make three or four simple puppets of characters in the book. Prepare a short puppet show to tell the story to the class.

Retell without Words - Retell your story to an audience without using any spoken or written words.

Sequel - Create an outline for a sequel to the book.

Time Line - After reading a book about history or a historical fiction, make a time line or calendar to show the important events of the story.

Top 10 Facts - After reading a factual book, make a list of ten important facts you found in the book.

Top 50 Smashing Words - After reading any book, make a list of 50 phrases or sentences that show effective word use.

Travel Poster - Make a travel poster inviting tourists to visit the settings of the book.

20 Questions - Prepare a list of questions to ask another reader to help find out if that person has a good understanding of the book.

Web Synopsis - Add a synopsis of the book to your website. Create illustrations to go along with the review.

Get Sharp: Literature Skills

READING PERFORMANCE ASSESSMENT GUIDE

Have student read a sample orally. Then check the following areas of performance. The performance descriptions given indicate a level of high competency in each area.

ORAL READING PERFORMANCE

Pace   Pace mostly or always matches a pace of normal conversation.

Flow   Reading is consistently smooth with few disruptions.
Student corrects errors quickly and smoothly.

Phrasing   The phrasing and breathing are natural.

The student mostly or consistently uses appropriate-length phrases for conversing, including some long phrases.

The student includes natural expression within the phrases.

Does her reading flow smoothly?

RE-TELLING

Clarity   The retelling is very clear and organized, showing good understanding of the whole piece and the correct sequence.

Completeness   The retelling contains a clear and accurate telling of the main point or idea.

The retelling includes all the main events, points, or developments.
The retelling includes important details.
The retelling covers the story in the correct sequence.

ORAL RESPONSE to COMPREHENSION QUESTIONS

Main Idea   When questioned, the student can clearly explain the main idea or ideas.

Details   The student can identify specific details that support the main idea, or that describe characters, setting, or plot development.

Personal Connection   The student can relate events, situations, or feelings from the piece to her/his own life experiences.

Can he tell the main idea?

Inference & Evaluation   The student can make generalizations from text ideas to situations outside of the text.

The student can make predictions with good text evidence to support them.
The student can draw conclusions with good text evidence to support them.

WRITTEN RESPONSE to PASSAGE

Comprehension

Student's response shows an understanding of the main point(s) or ideas.

Student's response shows a clear understanding of the supporting details.

Student is able to use specific details from the text to support conclusions, interpretations, and opinions.

Student is able to reach conclusions and form inferences from the text to convey meaning.

Critical Analysis of Text

Student can identify the author's purpose.

Student can identify the author's biases and give specific evidence from the text to demonstrate the biases.

Student can identify specific techniques of style used by the author to convey the message, and explain how those techniques are (or are not) effective in accomplishing the author's purpose or conveying the intended message.

Student uses specific details or evidence to support the inferences, conclusions, and judgments made about the author's style and the effectiveness of the text.

Making Connections

Student's response makes insightful connections between the ideas or message of the passage to events and circumstances in the world outside of the text.

Student's response shows that the student has thoughtfully connected the ideas and conclusions of the passage to his/her own life situations.

Student can relate personal experiences or feelings that show similarities or differences to events, feelings, or messages from the text.

Student's response relates the lives or circumstances or feelings of specific characters in the text to real-life situations.

Student's response shows that the student has thoughtfully connected the ideas and conclusions of the passage to conclusions and ideas from other written texts.

Student's response relates the lives or circumstances or feelings of specific characters in the text to those in other written texts.

Student's response shows that student understands how personal, cultural, or historical factors in the author's life may have affected the style, opinions, message, or purpose.

Get Sharp: Reading Literature Skills

Finding Meaning from Context

You're reading along and come across a word that stumps you—you are not sure what it means. You may need to head for the dictionary or glossary to learn the word's meaning. However, you may just be able to figure it out from the context (setting) of the word in the sentence or line. Often the sentence or paragraph that is home to a word will have clues to the word's meaning. Pay attention to those clues, and you'll increase your understanding of new words.

**Get Sharp
Tip # 19**
Watch for words in the sentence that seem to be synonyms for the unknown word. They'll help you get the meaning.

Context Clues in Sentences

Weary skiers **trudged** painfully through deep snow for hours.

The words *weary, painfully,* and *deep snow* give a clue that *trudge* means *to walk heavily and slowly.*

The plants and animals that were brought in from other regions were harmful to the **endemic** plants of the valley.

The plants and animals from other places give a clue that the endemic plants are opposite to them—helping you see that **endemic** means *natural to a location.*

With great **trepidation**, and against my better judgment, I'm going to try this frightful, dangerous sport of bungee-jumping.

The speaker uses the words *frightful* and *dangerous,* and shows she is doubtful about bungee-jumping. This can help you guess that **trepidation** means *fear.*

Benjamin was devastated and angry when he learned that an old rival, wanting to get revenge for a past disagreement, had **traduced** his reputation.

Devastated, angry, and revenge give you clues that the old rival was saying something harmful. This helps you conclude that **traduced** means *damaged or trampled.*

Let's get that muscular weight lifter to help us with this **herculean** task of carrying the bathtub.

You can guess that a weight lifter has huge muscles. This (along with the idea of carrying a bathtub) can lead to the assumption that a **herculean** task is one *requiring great strength or effort.*

After the storm, the ocean was **turbid**, filled with dirt and mud.

Filled with dirt and sand is a clue that the ocean was *murky.*

Context Clues in Paragraphs or Stanzas

Sometimes it takes more than one sentence to give you sufficient context clues for solving the mystery of a word meaning. Look for the clues in these longer passages to the meanings of the bold words.

Let's avoid that **macabre** new movie. I want to see something less ghastly.

I tried a number of arguments.
I thought they'd make him see.
My sharp-tongued friend was fast,
His responses came instantly.
I lost the ears of the listeners.
They couldn't stick with me
As each point I made was quickly trounced
By a clever **repartee**.

I was so sure the whole class would support this pep rally. How could I have guessed that over half the class would **boycott** the rally and party at the beach instead?

Last year, there was a **paucity** of food at this event. I went home starved. This year, there is a **plethora** of delicious choices.

Chester hates water. He hates sunshine. He hates sand. Therefore, his friends were **confounded** when he showed up for the beach party.

I heard this concert was sold out months ago. I've been trying for six weeks to find a way to get tickets. So how did you manage to **procure** three tickets today?

Yes, there's a **dearth** of tickets available. That's why I feel so lucky. Today I ran into an old friend who had these tickets and was **loath** to part with them, but she needed money so badly that she agreed to sell them to me.

The auctioneer is just not working out! He sounds too timid and bland. No one is even paying attention.

Send someone else—someone with a **stentorian** voice!

Better Grades & Higher Test Scores / READING & LANGUAGE
Copyright ©2003 by Incentive Publications, Inc., Nashville, TN.

Get Sharp: Vocabulary & Word Meaning

100 Great Vocabulary Words to Know

abase – to humiliate
abhor – hate
acrimony – bitterness

amicable – peaceable, friendly
assail – attack with words
audacious – bold
avarice – greed
bellicose – hostile, warlike
benevolence – act of doing good
brawn – strong, muscular
brusque – abrupt
cache – something hidden away
callow – immature
capitulate – surrender
churlish – grumpy
clemency – forgiveness
contemptuous – scornful
cozen – deceive
dearth – short supply
deduce – reason from facts
deride – ridicule
disparage – discredit, belittle
docile – obedient, submissive
doleful – sad
ebullient – enthusiastic
elicit – to draw forth
emulate – imitate
endemic – native to
erudite – scholarly

fatuous – foolish
fetid – rotten-smelling
frenetic – frantic
furtive – sneaky
garrulous – talking too much
gauche – lacking grace
gourmand – big eater
hoodwink – deceive
illicit – illegal
illusory – imaginary
impeccable – without flaw
impetuous – impulsive
impunity – freedom from punishment
indelible – permanent
indict – charge with a crime
jocose – playful
jurisprudence - system of laws
languid – listless, indifferent
loath – reluctant to do something
lurid – sensational
macabre – gruesome
malevolent – evil
mediocre – average, ordinary
mellifluous – pleasing sound
moniker – nickname
morose – dark and gloomy
nefarious – evil
noxious – harmful to health
obstreperous – stubborn
obtuse – blunt
onus – blame
ostentatious – showy
pallid – pale
petulant – impatient
placid – tranquil
plethora – excess
prerogative – special privilege
pretense – pretended intention

proclivity – natural tendency
quandary – doubt
query – question
rampant – widespread
rancor – deep spite or malice
requisite – required
sagacity – wisdom
savory – tasty
scrupulous – conscientious
specious – seeming genuine, but actually false
strident – shrill, harsh-sounding
sullen – gloomy
surfeit – excess

tenuous – flimsy
timorous – shy
truncate – to shorten by cutting
turgid – swollen
upbraid – to rebuke harshly
uncouth – unrefined, awkward
urbane – refined
undulate – move in waves
unseemly – indecent
vacillate – fluctuate
vacuous – empty
veritable – true
vindicate – clear from blame
wane – lessen, shrink
wraith – a ghost
yore – a time long past
zenith – highest point

Connotation & Denotation

The **denotation** of a word is its dictionary definition.

The **connotation** is all the ideas and images suggested by a word. The connotation may be different for different readers. When you read, connotation helps you imagine a rich context for a simple word.

The **denotation**
of *pirate* . . .

*one who robs
on the high seas.*

The **connotation** is much broader.
The word *pirate* stirs up all kinds of
images and ideas of . . .

*adventure, danger, mystery, swords, wooden
legs, canons, people walking planks, famous
pirates from literature, big black ships, buried
treasure, gold, silver, colorful parrots, patches
over the eye, a skull and crossbones flag, etc.*

GIANT

denotation – a person or thing of great size and strength

connotation – a huge, frightening hairy creature that looks strange, growls, and threatens people

MUSIC

denotation - the science of ordering tones

connotation – wonderful, colorful, and pleasing rhythmic sounds for dancing

ROLLER COASTER

denotation – a steep, sharply-banked elevated railway with small open passenger cars operated as an attraction at amusement parks and fairgrounds

connotation – a wild, terrifying amusement park ride that speeds up and down hills, jerking screaming passengers and upsetting stomachs

GOSSIP

denotation– petty and groundless rumors, usually of a personal nature

connotation – juicy secrets and harmful stories whispered behind someone's back

> **Get Sharp
> Tip # 20**
>
> When you write,
> make sure you choose
> the right word for a
> connotation.
>
> Example: Look at the
> _____ fireworks
> splattering the sky!
> *Spectacular* would be right
> for this connotation.
> *Handsome, graceful*, or
> *elegant* probably would not
> be right, although they
> have similar denotations.

Get Sharp: Vocabulary & Word Meaning

Meanings of Prefixes

prefix	meaning	examples
a-	not	*atypical, atheist*
ab-	away, from	*abnormal, abound*
alti-	high	*altitude, alto, altar*
ante-	before	*antecedent, anterior*
anti-	against	*antibody, antifreeze*
auto-	self	*autobiography*
bi-	two	*bicycle, biannual*
cent-	hundred	*century, centimeter*
circum-	around	*circumference*
co-	together, with	*coexist, cooperate*
con-	together, with	*concert, connect*
contra-	against	*contradict, contrast*
counter-	against	*counteract*
de-	away, down	*depart, dehumanize*
dec-	ten	*decade, decagon*
deci-	tenth	*decimal, decibel*
di-	two	*dissect, diagonal,*
dis-	apart from	*dislocate, distance*
dis-	not, opposite	*disallow, disapprove*
equi-	equal	*equilateral*
ex-	from	*expel, exit, exclude*
extra-	beyond	*extracurricular*
fore-	in front	*forward, forefinger*

prefix	meaning	examples
hyper-	above, over	*hypersensitive*
hypo-	under, below	*hypodermic*
il-	not	*illegal, illegible*
im-	not	*immature, imperfect*
in-	not	*inactive, incomplete*
inter-	between, among	*interact*
ir-	not	*irrational, irregular*
kilo-	thousand	*kilometer, kilowatt*
micro-	small	*microphone*
mid-	middle	*midair, midnight*
mill-	thousandth	*millimeter, milliliter*
mis-	wrong	*misfortune, misspell*
mono-	one	*monotone, monolith*
multi-	many	*multitude, multiply*
non-	not	*nonsense, nonsmoker*
over-	over	*overactive, overspend*
para-	beyond, beside	*parallel, paramedic*
poly-	many	*polygraph, polygon*
post-	after	*postdate, postscript*
pre-	before	*precaution, prefix*
pro-	before, forward	*produce, pronoun*
quad-	four	*quadrilateral*
re-	again	*reclaim, redo, repaint*
retro-	backwards	*retrograde, retrofit*
se-	aside, apart	*seclude, segregate*
semi-	half	*semicircle, semigloss*
sub-	under	*submarine, subplot*
super-	over	*supercede, superego*
tele-	far away	*telegram, telescope*
trans-	across	*transplant, transpolar*
tri-	three	*triangle, tripod*
ultra-	beyond	*ultramodern*
un-	not	*unclear, uneven, unfair*
uni-	one	*unicorn, unicycle*
with-	against	*withhold, withdraw*

It's true! I was **abducted** by a **multitude** of **extraterrestrial paramedics**. They were **super-sized quadrupeds** who carried **automatic** weapons and were intent on **exterminating** me. You can believe that I **cooperated** fully; I did nothing to **provoke** them.

Better Grades & Higher Test Scores / READING & LANGUAGE
Copyright ©2003 by Incentive Publications, Inc., Nashville, TN.

Meanings of Suffixes

suffix	meaning	examples
-able	tending to able to	enjoyable, lovable, payable, perishable, conquerable
-age	state of being, place of result of	anchorage, orphanage, shrinkage, wastage
-al	relating to	electrical, theatrical
-an	belonging to	American, urban
-ance	state of being	importance
-ant	one who	immigrant, occupant
-ar	one who	beggar, scholar
-ary	one who	missionary, visionary
-ate	to make	irrigate, saturate
-cy	state or quality of	lunacy, piracy
-en	have nature of	ashen, broken, earthen, golden
-en	to make or become	blacken, fatten, lengthen, whiten
-ence	state of	difference, excellence
-ent	one who	resident, president
-ery	place where	bakery, nursery
-er	more	faster, lighter, nicer
-er	one who	baker, preacher
-est	most	cleanest, deepest
-ful	characterized by, full of	awful, beautiful, helpful, masterful, plentiful
-fy	make or form into	clarify, glorify, horrify
-hood	state of rank	adulthood, falsehood
-ible	like, or capable of being	terrible, audible permissible, visible, impossible, reversible
-ic	pertaining to, like	angelic, artistic, athletic, classic
-ical	pertaining to, like	magical
-ish	having nature of	bluish, childish

suffix	meaning	examples
-ism	act or quality of	heroism, pessimism
-ist	one who	artist, biologist
-less	without	friendless, ageless
-like	resembling	childlike, lifelike
-ly	in the manner of	actively, happily
-ment	resulting state action or process	amazement, commitment
-most	most	aftermost, foremost
-ness	state of being	blindness, gladness
-or	person who	actor, auditor, debtor
-ous	state or condition, having quality of	courageous, prosperous
-ry	state of being	rivalry, revelry, finery
-ship	office, profession, art, or skill	championship, fellowship, hardship
-some	resembling	handsome, lonesome
-ion	act, process, state	action, collection
-tion	act, process, state	clarification
-ure	act, process	adventure, failure

Max is so *theatrical*. That story is *certainly unbelievable*. His *imagination operates actively*, doesn't it! Poor Max has always been quite the *hopeless visionary*. This *obsession* with *heroism* is just his *latest adventure*.

219

Meanings of Common Roots

So you're the pyromaniac culprit! You were admonished many times about transferring heat to a flammable substance! Did you unwittingly ignite the dynamite?

root	meaning	example
act	act or do	*actor*
ami	friend	*amiable*
ann	year	*annual*
aqua	water	*aquatic*
astr	star	*astronaut*
brev	short	*brevity*
cap	head	*captain*
card	heart	*cardiac*
celer	fast	*accelerate*
chron	time	*chronology*
clam	cry out	*exclaim*
crypt	hidden	*cryptic*
cycle	circle, wheel	*tricycle*
cir	circle, wheel	*circumvent*
cit	speak, talk	*citation*
civ	city	*civilian*
cred	believe	*credible*
culp	blame	*culprit*
dic	speak	*dictate*
don	give	*donate*
dorm	sleep	*dormant*
dom	rule	*dominate*
dox	opinion	*orthodox*
duc	lead	*conductor*
dur	hard	*durable*
dynam	power	*dynamite*
fer	bring, carry	*transfer*
fin	end	*final*
flam	fire	*flammable*
form	shape	*format*

root	meaning	example
fract	break	*fracture*
frag	break	*fragment*
fug	flee	*fugitive*
geo	earth	*geology*
glyph	carving	*hieroglyphics*
graph	write	*autograph*
grat	pleasing	*gratitude*
greg	crowd	*congregation*
gyr	whirl	*gyrate*
ign	fire	*ignite*
ject	throw	*eject*
labor	work	*laboratory*
lib	book	*library*
lith	stone	*lithograph*
loc	place	*locate*
lucr	money	*lucrative*
lum	light	*luminous*
lun	moon	*lunar*
manu	hand	*manufacture*
mar	sea	*marine*
morph	sleep	*morphine*
mort	death	*mortal*
mob	move	*mobile*

I'm **petrified**! This is my worst nightmare—to be **suspended**, **rotating** above a **tortuous** and **turbulent inferno**!

root	meaning	example
radi	ray	radiate
rot	turn	rotate
scend	climb	descend
sci	know	science
scrip	write	transcript
sculpt	carve	sculptor
sect	cut	dissect
sed	sit	sedentary
sol	sun	solar
son	sound	sonar
soph	wise	philosopher
strict	bind	restrict
stat	stand	stationary
tang	touch	tangible
tard	slow	tardy
tele	far	telephone
tempor	time	temporal
term	end	terminate
terr	earth	territory
therm	heat	thermal
tort	twist	torture
turb	spin	turbulent
vac	empty	vacate
vali	strong	valiant
vanqu	conquer	vanquish
verb	word	verbose
view	see	review
vict	conquer	victory
vid	see	video
vis	see	visible
vit	life	vitality
viv	life	revive
volv	roll	revolve
wit	know	wittingly

root	meaning	example
mon	warn	admonish
mot	move	remote
mov	move	movement
mur	wall	mural
mut	change	mutate
noct	night	nocturnal
nat	born	native
nom	name	nominate
oper	work	operator
pac	peace	pacify
ped	foot	pedal
pel	push	propel
pend	hang	suspend
petr	stone	petrify
phon	sound	phonics
pod	foot	podiatry
pop	people	popular
port	carry	portage
posit	place	position
pus	foot	octopus
pyro	fire	pyrotechnics

Get Sharp: Vocabulary & Word Meaning

Confusing Words

ability (power) - **capacity** (condition)

accede (agree) - **exceed** (surpass)

accept (receive) - **except** (exclude)

adapt (adjust) - **adopt** (accept)

all ready (completely prepared) - **already** (previously)

allude (to refer to) - **elude** (escape)

assure (to set a person's mind at ease) - **insure** (guarantee life or property against harm)
     ensure (to secure from harm)

avenge (to achieve justice) - **revenge** (retaliation)

averse (opposition on the subject's part) - **adverse** (opposition against the subject's will)

avoid (shun) - **avert** (turn away)

between (refers to two persons, places, or things) - **among** (refers to more than two)

clench (to grip something tightly, as hand or teeth) - **clinch** (to fasten firmly together)

complement (something that completes) - **compliment** (an expression of praise)

confidant (one to whom secrets are told) - **confident** (assured of success)

credible (plausible) - **creditable** (deserving commendation) - **credulous** (gullible)

deny (contradict) - **refute** (to give evidence to disprove something)

elicit (to call forth) - **illicit** (unlawful)

eminent (prominent) - **imminent** (soon to occur)

222

Better Grades & Higher Test Scores / READING & LANGUAGE

fatal (causing death) - **fateful** (affecting one's destiny)

graceful (refers to movement) - **gracious** (courteous)

impassable (impossible to traverse) - **impassive** (devoid of emotion)

imply (to hint or suggest) - **infer** (to draw conclusions based on facts)

incredible (unbelievable) - **incredulous** (skeptical)

insignificant (trivial) - **tiny** (small)

insinuate (to hint covertly) - **intimate** (to imply subtly)

invoke (to call upon a higher power for assistance) - **evoke** (to elicit)

judicial (pertaining to law) - **judicious** (exhibiting sound judgment)

latter (the second of two things mentioned) - **later** (subsequently)

mania (craze) - **phobia** (fear)

nauseated (to feel queasy) - **nauseous** (causing queasiness)

obliged (to feel a debt of gratitude) - **obligated** (under specific direction to follow a certain course)

official (authorized by a proper authority) - **officious** (extremely eager to offer help or advice)

older (refers to persons and things) - **elder** (refers to only one person)

persecute (to oppress or harass) - **prosecute** (to initiate legal or criminal action against)

piteous (pathetic) - **pitiable** (lamentable) - **pitiful** (very inferior or insignificant)

practically (almost) - **virtually** (to all intents)

precipitant (rash, impulsive) - **precipitate** (to hurl downward) - **precipitous** (extremely steep)

principal (chief) - **principle** (basic law or truth)

raise (to move upward; to build; to breed) - **rear** (to bring up a child) - **rise** (to ascend)

rare (of unusual value and quality, of limited supply) - **scarce** (refers to temporary infrequency)

ravage (to devastate or despoil) - **ravish** (to take away by force)

regretful (sorrowful) - **regrettable** (something that elicits mental distress)

reluctant (unwilling) - **reticent** (refers to a style that is characteristically silent or restrained)

repel (drive off; cause distaste or aversion) - **repulse** (drive off; reject by means of discourtesy)

respectfully (showing honor and esteem) - **respectively** (one at a time in order)

restive (resistance to control) - **restless** (lacking repose)

specific (explicitly set forth) - **particular** (not general or universal)

stationary (immovable) - **stationery** (matched writing paper and envelopes)

Get Sharp
Tip # 21
Pay special attention to the differences *(in meaning)* between those words that sound a lot alike.

Homophones

Homophones are words that sound alike, but have different meanings. Here are a few of the hundreds of homophones in the English language.

acclamation - acclimation	but - butt	find - fined
acts - axe	bye - by - buy	fir - fur
ail - ale	caller - collar	flew - flue
air - heir	canon - cannon	flea - flee
aisle - I'll - isle	canopy - canapé	flour - flower
all - awl	canvas - canvass	for - four - fore
aloud - allowed	capital - capitol	forth - fourth
ant - aunt	cache - cash	fowl - foul
arc - ark	carrot - carat	gait - gate
ascent - assent	ceiling - sealing	gamble - gambol
assistance - assistants	cell - sell	gilt - guilt
ate - eight	cellar - seller	gnu - new - knew
attendance - attendants	census - senses	grate - great
aught - ought	cent - sent - scent	grisly - grizzly
aye - eye	chance - chants	grater - greater
bail - bale	chord - cord	groan - grown
bait - bate	cite - sight - site	hail - hale
bald - bawled	close - clothes	hair - hare
bare - bear	coarse - course	hall - haul
bard - barred	colonel - kernel	hay - hey
baron - barren	compliment - complement	heal - heel
bass - base	concur - conquer	hear - here
beech - beach	coral - choral	heard - herd
beet - beat	caught - cot	higher - hire
bee - be	council - counsel	him - hymn
beau - bow	creak - creek	holy - holey - wholly
berry - bury	cruise - crews	hole - whole
berth - birth	currant - current	hour - our
better - bettor	cymbal - symbol	idol - idle
bier - beer	days - daze	incidents - incidence
billed - build	dense - dents	in - inn
blue - blew	descent - dissent	
bore - boar	do - due - due	
bowled - bold	die - dye	
border - boarder	doe - dough	
burrow - borough	draft - draught	
bow - bough	dual - duel	
breach - breech	earn - urn	
break - brake	elicit - illicit	
bred - bread	ewe - you - yew	
bridle- bridal	fete - feet	

A writer has his own "rite of passage," right?

Get Sharp: Vocabulary & Word Meaning

Better Grades & Higher Test Scores / READING & LANGUAGE
Copyright ©2003 by Incentive Publications, Inc., Nashville, TN.

knap - nap	pried - pride	
knead - need	principal - principle	
knight - night	prints - prince	
knot - not	profit - prophet	
know - no	rain - rein - reign	
knows - nose	raise - rays - raze	
lead - led	rap - wrap	
leak - leek	read - red	
lean - lien	read - reed	
leased - least	real - reel	
liar - lyre	right - write - rite	
lie - lye	ring - wring	
lone - loan	rowed - rode - road	tacks - tax
maid - made	roe - row	tail - tale
mail - male	rose - rows	taut - taught
main - mane - Maine	rote - wrote	team - teem
manner - manor	rot - wrought	tear - tier
marshal - martial	rung - wrung	tear - tare
meddle - medal - metal	rye - wry	teas - tease
miner - minor	sail - sale	tense - tents
mite - might	scene - seen	their - there
morning - mourning	scent - sent - cent	threw - through
navel - naval	scull - skull	throne - thrown
nay - neigh	sea - see	thy - thigh
none - nun	sealing - ceiling	thyme - time
or - oar - ore	seam - seem	tide - tied
ode - owed	seas - sees - seize	toad - towed
one - won	seed - cede	toe - tow
oh - owe	seen - scene	told - tolled
owed - ode	sense - scents - cents	too - to - two
paced - paste	serf - surf	vale - veil
packed - pact	sew - sow - so	vane - vain - vein
pail - pale	shear - sheer	wade - weighed
pain - pane	shoe - shoo	wail - whale
palate - palette	shone - shown	wait - weight
patience - patients	side - sighed	wave - waive
paws - pause	shoot - chute	way - weigh - whey
piece - peace - peas	slay - sleigh	weak - week
peak - peek - pique	soar - sore	wear - where - ware
peal - peel	soared - sword	were - whir
pear - pair - pare	some - sum	whether - weather
peer - pier	son - sun	which - witch
plain - plane	stair - stare	whole - hole
pole - poll	stake - steak	while - wile
pore - pour	stationary - stationery	whine - wine
pray - prey	steel - steal	wood - would
prays - praise	straight - strait	wrapping - rapping
		yolk - yoke

Speech bubble: Paying this tax is as painful as sitting on tacks!

Analogies

An analogy shows relationships between words in two pairs of words. In each pair, the words must have the same relationship. To solve an analogy with a missing word you must first discover the relationship in the completed pair. There are many different kinds of relationships used in analogies. Some of them are shown here.

Synonyms

Insipid is to *uninteresting* as *rebuff* is to *rebuke*.
Peril is to *danger* as *hectic* is to *chaotic*.
Noisy is to *clamorous* as *splendid* is to *superb*.
Impeccable is to *faultless* as *mimic* is to *imitate*.
Savory is to *tasty* as *boring* is to *dull*.
Fetid is to *malodorous* as *shun* is to *avoid*.
Parsimonious is to *stingy* as *scoundrel* is to *crook*.
Vindicate is to *exonerate* as *morass* is to *swamp*.
Brusque is to *abrupt* as *faze* is to *disturb*.

Sullen is to glum...

...as timid is to timorous.

Antonyms

Mania is to *sanity* as *slander* is to *truth*.
Novice is to *professional* as *perpetuate* is to *cease*.
Insolvent is to *wealthy* as *penniless* is to *flush*.
Languid is to *energetic* as *instigate* is to *stop*.
Subtle is to *garish* as *credible* is to *implausible*.
Inept is to *graceful* as *benefactor* is to *sycophant*.
Voracious is to *satiated* as *waxing* is to *waning*.
Disapprove is to *condone* as *avarice* is to *generosity*.
Adroit is to *clumsy* as *haughty* is to *friendly*.

Categories

Physician is to *professional* as *miner* is to *laborer*.
Cedar is to *evergreen* as *oak* is to *deciduous*.
Wrench is to *jackhammer* as *scapula* is to *tibia*.
Sleet is to *precipitation* as *hurricane* is to *storm*.
Dolphin is to *vertebrate* as *anemone* is to *invertebrate*.
Stomach is to *digestion* as *trachea* is to *respiration*.
Rigatoni is to *pasta* as *shrimp* is to *crustacean*.

Degree

Flurries is to *blizzard* as *sprinkles* is to *downpour*.
Warm is to *scalding* as *cool* is to *freezing*.
Death is to *injury* as *disastrous* is to *troublesome*.
Fawn is to *buck* as *kid* is to *goat*.
Comical is to *hilarious* as *serious* is to *critical*.
Evening is to *night* as *dawn* is to *morning*.

Function

Mitt is to *baseball* as *bucket* is to *drip*.
Wrench is to *faucet* as *drill* is to *cavity*.
Umbrella is to *rain* as *awning* is to *sunshine*.
Vocal chords are to *voice* as *strings* are to *piano*.
Siren is to *sound* as *chocolate* is to *taste*.
Welder is to *torch* as *dentist* is to *drill*.

Location

Femur is to *patella* as *ulna* is to *elbow*.
Channel is to *television* as *station* is to *radio*.
Squid is to *ocean* as *antelope* is to *tundra*.
Laces are to *shoes* as *buttons* are to *shirt*.
Aria is to *opera* as *motion* is to *courtroom*.
Coiffure is to *head* as *stone* is to *kidney*.

Goose is to geese...

...as artichoke is to artichokes.

Word Structure

Mice is to *mouse* as *berries* is to *berry*.
Worried is to *worry* as *frenzied* is to *frenzy*.
Boyhood is to *boy* as *neighborhood* is to *neighbor*.
Semiconductor is to *conductor* as *extraterrestrial* is to *terrestrial*.
Unfriendliness is to *friend* as *nonsensical* is to *sense*.
Fruitcake is to *cake* as *sandstorm* is to *storm*.

Other Relationships

Centimeter is to *meter* as *inch* is to *yard*.
Hiss is to *snake* as *growl* is to *tiger*.
Yellow is to *banana* as *green* is to *celery*.
Smoke is to *fire* as *rain* is to *clouds*.
Candidate is to *campaign* as *detective* is to *investigate*.
Diamond is to *rigid* as *copper* is to *malleable*.

Get Sharp: Vocabulary & Word Meaning

Idioms

Idioms are "sayings" peculiar to a particular language or group. The meaning of the expressions cannot necessarily be understood from the words themselves. The meanings have come to be understood over time—often to mean something very different from what the words actually say. Here are a few of the thousands of idioms in the English language.

a bad egg

a bee in your bonnet

a bone to pick

a drop in the bucket

a finger in every pie

a flash in the pan

a lion's share

a long row to hoe

a pain in the neck

a splitting headache

almighty dollar

an ace in the hole

an axe to grind

back to square one

bark up the wrong tree

bats in the belfry

be a good egg

be on top of the world

between the devil and
the deep blue sea

behind the 8 ball

bite the bullet

bite the dust

bite your head off

blows my mind

blow off steam

blow the test

break the ice

bring home the bacon

burn the candle at both ends

bury the hatchet

by the skin of my teeth

call her on the carpet

carry a torch for her

chew the fat

chicken out

chip off the old block

chip on your shoulder

come in out of the rain

cook your goose

cry your eyes out

I cried my eyes out when he died with his boots on.

deep in thought

died with his boots on

doesn't amount to
    a hill of beans

don't beat a dead horse

don't bite off more than
    you can chew

don't cry over spilt milk

don't cry wolf

don't give me any lip

don't make a mountain
    out of a molehill

dressed to the nines

eager beaver

easier said than done

eat crow

eat humble pie

eye to eye

face the music

fly the coop

get cold feet

get it off your chest

get forty winks

get off my back

get off my case

get on board the gravy train

get on your high horse

give a tongue lashing

got an earful

have your cake and eat it, too

hit it off

hit the nail on the head

hold a candle to

hold your horses

hold your tongue

in a pretty pickle

in hot water

in the bag

in the doghouse

in the nick of time

in the pink

in the red

it's right down my alley

jump the gun

just under the wire
keep a stiff upper lip
keep your shirt on
kick the bucket
kick up your heels
knock it off
lay an egg
left holding the bag
lend me a hand
let the cat out of the bag
lie through your teeth
look a gift horse in the mouth
lose your cool
lose your head
lose your shirt
lost his marbles
mad as a hatter
make a beeline
make hay while the sun shines
make no bones about it
make your mouth water
mint condition
more fun than a barrel
    of monkeys
more than one way
    to skin a cat
nose to the grindstone
not worth a hill of beans
nothing to shake a stick at
off the record
on the bandwagon
on the money
on the nose
on top of the world
once in a blue moon
out of the frying pan
    into the fire

out on a limb
out to lunch
paint the town red
pass the buck
pay through the nose
plain as the nose
    on your face
pull strings
pull the wool over
    your eyes
put a sock in it
put on the dog
put your foot in
    your mouth
puttin' on the Ritz
raining cats and dogs
rake over the coals
read you the riot act
red letter day
right up my alley
run it into the ground
sadder but wiser
see eye to eye
shoot the breeze
shoot the bull
skeleton in your closet
skin the cat
sleep like a top
sour grapes
spill the beans
split hairs
spring a leak
stab someone in the back
stay until the bitter end
stick your neck out
straight from the horse's mouth
swallow it hook, line, and sinker

sweating bullets
take heart
takes the cake
talk through your hat
talk turkey
the apple of my eye
the black sheep
the handwriting's on the wall
the lady is a fox
things are touch and go
tickled pink
till the cows come home
too many irons in the fire
under her thumb
under the gun
up the creek without a paddle
upset the apple cart
wants cash on the barrel
wear your heart on your sleeve
went bananas
wolf in sheep's clothing
worth his salt
yell your head off

If you see a wolf in sheep's clothing— yell your head off!

Get Sharp: Vocabulary & Word Meaning

Puns & Proverbs

pun – a word or a phrase used in a way that gives a funny twist to the words. Puns often make use of double meanings of words.

Is it any surprise that a girl named Robin Steale would grow up to be a thief?
It's a drain on our budget to hire a plumber.
"Don't drop the eggs!" cracked the grocer.
A clockmaker works overtime.
Our new Phys Ed teacher is Jim Schorts.
That Dracula movie was a pain in the neck.
My surgeon is so funny; she keeps me in stitches!
Is a barber who works in a Library called a Barbarian?
Our optometrist is Seymore Clearly
Claude Severely is an ex-lion tamer.
To win a relay race, swimmers pool their efforts.

proverb – a brief saying that presents a truth or some bit of useful wisdom

A bird in the hand is worth two in the bush.
A fool and his money are soon parted.
An apple a day keeps the doctor away.
A stitch in time saves nine.
Absence makes the heart grow fonder.
Better safe than sorry.
Blood is thicker than water.
Cleanliness is next to godliness.
Curiosity killed the cat.
Don't change horses in the middle of the stream.
Don't count your chickens until they're hatched.
Don't cut off your nose to spite your face.
Don't air your dirty linen.
Every family has a skeleton in its closet.
Fish and visitors smell in three days.
Fools rush in where angels fear to tread.
Good fences make good neighbors.
He who hesitates is lost.
It is no time to send for the doctor
   when the patient is dead.
When it rains, it pours.
It takes two to tango.
Laughter is the best medicine.

Let sleeping dogs lie.
Look before you leap.
Money is the root of all evil.
Never look a gift horse in the mouth.
No news is good news.
Practice what you preach.
Rats desert a sinking ship.
Spare the rod and spoil the child.
Strike while the iron is hot.
The early bird gets the worm.
There's more than one way to skin a cat.
Too many cooks spoil the broth.
Two heads are better than one.
You can lead a horse to water, but you can't
   make him drink.
You can't tell a book by its cover.
Where there's smoke, there's fire.

Fish and visitors smell in three days.

Oxymorons & Palindromes

oxymoron – a combination of two words which seem to contradict each other

act naturally
airline food
almost exactly
alone together
bittersweet
black light
cafeteria food
calm wind
childproof
civil war
clearly misunderstood
deafening silence
definite maybe
designer jeans
double solitaire

exact estimate
even odds
found missing
freezer burn
fresh-frozen
friendly fire
good grief
jumbo shrimp
half naked
holy war
ill health
industrial park
minor crisis
minor miracle
modern history

more perfect
old news
open secret
original copies
plastic silverware
pretty ugly
sanitary landfill
seriously funny
silent scream
small crowd
terribly pleased
unbiased opinion
vaguely aware
virtual reality
working vacation

palindrome – a word or phrase that reads the same forwards and backwards

a nut for a jar of tuna
a Santa at NASA
a Toyota
Ana, nab a banana.
bird rib
Bob, level Bo.
Boston, O do not sob.
Dee saw a seed.
Del saw a sled.
deified
Delia failed.
Do geese see god?
Don't nod.
Dot saw I was Tod.
Dot sees Tod.
Dr. Awkward
Dumb mud.
Ed is on no side.
Evade me, Dave.
Eve
God saw I was dog.
He stops spots, eh?
I did, did I?

I prefer pi.
I saw I was I.
I'm, alas, a salami!
kayak
Lepers repel.
level
Ma has a ham.
Ma is a nun, as I am.
Mad am I, Adam!
Madam, I'm Adam.
Name no one man.
Never odd or even
Niagara, O roar again.
No devil lived on.
No garden, one dragon.
No lemons, no melon.
Olson is in Oslo.
Pa's a sap.
party-trap
peep
Poor Dan is in a droop.

radar
racecar
re-paper
Rise to vote, sir.
senile felines
solos
so many dynamos
star comedy by democrats
Stella won no wallets.
Step on no pets.
straw warts
Too bad, I hid a boot.
too hot to hoot
top spot
tuna nut
Warsaw was raw.
Was it a bat I saw?
Was it a cat I saw?
Was it a rat I saw?
we few
We panic in a pew.
Wontons? Not now.
Yreka bakery

Lil? Mom, Dad, Bob, and Eve went off in a kayak! Is that a racecar?

Get Sharp: Vocabulary & Word Meaning

Common Acronyms & Abbreviations

AC	alternating current
A.D.	anno Domini (Latin for "in the year of the Lord" or "since the birth of Christ")
a.m.	ante meridiem (midnight to noon)
Amer.	American
anon.	anonymous
apt.	apartment
ASAP	as soon as possible
assoc.	association
asst.	assistant
atty.	attorney
A.S.P.C.A.	American Society for the Prevention of Cruelty to Animals
B.A.	Bachelor of Arts (college degree)
B.C.	before Christ
B.C.E.	before the Christian era
bps	bits per second
B.S.	Bachelor of Science (college degree)
C	centigrade (or Celsius)
c.	copyright
cal.	calories
CD	compact disc
cent.	century
C.I.A.	Central Intelligence Agency
cm	centimeter
C.O.D.	cash on delivery
C.P.A.	certified public accountant
CPR	cardiopulmonary resuscitation
CPU	central processing unit
CST	Central Standard Time
D.A.	district attorney
DC	direct current
D.D.S.	doctor of dental surgery
dept.	department
DNA	deoxyribonucleic acid (basic genetic material)
doz.	dozen
DVD	digital video disc
ed.	editor, edition
e.g.	for example (exempli gratia)
email	electronic mail
enc.	enclosure, encyclopedia
ESP	extrasensory perception
EST	Eastern Standard Time
esp.	especially
et al.	and others (et alia)
etc.	and so forth (et cetera)
F	Fahrenheit
FAQs	frequently asked questions

F.B.I.	Federal Bureau of Investigation
ft.	foot, feet
govt.	government
i.e.	that is (id est)
I.Q.	Intelligence Quotient
I.R.S.	Internal Revenue Service
K	kilo (1000)
k.	karat
kg	kilogram
l	liter
lb.	pound
M.D.	Medical Doctor
min.	minute
ml	milliliter
mm	millimeter
mph	miles per hour
mpg	miles per gallon
no.	number
oz.	ounce
p.	page
p.m.	post meridiem (noon to nidnight)
POW	prisoner of war
P.S.	post script
pt.	pint
qt.	quart
R.F.D.	rural free delivery
R.N.	registered nurse
RR	railroad
R.S.V.P.	please respond
S.A.S.E.	self-addressed, stamped envelope
St.	street, saint
t.	ton
UFO	unidentified flying object
UHF	ultrahigh frequency (radio wave)
URL	Uniform Resource Locator
v. or vs.	versus
VCR	videocassette recorder
VHF	very high frequency (radio wave)
w	watt
www	world wide web (Internet)

I'm going to buy a CD ASAP.

Get Sharp: Vocabulary & Word Meaning

INDEX

Index

Better Grades & Higher Test Scores / READING & LANGUAGE
Copyright ©2003 by Incentive Publications, Inc., Nashville, TN.

Better Grades & Higher Test Scores / READING & LANGUAGE
Copyright ©2003 by Incentive Publications, Inc., Nashville, TN.

Index

U

Understatement, 206
usage, 96-105
 do's and don't's', 100-101
 double negatives, 100
 double subjects, 100
 infinitives, 101
 mix-ups, 102-105
 participles, 101
 pronouns, 98-99
 subject-verb agreement, 96-97

V

verbals, 74
verbs, 74-79
 helping, 79
 intransitive, 78
 irregular, 75, 77
 linking, 79
 regular, 76
 tenses, 76-77
 transitive, 78
vocabulary words, 216
voice, 160, 206

W

webs, 149
word meaning, 214-232
 abbreviations, 232
 acronyms, 232
 analogies, 226-227
 confusing words, 222-223
 connotation, 217
 context from paragraph, 214
 context from sentence, 215
 denotation, 217
 homonyms, 224-225
 idioms, 228-229
 oxymorons, 231
 palindromes, 231
 prefixes, 218
 proverbs, 230
 puns, 230
 roots, 220-221
 suffixes, 219
 vocabulary words, 216
word use, 136
words, 150-151
 active, 150
 precise, 150
 effective, 150-151

writing
 advice to parents, 144-145
 assessment, 146-147
 beginnings, 156, 158, 167
 checking mechanics, 143
 closings, 156, 158
 collecting, 142, 148
 compositions, 156-159
 conclusions, 156, 159
 content and organization, 136
 devices, 138-141
 drafting, 142
 editing, 137, 161-163
 effective, 135
 effective words, 150-151
 endings, 156, 159
 essays, 157
 forms, 128-129
 genres, 128-129
 headlines, 167
 helping students with, 144-145
 letters, 170
 modes, 130-131
 news articles, 167
 paragraphs, 154-155
 polishing, 143, 162
 praises, 142, 161
 process, 137, 142-143
 openings, 156, 158, 167
 organizing, 142, 149
 outlines, 149, 165
 P-Q-P Plan for Editing & Revising
 Writing, 161-162
 proofread, 143, 166
 questions, 143, 162
 reports, 58-61, 164-166
 reviewing, 143
 revising, 137, 143, 161-163
 romancing, 142
 scoring guide, 146-147
 sentences, 152-153
 sharing, 143
 short stories, 168-169
 showing off, 143
 skills, 136-137
 techniques, 137, 138-141
 tips, 145
 transitions, 155
 webs, 149
 voice, 160
 words, 150-151